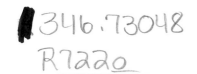

Open Source Licensing

D1302573

Open Source Licensing

Software Freedom and Intellectual Property Law

Lawrence Rosen

PRENTICE HALL PTR
Upper Saddle River, NJ 07458
www.phptr.com

Cataloging-in-Publication Data is on file with the Library of Congress

Publishing partner: *Mark Taub*
Editorial assistant: *Noreen Regina*
Marketing manager: *Robin O'Brien*
Production: *BooksCraft, Inc., Indianapolis, IN*
Cover designer: *Mary Jo DeFranco*

Original book © Copyright 2005 Lawrence Rosen
Foreword copyright © 2005 Lawrence Lessig

 Publishing by Prentice Hall Professional Technical Reference
Upper Saddle River, New Jersey 07458

Prentice Hall books are widely used by corporations and government agencies for training, marketing, and resale.

For information regarding corporate and government bulk discounts please contact:

Corporate and Government Sales (800) 382-3419 or
corpsales@pearsontechgroup.com

Company and product names mentioned herein are the trademarks or registered trademarks of their respective owners.

Printed in the United States of America
First printing, July 2004

ISBN 0-13-148787-6

Pearson Education LTD.
Pearson Education Australia PTY, Limited
Pearson Education Singapore, Pte. Ltd.
Pearson Education North Asia Ltd.
Pearson Education Canada, Ltd.
Pearson Educación de Mexico, S.A. de C.V.
Pearson Education—Japan
Pearson Education Malaysia, Pte. Ltd.

For Harry Adams
who shared this open source madness
with me

Acknowledgments

I will be forever grateful for the encouragement and assistance of Michael Einschlag, my mentor, my law partner, and my friend of many years. He's the most brilliant attorney I know, and his counsel about patent and contract law through many drafts of this book was invaluable.

We stand on the shoulders of giants. I had the good fortune to learn about open source from the leaders who created it. I want to thank them all but can only name a few special ones who influenced me and taught me about software freedom and open source: Bruce Perens, Peter Deutsch, Eric Raymond, Russell Nelson, Brian Behlendorf, Richard Stallman, Eben Moglen, Danese Cooper, Guido van Rossum, and Michael Tiemann. Anyone who knows these players knows that we disagree among ourselves about more than a few licensing matters, but we all agree that software freedom is a grand goal. I couldn't and wouldn't have written this book without them.

It is impossible to name all the contributors to the various licensing lists I monitor, but thank you all for expressing yourselves so eloquently. I've stolen many of your (unpatentable) ideas for this book. Special thanks go to John Cowan, Mårten Mickos, Scott Peterson, Mark Webbink, Dietmar Tallroth, Tim O'Reilly, Brian Fitzgerald, Dan Ravicher, and Rod Dixon, who may not realize how important their help and inspiration have been for writing this book. Thanks.

Contents

Foreword
by Lawrence Lessig[†]

Open source resources are completely common within our society. Yet open source and free software remain a mystery. Science, public highways, city parks, language—these are at the core of any free society. Commerce gets built upon them. Culture flourishes through them. Yet the same ideas applied to software puzzle many people. Language can be free, and the results of science open to all, yet to many, software is, or should be, proprietary.

Why code must be proprietary is a question whose answers have changed over the past ten years. At first, the reasons were technical: no free or open source project, it was said, could develop the highly complex and robust code necessary for modern software applications. But when the GNU/Linux project began to produce an operating system that rivaled Microsoft's in robustness and efficiency, this technical argument began to fade.

† Professor of Law, Stanford Law School, and author of *Code and Other Laws of Cyberspace* (Basic Books, 2000); *The Future of Ideas: The Fate of the Commons in a Connected World* (Vintage Books, 2002); *Free Culture: How Big Media Uses Technology and the Law to Lock Down Culture and Control Creativity* (Penguin Press, 2004).

In its place, many offered an argument of commercial necessity: No free or open source project could survive commercially, given the high costs of quality programming, and the inability to exclude others from the benefits of that quality. But again, when companies such as IBM and HP began to invest billions in free software development, this argument too began to weaken. And as the embedded systems market began to take off, built as it is upon open and free software, it became clear to most disinterested observers that open source and free software were elements of a different business model, not opponents to business. Whether this different business model will produce more profits for the technology sector generally is an empirical question we rely upon markets to resolve. But that it does make money for some is no longer subject to doubt.

Having failed to convince the world that propriety software is technically necessary, or commercially necessary, the opponents of free and open source software now argue against it on the basis of legal necessity. At the most extreme (and absurd), SCO President Darl McBride argues that free software licensed under the GPL is "unconstitutional." At the center are those allied with Microsoft, who argue that the licenses supporting the most popular free and open source projects are "dangerous" and "unproven."

In this beautifully clear and accessible work, Lawrence Rosen defuses this last, and equally fallacious, argument against open source and free software. While he doesn't waste trees responding to the ridiculous claims of McBride, this book builds a framework within which the family of free and open source licenses can be understood. And in a rare talent for a lawyer, Rosen succeeds in making these points about the law meaningful and understandable to anyone at all.

This is the great value of this perfectly timed book. As open source software is among the fastest growing and most important software produced, it has become necessary for a wide range of people to understand the foundations upon which it is built. Businesses and investors, as well as technologists and scientists, need to understand how pedestrian the legal framework is within which open source and free software are grounded. Policymakers need to see that this distinctive model for creating and spreading knowledge about code is neither communism come to the digital age, nor a binary version of Thomas More's *Utopia*.

The need for this understanding was never more clear to me than when I read about our own government's view about open source and free software. In July 2003, the United States government vetoed a request that the World Intellectual Property Organization (WIPO) hold a meeting to discuss "open collaborative models for producing public goods," including open source and free software. Lois Boland, director of international relations for the U.S. Patent and Trademark Office, explained "that open-source software runs counter to the mission of WIPO, which is to promote intellectual-property rights." As she is quoted as saying, "To hold a meeting which has as its purpose to disclaim or waive such rights seems to us to be contrary to the goals of WIPO."

This statement is astonishing on a number of levels, and Rosen's book demonstrates why. Most obviously, open source and free software is not "counter to the mission of" an organization that "promote[s] intellectual property rights," as open source and free software generally relies upon intellectual property to achieve their effect. The most important open source and free software is not software in the public domain. It is instead, like Microsoft's software, software protected by intellectual property law and licensed to users on the terms chosen by the property owner.

No doubt the property owners in an open source and free software project "disclaim or waive" some of their rights. But again, it is puzzling why property owners choosing how to exercise their rights could ever be "contrary to the goals of WIPO." Is it against the property system generally when Bill Gates gives $20 billion to help the poor in Africa? Are public highways latent communism?

Boland's view is grounded in a mistaken understanding of the way open source and free software function. In my view, no one who understands what this book teaches could have any principled opposition to this business model competing with any other. There will be a great deal of social wealth created by this family of licensing. There will be an even greater amount of knowledge and freedom that is spread by this legal arrangement. Rosen has done us all a great service by making understandable the legal tools that make these goods possible.

Preamble

In February 1989, Richard Stallman first released his GNU project software for UNIX under version 1.0 of the GNU General Public License (GPL). In June of that same year, Bill Joy first released a free version of UNIX software under the University of California's Berkeley Software Distribution (BSD) license. These relatively quiet events signaled a new era in software licensing. Almost imperceptibly at first, but with increasing speed and energy, this licensing revolution, now widely referred to as open source, spread around the world.

By the first year of this century, approximately 17,000 open source projects were active on the SourceForge servers (*www.sourceforge.org*). Four years later there are over 74,000 such projects and more than 775,000 registered SourceForge users. The majority of that open source software is currently licensed under the GPL or BSD licenses; the rest use one of about fifty other licenses based on the same open source principles.

Open source is now dominating many of the market conversations in the software industry. While software companies continue to release valuable and high-quality products under proprietary licenses, most are also embracing open source product development and distribution models as well as the software licenses that make those models possible.

This book is about the law but it is not written for lawyers. You will not find citations to case law or rigorous academic analyses suitable for publication in a law journal. This book is written for my friends in the open source community who write and distribute software and who are confused about which licenses to use. It is also written for our customers who are concerned about how software licenses may affect them and their businesses. It seeks to dispel myths and fears about open source software licensing and to explain the legal context in which open source software exists.

Open source is built upon a foundation of intellectual property law, particularly copyright law. Open source software is owned by its authors, who license it to the public under generous terms. Open source licenses do not seek to destroy or steal intellectual property. The first chapters of this book explain the intellectual property laws that make open source licensing possible.

The following chapter describe the first broad category of open source licenses, what I call academic licenses to acknowledge their heritage in universities. These academic licenses allow software to be used, copied, modified, and distributed, even with proprietary software—and their source code is included. These licensors generously donate their software to the public for use by anyone.

The GPL—and the MPL, CPL, and OSL licenses that followed it—strike what I call a reciprocal bargain. Licensor and licensees share a public commons of open source software, but any modifications to that software must be distributed under the same license. These four licenses are much more complex than the academic licenses and so I devote a chapter to each of them.

Choosing a license to apply to your open source software is not an easy decision and so I devote an entire chapter to it. The answer depends intricately upon your business model, on your software and product architecture, and on understanding who owns the intellectual property in your products. If you expect a checklist method to select a license, don't bother reading this chapter; it cannot be so easy.

Eventually, a licensor or licensee may need to enforce the terms and conditions of an open source license. I devote an entire chapter to satisfying the curiosity of those who may want to sue—or who are afraid of being sued—under an open source license.

Finally, I begin to address a potentially bigger issue than open source. Open standards are really the battlefield on which we will determine whether software can truly be free and open. That topic deserves a book of its own someday; this isn't it, but I'm making a start.

Turning a software license into interesting reading is probably an insurmountable challenge. There is no other way than reading the words of a license to understand what it means. And so, for those of you who won't actually plod your way through the detailed explanations of licenses herein, I want to give you the conclusion.

As a user of open source software you may go forth and live free. None of the licenses in this book restrict in any way your use of open source software.

But if you are more directly involved in the creation, modification, or distribution of software, or if you manage or advise the in-licensing of software into your company, you should at the very least consult your attorney to make sure you don't commit to more than you're willing to deliver. This book may help you ask your attorney the right questions.

1

Freedom and Open Source

The Language of Freedom

Open source licenses promise to everyone what many in the community refer to as *software freedom*. The terminology of *freedom* is emotionally satisfying, but it has proven to be very confusing.

Freedom is an important subject in law school. Constitutional law courses address such topics as the *free speech* clause of the First Amendment to the U.S. Constitution. But freedom seldom comes up as a topic in classes devoted to business issues such as contract or tort law, or software licensing. Law school courses on intellectual property deal with copyright and patent, but they don't teach about freedom, referring instead to the *rights* of the owners of those legal monopolies. As a result, there is no easy conceptual basis for integrating the language of freedom into the legal language of software licenses. For example, where the word *free* is currently used in software licensing contexts, it usually means *zero*, as in *free of charge* or *free of defects*. Neither of these meanings is intended by open source licenses.

Not that *software freedom* isn't definable. The Free Software Foundation lists four essential kinds of software freedom:

1

1. The freedom to run the software for any purpose

2. The freedom to study how the software works
    and to adapt it to your needs

3. The freedom to redistribute copies of the
    software

4. The freedom to improve the software and
    distribute your improvements to the
    public

That list, it turns out, can be satisfied by many different software licenses. Both the GPL and the BSD licenses, the earliest open source examples from the late 1980s, ensure those four kinds of software freedom, although they do it in vastly different ways.

Proprietary software vendors love the software freedom provided by the BSD license, but some of them hate and fear the software freedom guaranteed by the GPL. So once again, the concept of *freedom* by itself is only marginally helpful to understanding open source licensing.

Defining Open Source

Confusion about the term *freedom* was the very reason the term *open source* was created. The newer term refers to an important concept well understood by anyone who has ever written computer software: Programmers write *source code* to direct computers to perform specific tasks, while the computer itself takes care of the routine task of translating the source code into an executable program. For a computer programmer, understanding and modifying software requires access to the source code. The source code must be *open*—made available for all to see—in order that the software can be studied, changed, and improved.

Open source code is an essential requirement for software freedom, a technical prerequisite. *Software freedom* is the goal; *open source* is the means to that goal.

The term *open source* has caught on in the media and in public discourse. It is now possible to ensure that open source licenses promote software freedom without using the confusing word *freedom* at all. We now mostly refer to *open source software* when we also mean *free software*.

Simply changing the name we call something, however, doesn't eliminate existing ambiguities. We still need a definition—a brief set of open source principles—that summarizes what open source means and provides guidelines for open source licenses.

In 1997, Bruce Perens proposed the Debian Free Software Guidelines to reflect the new open source terminology, to avoid confusion about the term *free software*, and to clarify certain other issues about acceptable licenses. Those guidelines were refined in a month-long email discussion and finally adopted by consensus as the Open Source Definition. (Perens wrote about this history in *Open Sources: Voices from the Open Source Revolution*. [O'Reilly 1999].) Originally consisting of nine criteria for licenses, the Open Source Definition had a tenth guideline added in 2002.

Licenses that meet these criteria are approved by the Open Source Initiative (OSI) board of directors. Software that is distributed in source form under such approved licenses is *OSI Certified open source software*. License approval has become a prerequisite for widespread adoption of software by the open source community; such organizations as SourceForge, for example, will only permit software licensed under an OSI-approved license to be hosted on their website.

Here, in summary form, is the most recent version of the Open Source Definition (OSD) from the website of OSI, *www.open-source.org*.

1. Free Redistribution

The license shall not restrict any party from selling or giving away the software as a component of an aggregate software distribution containing programs from several different sources. The license shall not require a royalty or other fee for such sale.

2. Source Code

The program must include source code, and must allow distribution in source code as well as compiled form. Where some form of a product is not distributed with source code, there must be a well publicized means of obtaining the source code for no more than a reasonable reproduction cost, preferably downloading via the Internet without charge. The source code must be the preferred form in which a programmer would modify the program. Deliberately obfuscated source code is not allowed. Intermediate forms such as the output of a preprocessor or translator are not allowed.

3. Derived Works

The license must allow modifications and derived works, and it must allow them to be distributed under the same terms as the license of the original software.

4. Integrity of the Author's Source Code

The license may restrict source code from being distributed in modified form only if the license allows the distribution of "patch files" with the source code for the purpose of modifying the program at build time. The license must explicitly permit

*distribution of software built from modified source code. The
license may require derived works to carry a different name
or version number from the original software.*

5. No Discrimination Against Persons or Groups

*The license must not discriminate against any person or
group of persons.*

6. No Discrimination Against Fields of Endeavor

*The license must not restrict anyone from making use of the
program in a specific field of endeavor. For example, it may
not restrict the program from being used in a business, or
from being used for genetic research.*

7. Distribution of License

*The rights attached to the program must apply to all to
whom the program is redistributed without the need for execution of an additional license by those parties.*

8. License Must Not Be Specific to a Product

*The rights attached to the program must not depend on the
program's being part of a particular software distribution. If
the program is extracted from that distribution and used or
distributed within the terms of the program's license, all parties to whom the program is redistributed should have the
same rights as those that are granted in conjunction with the
original software distribution.*

9. License Must Not Restrict Other Software

*The license must not place restrictions on other software that
is distributed along with the licensed software. For example,
the license must not insist that all other programs distributed
on the same medium must be open source software.*

10. License Must Be Technology-Neutral

No provision of the license may be predicated on any individual technology or style of interface.

This Open Source Definition has itself created some confusion. It replaced certain vague concepts in the Free Software Guidelines with some equally vague concepts about discrimination, authors' integrity, and software redistribution. Public discussions about license approval sometimes become arguments about what the OSD itself means.

Lawyers point out that the OSD uses words like *shall not* and *must* and *may* in inconsistent ways. For example, the phrase *must allow* means different things in the two places it is used in one sentence.

The license must allow modifications and derived works,
and must allow them to be distributed under the same terms
as the license of the original software. (OSD # 3.)

The first part of this provision is interpreted to mean that a license *must allow a licensee to create derivative works.* The second part, however, is interpreted to mean that a license *may require (but need not require)* that the same license be used to distribute those derivative works and also that a license *may not forbid* licensing derivative works under the same license.

Even the two sentences of OSD # 1, with their uses of *shall not restrict* and *shall not require*, confuse many new visitors to open source. One of the most frequent first questions people ask is, "Is all open source software zero price?" No. Most open source licensees will be glad to take your money for your first copy of a piece of software. But you never have to pay a royalty or license fee for the right to make copies. It would be better if OSD # 1 phrased this point better.

The Open Source Definition is in some respects mandatory (e.g., under OSD # 1 and 2, licenses *must* permit copying of the software and the creation of derivative works) and in some respects permissive (e.g., under OSD # 4, a license *may* provide mechanisms to protect the author's integrity). Some suggest that an OSD provision that is merely permissive should be left to market forces and should not be part of a definition of what constitutes *open source*.

The word *discrimination* in various places in the OSD is also confusing. Every software license discriminates in favor of those who accept and honor its terms (the *licensees*) and discriminates against those who use the software but don't accept and honor its terms (the *infringers*). The word *discrimination* has colloquial meanings that may not have been intended by the OSD. For example, because certain reciprocal licenses like the GPL are unacceptable to certain proprietary software companies, the license has been said to *discriminate* against those proprietary software companies; others say that is merely discriminating against nonlicensees who refuse to accept the license terms and conditions.

While most in the open source community agree that non-discrimination is a commendable goal in the abstract, the community has been unable to agree about what constitutes discrimination. In many jurisdictions around the world, discrimination on the basis of race, age, religion, national origin, sex, sexual orientation, health status, and other personal characteristics is always illegal. How does discrimination against field of endeavor in OSD # 6 fit into that list? The laws of some countries may prohibit the use of certain software by persons or groups (e.g., the export control laws of the United States are discriminatory on purpose); don't such laws mandating discrimination override the anti-discriminatory provisions of a mere software license? Is such software still open source?

Certain provisions of the OSD have proven to be of no great importance. In OSD # 7, because the reference is to an *additional license*, it is not clear what role this OSD provision can ever play, as a practical matter, when reviewing *this license* for approval. As to OSD # 8, the Open Source Initiative website mysteriously says only that this provision "forecloses yet another class of license traps." This issue has never arisen concerning any present open source license. Furthermore, OSD # 9 is probably unnecessary because it protects against something that would probably be illegal on antitrust grounds wherever it really mattered. Its use of the phrase *other programs distributed on the same medium* is far too narrow to adequately describe what a distributor actually does with software.

Many OSD provisions deal with the *distribution of software*. Some have criticized the OSD because it doesn't directly address the *use of software*. This is not entirely valid because the rights to copy, to create derivative works, and to distribute are essential for the use of open source software. But nothing in the OSD actually makes that point directly.

Open Source Principles

In preparing this book, I found that the official Open Source Definition was simply too confusing to focus readers on what really matters most about open source licenses. Therefore, I have chosen to rely on a somewhat different set of Open Source Principles to describe software that is *open source*.

These Open Source Principles are different from but consistent with the official Open Source Definition and with the Free Software Guidelines quoted earlier.

They guide us to what I believe are the key things to look for in open source licenses—and the key things we'll find missing in non–open source licenses.

It will be useful to keep these Open Source Principles in mind as I describe specific open source licenses later in this book. You may also find the brief explanations of each principle helpful later in this book as I explore various actual open source license provisions and the laws relating to licenses and contracts.

1.
Licensees are free to use open source software for any purpose whatsoever.

An open source license may not interfere in any way with the use of the software by licensees. Restrictions on use, such as "for research and noncommercial purposes only," are not allowed in open source licenses. The phrase *free to use* is also intended to mean "without any conditions that would impede use," such as a requirement for the licensee to report uses to the licensor, or to disclose the means or manner of internal uses of the software. Note also that the first word, *licensees,* means that *open source software is only available under the terms of a license to which each licensee must agree.*

2.
Licensees are free to make copies of open source software and to distribute them without payment of royalties to a licensor.

This principle does not mean that a licensor cannot sell open source software. It merely says that a licensee need not pay the licensor for additional copies he makes himself, even if those copies are distributed to others. As a practical matter, this open source principle drives the price of mere copies of open source software toward its marginal cost of production and distribution.

3.

Licensees are free to create derivative works of open source software and to distribute them without payment of royalties to a licensor.

Quality software is built upon the foundations of earlier software. Many advocates of free and open source software contend that the requirement for open source licenses to permit the unhindered creation and distribution of *derivative works* is essential to meet the goal of the intellectual property laws as stated in the U.S. Constitution, "to promote the progress of science and the useful arts." Under this open source principle, a licensor cannot charge a royalty for the privilege to create and distribute derivative works, or require a licensee to pay a royalty for copies of a derivative work that are distributed, or impose any restrictions on the type or character of those derivative works.

4.

Licensees are free to access and use the source code of open source software.

Source code is written in a human language to instruct a computer how to perform certain functions. Since the source code must be changed in order to instruct the computer to perform different functions, access to the source code is essential to make the third open source principle—the freedom to create derivative works of open source software—a practical reality. Source code is a means to an end, not the end itself. The phrase *free to access* merely requires the licensor to make source code available to licensees upon request at zero price, not necessarily to distribute the source code to everyone.

5.
Licensees are free to combine open source and other software.

Open source licenses may not impose conditions or restrictions on other software with which the licensed software is merely combined or distributed. This prevents restrictions regarding what other software can be placed on computer storage media or in computer memory. Open source is but one of many possible business and licensing models for software distribution, and customers must be free to select and use those software alternatives. This open source principle does not mean that licensors cannot impose reciprocal conditions upon licensees who create and distribute derivative works, for the activity of creating derivative works is not the same as merely combining software on media or on computers.

2

Intellectual Property

Dominion Over Property

Software isn't *free*, as in the expression "the birds are free to fly." Software is someone's property, and you can't use another person's property—to fly or to do anything else—without that owner's permission.

And so this explanation of the law relating to software freedom actually starts with the other side of the coin, property rights.

Most people think of property as something tangible, discernible by touch. We exercise dominion over tangible land and call it our *real property.* We put personal things on our land and call that tangible stuff our *personal property.* We expect to have wide-ranging rights to use our property for our own benefit and enjoyment, with minimal interference from others. We assert that we *own* our property, and we often have the deeds or purchase receipts to prove it. We believe we have the right to prevent others from trespassing upon or taking our property.

In common usage, we also treat computer software as tangible personal property. We go to stores to *buy* software and pay for it with the same credit card we use to buy mouse pads in the next aisle. We take our new software home, put it in our computer, and it does our bidding.

But this concept of software as personal property is incomplete. There is much more to software than the disk it comes on. As one California court wrote in 1948, property is a very broad concept that includes not only the tangible but also "every intangible benefit and prerogative susceptible of possession or disposition." Computer software is this kind of intangible property because, under the law, it comes with specific but intangible benefits and prerogatives that can be separately owned and disposed of.

Software is a product of human intellect, and therefore it is a kind of *intellectual property*. Intellectual property is a valuable *property* interest, and the law allows its owner to possess and control it. The programmer who writes software—or the company that hires that person to write software—is deemed to be the first owner of intellectual property embodied in that software. That owner may exercise dominion over that intellectual property. He can give it away, sell it, or license others to use it. That owner has the prerogative to create copies of the intellectual property, and he or she may prevent others from making, using, or selling those copies.

Because of these partly tangible and partly intangible aspects of computer software, it is possible to have different owners own (1) a tangible copy of software purchased at a computer store or downloaded from a website, and (2) the intellectual property embodied in that software.

Never confuse these two aspects of intellectual property, for the laws apply differently to each.

In most respects, intellectual property law is very different from the law of both real and tangible personal property but, in at least one respect, the laws are similar. An owner of any form of real or personal property, including intellectual property, may sell or gift it, dispose of it upon his death by will or trust, or have it taken from him by a bankruptcy court. I will discuss the effects on open source software of the laws of disposition of property at the appropriate places in this book.

The first task, however, is to identify the varieties of intellectual property that can be embodied in software. That will help explain why the owners of intellectual property in software do not have unlimited rights to its exploitation and use, but they often have enough rights to protect their property from unauthorized exploitation by others.

Right Brain and Left Brain

Art is said to be the product of our right brain, the right hemisphere of our cerebral cortex that supposedly controls feelings and emotions. Scientific creations, it is said, are the product of our left brain, the left hemisphere that uses logic. Whether true or not, this bicameral description of the two products of human intellect—art and science—is useful to help us understand what we do when we create software.

Intellectual property law distinguishes these two kinds of intellectual creations. Our right brain creations are in the nature of *expression*, most often found in painting, music, fiction, and poetry. Our left brain creations are in the nature of *idea*, found in our scientific and technical innovations. Expressions are subject to *copyright* law; ideas are subject to *patent* law. (A third form of intellectual property, *trademark*, will be discussed later.)

The boundary line between expression and idea is very fuzzy in computer software. There may be two hemispheres, but there is one brain, and ultimately the software products of our creative intellect are simultaneously art and science, simultaneously expression and idea.

I remember, for example, while a graduate computer science student reading Donald Knuth's *The Art of Computer Programming*, coming to appreciate that his programs (and a few of mine) were truly works of art in ways sometimes unrelated to the functions they performed. The way Knuth expressed a particular algorithm, for example, became an object of beauty to that young computer programmer. Only someone who has written a tight computer program that does something well can appreciate how much expression goes into writing a piece of software and how emotionally rewarding that creative process can be simply because of the elegance and precision of the code.

Soon after that, I began to write software for Stanford University. As I became immersed in the practical world of grant proposals, teaching, and other university activities, I realized that the functions performed by my programs were far more important to my customers than the beauty of my code. Still later, when I moved into the high technology industry and began to worry about how commercial products are designed, manufactured, distributed, and supported, the *art* of computer programming became less and less relevant. What was essential were the functions that the software performed, the *ideas* that it implemented.

Truth be known, both perspectives are correct. When we create software, we create both *copyrightable expressions* and *patentable ideas*. The best functioning software is often the best-written software. Elegant source code usually leads to elegant software that does amazing things.

The law didn't originally allow software to be treated as intellectual property, and neither copyright nor patent laws applied to software. Finally, after much debate, in 1980 Congress decided that software should be copyrightable, and in 1981 the U.S. Supreme Court decided that software-enabled inventions should also be patentable. Federal courts and the U.S. Patent Office have since broadened patent coverage of software to include *computer readable media that store software.* This means that software is patentable. Some still complain about those decisions, but that's the law, at least in the United States.

Other countries have similar laws and policies. Readers in other countries are encouraged to ask their local attorneys for legal advice about specific differences, since some countries do not allow some kinds of software to be patented.

A low level of expressive creativity is sufficient to create copyrightable software, but the standards for obtaining a patent in software are substantially higher. Notwithstanding that difference, the laws of copyright and patent do not require that all art be at the standard of Picasso or that all ideas be at the level of Einstein. Quality of expression and profundity of idea are the province of art critics and the marketplace. To obtain a copyright you must simply be an author of an original work; to obtain a patent you must merely be the first inventor of something new, useful, and unobvious.

Acquiring Copyrights and Patents

Copyright is said to subsist in an original work of authorship. An author need not undertake any formal act—other than the act of original creation and fixation—to obtain a copyright. This applies to software as well. Any original software that is written down is automatically protected by copyright.

Formalities still may be useful. You should mark an original work with a copyright notice in the form:

© Copyright <year> <author>

Such a notice is no longer required to obtain a copyright, but it provides added protection. If you mark your software with a prominent copyright notice, a defendant can't argue that he was unaware who owned the copyright on the work. Registering a copyright isn't strictly necessary to have a copyright, but registration *is* required to initiate litigation to enforce the copyright. Furthermore, early registration provides added protection in the form of statutory damages and attorneys' fees if litigation becomes necessary to enforce the copyright. If it becomes important to do so, registration involves filling out a short form and paying a small fee (currently $30) to the Library of Congress (similar processes apply in other countries). But as a matter of law and international treaty, neither a copyright notice nor registration is required *to have* a copyright. Copyright merely subsists.

For the most part, because of international treaties, a copyright in one country is a copyright in all countries.

Obtaining patents is far more time-consuming and expensive. An application must be submitted to the patent office of each country (or group of countries) where patent protection is sought, describing with specificity the invention being claimed. Trained patent examiners review the patent application and the prior art to determine whether the claimed invention meets patentability standards. If it passes tests of novelty and unobviousness—and other legal tests relating to patentability—a patent will be issued. Even then, a patent certificate from the government provides only a presumption of validity, a presumption that can be challenged in court.

Just as with copyright notices, there are advantages to marking products with patent notices identifying specific patents. Even the phrase "Patent Pending" can be useful to alert others that patent protection is being sought. Patent notices are not a mandatory prerequisite to patent enforcement, but using them may allow a patent owner to obtain damages for infringement starting prior to the date of filing of an infringement lawsuit.

Anyone who owns a copyright or patent may license the intellectual property rights to others.

Original Works of Authorship

Open source software always starts with one or more original authors and their original works of authorship. Copyright law describes an original work in the following broad terms:

> *Copyright protection subsists ... in original works of authorship fixed in any tangible medium of expression, now known or later developed, from which they can be perceived, reproduced, or otherwise communicated, either directly or with the aid of a machine or device.... (17 U.S.C. § 102.)*

Understanding this statute may be easier if you initially broaden your perspective beyond computer software. An original work of authorship can be many things, including literary works; musical works; dramatic works; pantomimes and choreographic works; pictorial, graphic, and sculptural works; motion pictures and other audiovisual works; sound recordings; and architectural works.

Here's one example: The tune that Windows plays when it first loads is copyrightable. The author of that tune (or the author's employer) owns the copyright. The fact that it is computer software that communicates that tune through your computer speakers is irrelevant. The fact that the musical score resides not on sheet music in your piano bench but as bits and bytes on your computer disk is irrelevant. Any original work of authorship, including that ubiquitous tune announcing the start of Windows, is copyrightable.

The source code that defines a computer program is copyrightable, as is the translated object code that actually executes on the computer. It makes no difference whether the program actually works. It makes no difference what programming language was used. Software is copyrightable if it is fixed on paper, on a disk drive or a CD-ROM, or even (for those who remember those technologies) on paper tape and punched cards. When future storage mechanisms are invented, software stored on those will also be copyrightable.

Original works of authorship include things that can be "perceived, reproduced, or otherwise communicated." Thus programs downloaded from the Internet are copyrightable, as are music, movies, photographs, and any form of literary work.

Because an author of an original work of authorship may transfer the copyright by sale, gift, will, or trust, it is sometimes more appropriate to refer to the owner of a copyright rather than simply to the author of the work. Whether the copyright is held by the original author or by a successor in interest, I will often refer to that person in what follows as the copyright owner.

Works Made for Hire

Not every author is the owner of his or her original works of authorship. Many works are prepared by employees within the scope of their employment; those are *works made for hire*. In most countries, such works are owned by the employer. It is the employer who can decide whether or how to dispose of the work. The employee has no right, title, or interest in the work once the work is done. Here's what the U.S. Copyright Act says:

> *In the case of a work made for hire, the employer or other person for whom the work was prepared is considered the author..., and, unless the parties have expressly agreed otherwise in a written instrument signed by them, owns all of the rights comprised in the copyright. (17 U.S.C. § 201[b].)*

Sometimes employees create software on their own time using their own computers, software that has nothing to do with their real jobs as employees. In the United States, as long as writing that software is outside the scope of his or her employment, the employee owns the software and can dispose of it as he or she wishes.

Copyright law deals with works for hire differently in different jurisdictions, and even within the United States each state has different rules concerning ownership of employees' creations. Be careful to consult an attorney.

Not everyone who writes software for someone else is an employee. Many programmers are independent contractors who move from company to company, or from assignment to assignment, writing software on demand. In most jurisdictions, the copyrights to original works prepared by contractors are owned by the contractors themselves, unless there is a written agreement between the parties specifying otherwise.

What happens if there is no written contract? In this situation, even though a contractor owns the copyrights to software written for someone else, the person who hired the contractor to write the software will be entitled to a nonexclusive license to use the software for its intended purpose. That is because he or she paid for the work; otherwise, contractors could hold their software hostage from the very companies that paid to have it developed.

The default law regarding ownership of employee and contractor inventions in the absence of a contract varies from jurisdiction to jurisdiction. Most companies protect their own interests by executing written invention agreements with their employees and contractors in order to contractually ensure that the rules of ownership for patents are similar to those for copyrights. If you want to be sure to own your creations, consult an attorney.

Exclusive Rights of Copyright and Patent Owners

Intellectual property, like other forms of personal property, is characterized by the things that nobody else can do without the owner's permission. If you own an automobile, for example, only you can drive it—unless you give others permission to do so. It is your prerogative to do what you want with your automobile, including keeping it in your garage for private showings if you are so inclined.

So too, if you own a copyright, you have an exclusive right to do certain things with your copyrighted intellectual property that others cannot do without your permission:

- You have an exclusive right to make copies.

- You have an exclusive right to prepare derivative works.

- You have an exclusive right to distribute copies of the original work or derivative works.

- In the case of certain kinds of works, including literary, musical, and motion picture works, you have an exclusive right to perform the work publicly.

- In the case of certain kinds of works, including literary, musical, pictorial, and sculptural works, you have an exclusive right to display the work publicly.

This list of exclusive rights is found in the U.S. Copyright Act, 17 U.S.C. § 106. A similar list is found in the copyright laws of most countries.

If you own a patent, you have a right to exclude others from doing certain things with your patented intellectual property:

- You have a right to exclude others from making products embodying your patented invention.

- You have a right to exclude others from using products embodying your patented invention.

- You have a right to exclude others from selling or offering for sale products embodying your patented invention.

- You have a right to exclude others from importing products embodying your patented invention.

This list of rights is found in the U.S. Patent Act, 35 U.S.C. § 154. A similar list is found in the patent laws of most countries.

You may have noticed that I described the rights of copyright and patent in two different ways. In the case of copyright, the owner *has an exclusive right to do* certain things; in the case of a patent, the owner *has a right to exclude others from doing* certain things.

This is an important distinction. Because copyright involves the affirmative act of creating an original work of authorship, it is a simple matter to determine if someone has copied, modified, or distributed that work. The copyright owner has an exclusive right to do those things, and he or she may license those rights to others.

However, the owner of a patent does not necessarily have the exclusive right to practice his own patented invention because someone else may have invented a necessary prerequisite or broader invention. The most that a patent owner can do is prevent someone else from practicing his or her invention. The patent owner usually can't guarantee that his or her own patents are sufficient to make, use, sell or offer for sale, or import the software. Additional patent rights from third parties may be necessary.

This difference manifests itself in open source licenses by the language of the copyright and patent grants. The copyright grant is an affirmative license to copy, modify, or distribute the software owned by the licensor. The patent grant is an affirmative license to practice patents necessary to make, use, sell or offer for sale, or import the software, but only to the extent of patent claims actually owned or controlled by the licensor. Additional third-party patent rights may interfere with the right to do things with the software, and the licensor does not have authority to grant that broader license.

Copies

The author of an original work of authorship (e.g., the owner of the copyright) has the exclusive right to make (or not make) *copies* of a copyrighted work. Others must seek the permission of the author, given in legal form by a license, before they may make copies.

All of the open source licenses in this book grant an unlimited right to create copies.

> *"Copies" are material objects ... in which a work is fixed by*
> *any method now known or later developed, and from which*
> *the work can be perceived, reproduced, or otherwise commu-*
> *nicated, either directly or with the aid of a machine or de-*
> *vice. The term "Copies" includes the material object ... in*
> *which the work is first fixed. (17 U.S.C. § 101.)*

Technology is always at least one step ahead of the copy-right law, so the word *copies* isn't limited to photocopies, or to CD-ROM duplicates, or even to binary images fixed for a time in a computer's memory. Any method of copying, now known or later developed, can be used to create a copy and still meet the definition in the law.

The original of a work is merely the first copy. Any dupli-cate made from it, by any means, is a copy. Every instance of computer software, as long as it is fixed in some tangible form, is a copy.

The copyright owner of software has the exclusive right to make, or to allow others to make, copies of that software.

Exceptions to the Exclusive Right to Make Copies

There are two important exceptions under the law to the rule that the copyright owner has an exclusive right to make (or not make) copies of that work. These exceptions apply only to computer software and it reflects the unique nature of that technology.

First, everyone understands that software can be used on a computer only if it is copied onto a computer disk or into memory. Therefore, the authorized owner of a copy of software is given the right to make a copy of that software "as an essen-tial step to the utilization" of the software "in conjunction with a machine." (17 U.S.C. § 117.) Without this exception, any-one purchasing a software program at a computer store would require an additional license to copy it to a hard disk and to the computer's memory, clearly a wasteful burden for someone who merely wants to run a program he or she *bought*.

Second, software is effective only if there is a way to back it up for archival purposes. Therefore, the authorized owner of computer software is given the right to make archival copies, with the added requirement that those archival copies must be destroyed in the event that continued possession of the computer software "should cease to be rightful." (17 U.S.C. §117.)

These limited exceptions are not intended as wedges into which to drive a high-speed copy machine. These exceptions only apply to an authorized owner of a copy, someone who has a license from the copyright owner. These exceptions in the law to the exclusive rights of a copyright owner to make copies do not excuse the making of other copies not intended for these limited purposes.

Collective and Derivative Works

The terms *collective works* and *derivative works* will be the subject of more rigorous explanation later in the book. For now, it is important only to understand these terms in the context of open source software, as a way of describing what the participants in open source development and licensing actually do.

Before I define these terms, note one thing: Collective works and derivative works are also original works of authorship, and copyright subsists in them. (17 U.S.C. § 103.)

> *The subject matter of copyright as specified by section 102 includes compilations and derivative works....*
> *(17 U.S.C. § 103.)*

> *The term "compilation" includes collective works. (17 U.S.C. § 101.)*

A collective work is:

> ...*A work ... in which a number of contributions, constituting separate and independent works in themselves, are assembled into a collective whole. (17 U.S.C. § 101.)*

In the nonsoftware context, think of a collective work as an encyclopedia or an anthology. In the software context, a collective work is usually an aggregation of separately written software that is distributed as a single package or on one disk. An office productivity suite, for example, may contain separately written components such as a word processor, a spreadsheet program, and an email client. Each of those components is an original work of authorship as is the collective office suite as a whole.

The copyright in a collective work is a reflection of the originality of the collection and its organizational structure rather than of the individual components. Most software is a copyrightable collection of modules. The arrangement and organization of the collection of individual modules are often the most original aspects of a software program.

A derivative work is:

> ...*A work based upon one or more preexisting works, such as a translation...or any other form in which a work may be recast, transformed, or adapted. (17 U.S.C. § 101.)*

Since there are so many varieties of derivative works, the statute merely lists examples of derivative works, including translations, editorial revisions, elaborations, modifications, or any other form in which a work may be recast, transformed, or adapted. This leaves it for the courts to sort out whether a specific work is or is not a derivative work. How the courts do that is the topic for much later in this book. For now, in the software context, think of derivative works as programs that have been improved or enhanced from earlier versions of a program. Distributors of open source software often create successive versions containing improvements contributed by many programmers. Those successive versions are derivative works of earlier versions, and each such version is itself an original work of authorship.

It may be helpful to view ownership of open source software as being represented by a *chain of title*. An original work of authorship is the first link in the chain. That chain is elongated during the collaborative open source development process. People take original works of software, aggregate them with other such works, and make modifications, in the process creating collective and derivative works—each a new original work of authorship.

Title to each successive aggregation or modification is subject to the ownership rights of the copyright owners of the previous contributions and modifications, as each new derivative or collective work forges the next link in the chain of title.

Software improves through such aggregation and modification. This dynamic, fluid evolution of expressions and ideas in the open source community, manifested by evolving collective and derivative works, results in the creation of ever more powerful software. That process is described eloquently in Eric Raymond's book, *The Cathedral and the Bazaar.* Its observations and predictions about software quality have been proven applicable in a wide variety of open source projects. All this has been made possible by the free creation of collective and derivative works authorized by open source licensors.

The Chain of Title for Copyright

Collective and derivative works are entitled to copyrights as original works of authorship, but that doesn't mean that those copyrights replace the earlier copyrights on the component parts. Here's how the Copyright Act describes it:

> *The copyright in a compilation or derivative work extends only to the material contributed by the author of such work, as distinguished from the preexisting material employed in the work, and does not imply any exclusive right in the pre-existing material. The copyright in such work is independent of, and does not affect or enlarge the scope, duration, owner-ship, or subsistence of, any copyright protection in the exist-ing material. (17 U.S.C. § 103[b].)*

Mature open source projects often consist of software passed through many such stages of aggregation and modifica-tion, their original works of authorship proudly displaying a long chain of title including the names of many individuals and organizations that preceded them.

The term *chain of title* is most frequently used to describe ownership of real property in the United States. Starting with the original land grant from the King of England (and usually ignoring completely the previous rights of the Native Ameri-cans who long preceded the king), it is possible to trace owner-ship of each parcel of land through the generations. As land is divided, easements are granted, and children inherit from their parents, title to the land passes from one owner to another. The current owner of the land holds that land subject to the restrictions and covenants agreed to by his forebears.

The chain of title becomes important in open source licens-ing when someone wants to create a collective or derivative work of a previous work that itself consists of contributions by many people. The new authors are subject to the licenses of previous authors who preceded them, and each of those con-tributions may have different license restrictions on its use.

That ever lengthening chain of title would appear to be an increasing burden on future generations of software developers, but the problem is not nearly so complex. Depending upon the open source licenses being used, it may only be necessary for new authors to ensure that they have licenses from their immediate predecessors and not all the way back to the first programmer writing the first version of the original contribution that started the chain.

The Chain of Title for Patents

Once again, a patent is a right to exclude others from making, using, selling or offering to sell, or importing a specific claimed invention. An inventor writes his claim in precise terms in a patent application and then a patent examiner reviews the claim for patentability. Only claims that meet a legal standard will be approved. The legal standard for patentability involves arcane criteria of novelty and unobviousness for which a qualified attorney is often indispensable. Upon approval of the patent application, the inventor (or his assignee) receives a limited monopoly right to prevent unauthorized practice of his patent.

A patent differs from a copyright in a fundamental way: A copyright prevents a third party from copying or modifying the original work, but a patent restricts everyone who uses the patented invention whether the invention has been copied or not. Even someone who independently creates the same invention and doesn't copy the first inventor still cannot make, use, sell or offer for sale, or import the patented invention because he's not the first inventor. It makes no difference whether the second inventor even knew of the first invention.

As with any other form of intellectual personal property, patent rights can be sold or given away, inherited, lost in bankruptcy, or licensed. In that sense, there can be a chain of title for a patent just like there is for a piece of real property. It is often possible to trace that chain of title using public documents on file with the government patent office.

Unlike copyright rights to *collective* and *derivative* works that are subject to the prior licenses for each of the contributions and modifications that preceded them, a patent has only one current owner we must worry about. (There may actually be multiple inventors or owners of a patent, or different owners of the exclusive rights in a patent. For our purposes, we can treat those multiple owners as one person.) There is no concept of a collective or derivative work in patent law. One either infringes a patent or one doesn't.

Before you can implement a patent claim in software, you need to determine who actually owns the relevant patent rights and whether you have a license to practice it. The patent owner may be the original author of the copyrighted work from which you're creating a collective or derivative work, but it may also be someone entirely different, perhaps someone neither you nor the copyright owner ever heard of before.

It is a complex and enormously expensive task to find all relevant patent claims and analyze them to determine whether you have the right to make, use, sell or offer for sale, or import your software. It is no wonder that most software authors—open source ones and proprietary ones—don't devote the time or money needed to undertake that search and analysis. They often merely wait to be surprised by bad news. If a patent claim by a third party is asserted against your software, you can simply stop using the patented invention, or challenge its validity in the patent office or in court. Another obvious choice is to seek a license to the patent.

A patent license can be narrow or broad, specific to a particular implementation, or broad enough to cover any possible implementation of the patent. Depending upon the specific terms of the patent license, it may not include the right to implement the patent in a collective or derivative work. There is no *free software* or *open source* definition for a patent license, and so each license must be analyzed to determine whether its terms are compatible with such software.

At least in theory, you must obtain a license from any patent owner whose patents are practiced in any software you make, use, sell or offer for sale, or import. In practice, hardly anyone bothers until it is too late. As I discuss various open source licenses later in this book, I will explain how each license handles—or doesn't handle—this potential patent problem.

Joint Works

Open source prides itself on being a cooperative development process. Communities of engineers work together over the Internet to write software. In this way, they may create collective works. But they may also, without realizing the difference, create an entirely different kind of work: The result of collaborative development may become a *joint work* rather than a *collective work*.

> A "joint work" is a work prepared by two or more authors
> with the intention that their contributions be merged into
> inseparable or interdependent parts of a unitary whole. (17
> U.S.C. § 101.)

Obviously, joint authors of a work don't have to collaborate on each word of the final product. They can divide their activities to create a unified work—perhaps chapter by chapter, perhaps plot line by plot line, perhaps one writes the music and the other the words, perhaps they cooperate in more subtle ways. They may intentionally decide not to reveal which author did which portion of the work. Joint authors usually manifest their intent to create a joint work by documenting in a contract between them the specific relationship that they intend to forge while working together on the work. Proof that something is a joint work requires proof of the intention of the authors, but that proof isn't always easy to provide for the authors who contribute to informal open source projects.

There is a very important legal difference between a collective work and a joint work. Each contribution to a collective work is owned by its author, and that author has the exclusive right to decide how that contribution is to be licensed. A contribution to a joint work is owned by all of its authors jointly.

In the United States, unless they agree otherwise, each of the joint authors may separately license a joint work—and all of its parts—without the consent of any of the other joint authors, and every author must account to the other authors for their share of the profits derived from the license. Consult local law to determine whether one owner of a joint work may license without the consent of the others or must account to the others for his or her licensing revenue.

For most projects, whether the software is a collective work or a joint work will be unimportant as long as the contributors all continue to agree on a licensing strategy. Only when disagreements occur and the licensing strategy is to be changed— what in open source circles is called *relicensing*—does it matter how the parties formally agreed to collaborate.

Relicensing a joint work is, in some ways, easier than relicensing a collective work because any one of the authors can do it without consulting the others, but it may leave some contributors angry with the results.

Assigning Ownership

This book is about licensing, but there is an alternative to licensing that is occasionally employed by open source projects to ensure that the projects themselves have the right to license contributions. Authors are encouraged to *assign* their entire ownership interest in open source software (and occasionally the ownership interest in any patents embodied in that software) directly to the project. This *assignment* is an effective way to ensure that the project itself has the authority to license the software.

You will recall that the owner of intellectual property may dispose of it as if it were real or personal property, including by sale or gift. Once transferred to a new owner, it is the new owner who has the exclusive rights described in this chapter.

This technique of copyright assignment is generally neither useful nor necessary, because an open source license can convey all rights as effectively as an assignment. There are only a few limited occasions when an assignment is preferable.

First, as I shall explain more fully in Chapter 12 on open source litigation, only the owner of a copyright, or an exclusive right under copyright, or the owner or exclusive licensee of a patent right (e.g., in an explicit territory or field of use) has the right to sue to enforce those rights or licenses. (17 U.S.C. § 501[b]; 35 U.S.C. § 281.) Second, since intellectual property is inheritable upon death of the owner, the owner may prefer to assign a valuable copyright or patent rather than burden his heirs with something they may not understand, appreciate, or know how to manage.

Copyright law in the United States requires that copyright assignments be in writing. (17 U.S.C. § 204[a].) Similar provisions apply to patent assignments. (35 U.S.C. § 261.) As an exercise in legal drafting, an assignment usually includes the formalities needed to satisfy the writing and filing requirements of copyright and patent law.

One risk to the original author of assigning a copyright is that the author loses the right to license it yet again under different terms to different licensees. (I discuss dual licensing strategies in Chapter 11.) Once copyright ownership is assigned, the new owner has the exclusive right to decide on licensing strategies, and the original owner has no rights left (unless he or she receives a license-back, about which I will say nothing more in this book).

Another risk of assignment is that many open source projects have informal structures, often without a legal corporate entity behind them. Assigning a copyright to an informal entity leaves in doubt just who has the authority to commit to licensing decisions. Indeed, if a project makes licensing decisions that the original copyright owner dislikes, that original owner will have no legal basis to object and will be obligated to honor the express provisions of the written assignment that he or she signed.

Other than the infrequent situations described above, there is little advantage to open source projects to receive assignment of copyrights and patents. Everything that an open source project needs, including the rights to make copies, create derivative works, and distribute the software, is provided by any of the open source licenses described in this book as readily as by an assignment. Contributors and the open source projects that receive those contributions can usually accomplish their objectives with an open source license instead of an assignment.

Since a license accomplishes much the same thing in open source as an assignment, I will not bother describing the special language that would be needed for an assignment to make

it legally effective. Nor will I describe how to draft an assignment that includes a license-back to the original owner. These
are questions best directed to your own attorney.

Duration of Copyright and Patent

There is another fundamental difference between most
forms of real and personal property and the intellectual property embodied in software. Real and personal property rights
generally last forever, but copyrights and patents are tempo-
rary ownership rights that terminate with the passage of time.

In the United States, the Constitution mandates that such
rights shall be granted "for limited times," a particularly vague
provision that allows Congress to define and change the terms
of the copyright and patent monopolies, which it frequently
does. Current U.S. law provides that, for new works, copyrights last for the life of the author plus 70 years or, for a work
of corporate authorship, the shorter of 95 years from publication or 120 years from creation. New patents last for 20 years
from the date the patent application is filed.

Upon expiration of the term of a copyright or patent, the
intellectual property is said to pass into the *public domain*. The
once exclusive rights of the owners of that intellectual property
become available for exercise by anyone who wants them,
freely and without charge.

The word *freely* is used here in a different way than when I
was describing *software freedom* in the open source definition.
Freedom under an open source license may be limited and
conditioned by the copyright and patent owners. But once
intellectual property enters the public domain, its owner can
no longer restrict its exploitation and use in any way.

Through the passage of time, the intellectual works of
Shakespeare, Mozart, and Newton have long since passed into

the public domain. That intellectual property is completely free for anyone to use. But the *free* intellectual property of Linux and Apache is still subject to the terms and conditions set by the owners of those original works of authorship, because those copyrights have not yet expired.

It is incorrect to suggest that open source licensing destroys intellectual property or is inconsistent with intellectual property laws. Quite the opposite. Open source software is owned by individuals and companies under the authority of the copyright and patent laws. Those owners license their software to the public. It is not public domain software. Or at least, it won't be public domain software until the copyrights and patents embodied in the software expire by the slow passage of time, as specified in the intellectual property laws.

Trademarks

It was presumptuous of me to suggest earlier in this chapter that the only two brains involved in creating successful software products are the right brain of copyright and the left brain of patent. This leaves out what is sometimes the most important brain of all—the one that captures consumer attention through effective marketing.

Often the keys to marketing success for open source projects are their product or brand names, or trademarks. More specifically, a trademark is a word, phrase, symbol, or design, or a combination of words, phrases, symbols, or designs that identify and distinguish the source of the goods of one person or company from those of others.

Trademarks are a form of intellectual property. Trademarks are owned, and they can be licensed. Consider, for example, the brand name *Linux*, a registered trademark owned by Linus Torvalds for:

*Computer operating system software to facilitate
computer use and operation. (U.S. Trademark
1916230.)*

It is inevitable that more people recognize the Linux operating system by its trademark than would recognize even a single line of its copyrightable code or any patent claims it embodies. The success of Linux in the marketplace, while made possible by the underlying copyrightable and patentable subject matter, is largely now due to good brand recognition and the aura of accomplishment that the brand engenders in the public. As long as the contributors and distributors responsible for Linux software continue to focus on quality and reliability, the Linux brand name will prosper.

Other open source projects and companies also rely on trademark protection. Brand names such as Apache, MySQL, Open Office, JBoss, Red Hat, and Debian identify quality products to open source customers. And now that major software companies are becoming open source contributors and distributors, brand names like IBM, HP, Apple, Sun, Oracle, Novell, and Nokia adorn open source products.

As a matter of trademark law, a trademark would be lost if it were licensed under typical open source license terms. This is because a trademark owner must maintain control over the quality of the goods bearing his or her trademark when the trademark is licensed to others. But an open source licensor cannot control the quality of the licensees' derivative works. (Open Source Principle # 3.)

Because of that incompatibility between trademark law and open source principles, no open source license includes a trademark license. Some open source licenses even contain an explicit exclusion of trademark license. I will discuss such provisions in due course.

Exceptions to Intellectual Property Protection

Not everything in software is subject to copyright or patent protection. It is possible to write software that is not protected by either. For our present purposes, these are the two most important exceptions:

1. You cannot use copyright law to prevent someone from practicing the underlying ideas in the software. Copyright protects only expression. If there is only one way to implement an idea in software, anyone can copy the software unless it is also protected by patent (or by a trade secrecy restriction, something that never applies to open source software whose source code is published).

2. Before you can use patent law to prevent someone from practicing the underlying ideas in the software, you must actually apply for and obtain a valid patent. That can be both expensive and difficult. The validity of a patent can be challenged in court. If the author of the software doesn't have a patent, anyone can build equivalent software from scratch without asking the original author's permission.

These exceptions to copyright and patent, and a few others, often become important in intellectual property litigation. Authors of software always claim that they own intellectual property in the form of copyrights and patents, but at the end of the day, they may still have to prove in court that their software isn't one of those unprotected exceptions. I'll describe how that plays out in court when I discuss open source litigation in Chapter 12.

3

Distribution of Software

Contributors and Distributors

Open source software is written by computer programmers who generously distribute it to their friends, employers, or customers. Often these programmers work for companies that aggregate code written by many programmers into a functional whole; those companies then distribute the aggregated work to the world. Important computer software is usually too big and complicated to be written by one person acting alone—although each component of software always starts with one person acting alone—and it almost always requires collaboration and joint development.

This is not a unique process to open source. Commercial software has long been created and distributed collaboratively. What is unique about the open source process is that once software has been licensed under an open source license, the collaborative process is no longer tied to a single individual or company. Because software freedom is promised by every open source license, users are free to take control of the software and do whatever they want with it. Everyone is free to become a contributor to or distributor of open source software, starting from anyone's open source software. At least that is the promise, although incompatibilities between open source licenses are preventing that goal from being completely met. License compatibility is discussed in Chapter 10.

Distribution

I have thus far used the word *distribution* as if it had obvious meaning in the software world. Certainly it means selling or giving copies of software away to others. It also may include such arrangements as incorporating software into consumer or industrial products and selling those products to others. For some software, it may also include making the software available across a network for execution by others.

In the proprietary software world, before a company may become a distributor it must negotiate a formal business arrangement with the owner of the software. These contracts typically establish marketing arrangements, territorial limitations, pricing structures, and other business terms.

None of this is needed for open source software. Because of the objective to provide software freedom as specified in the open source definition, the distribution of open source software cannot be restricted in those ways. (See Open Source Principles # 2 and 3.) An open source license must grant everyone permission to make copies, to create derivative works, and to distribute those copies and derivative works. Anyone, anywhere, for any reason, may become a distributor of open source software.

There may be no time, place, or manner limitations on distribution in an open source license—but this does not mean that there may be no conditions on distribution at all. Open source licenses may condition the distribution of derivative works on reciprocity of licensing, an important device first used in the GPL. (Reciprocal licenses are introduced in Chapter 6.) Certain open source licenses include an obligation to provide a reference implementation of derivative works that are distributed, so that standards can be enforced. (The Sun Industry Standards License is discussed in Chapter 13.) And finally, open source licenses can use their own definitions of the term *distribution* to include or exclude network execution of software, the so-called *application service provider* exception. (The OSL and AFL licenses described in Chapter 9 have such a provision.) These qualifications and limitations to the term *distribution* are explained in due course when specific open source licenses are described.

Open Source Collaboration

Open source software is distinguished from most other commercial software because its development frequently takes place collaboratively among many individual developers, working alone or for different companies, without contracts or other formal arrangements among them. Worldwide communities of software engineers dynamically form and grow on the Internet. Participants discuss among themselves what needs to be implemented; allocate the design, programming, and documentation tasks to those who volunteer to do them; and eventually publish one or more working programs for all to use. That is how major open source programs like the Linux operating system and the Apache web server were initially developed.

In the case of Linux, that open source development project is coordinated by an overall project leader, Linus Torvalds. The Linux team and Torvalds evaluate the quality of contributions they receive from around the world, and they decide whether to include those contributions as a part of Linux. The Linux project has formal mechanisms for evaluating and testing contributions, and there is a collective rather than dictatorial decision process, as befits the importance of Linux to the computing community and the collaborative bent of the project leaders.

Torvalds continues to lead the Linux development project. He effectively controls the main intellectual property of the Linux operating system, such as the Linux trademark, although many thousands of programmers and companies are always deeply involved in its development and distribution.

In contrast, a board of directors coordinates the development activities of the Apache Software Foundation, a non-profit corporation that is the distributor of the Apache web server and many other open source packages. Many of the leaders of the Apache project work for software companies that donate their employees' time and software to the Apache Foundation. Important decisions relating to Apache are decided by open vote and consensus.

These are only two of a wide variety of successful open source development models. Many open source projects are now managed by private companies that have found ways to turn software freedom into profitable enterprises, and by non-profit foundations that serve the "public interest." But that remarkable and evolving story is not the subject of this book. Open source business models are topics for other books entirely.

Contributors to open source software can be individuals or companies. Their contributions are combined at the project level with the contributions of other individuals and companies into larger works. Those larger open source works, with their many contributions, are then distributed to the public. Some companies take software distributed by open source projects and aggregate it still further into their own open source products, which they then distribute. A single operating system like Linux, a single web server like Apache, or a single commercial product like a cell phone or a television recorder that includes Linux and Apache may be the result of many contributions by many original authors and distributors along the way.

It is not always easy to distinguish between a contributor and a distributor of open source software, because people aggregate software into larger systems at each step of the development and distribution process. A distributor becomes a contributor to the next higher level of the food chain, just as fish in the ocean become food for larger fish.

The roles and rules for contributors and developers, sometimes the same and sometimes different, are important topics for open source licensing to which I shall return frequently.

Contributor Agreements

Why do contributors contribute? There are certainly as many answers to that question as there are contributors. But one thing is certain: People contribute to open source projects whose goals they share. There is usually camaraderie among project members, whether the project is structured as a loose confederation, a formal nonprofit corporation, or a corporate-sponsored activity. When camaraderie fails—for either technical or personal reasons—projects may fork into rival projects. Open source contributors are free to join either fork or leave altogether. Such forks, by the way, have proven to be very rare in open source projects.

Contributors may leave a project but their contributions remain. Once software is made available to a project under an open source license, the project may continue to copy the software, create derivative works from it, and distribute it even after the contributor's participation ends. That is because open source licenses are perpetual, even though most licenses don't expressly say so. As long as the project continues to honor the terms of the licenses under which it received contributions, the licenses continue in effect. There is one important caveat: Even a perpetual license can be revoked. See the discussion of bare licenses and contracts in Chapter 4.

For most projects, receiving contributions under an appropriate open source license from the contributor provides more than enough authority to do what they need to incorporate the contribution into the project's software. That, after all, is what the Open Source Principles stand for.

As long as each contributor's license is compatible with the project's open source license used for its distributions, then the contributor/distributor food chain evolves as I described in the previous section. This is always the case when identical licenses are used for contributions and for the project's derivative works. For example, if a project accepts contributions under the BSD license, it can then license derivative works under the BSD license; if it accepts contributions under the GPL, it can then license derivative works under the GPL.

But compatibility encompasses much more than simply identical licenses. A contributor license for his contribution is compatible with a project license for its collective or derivative work if the contributor's license contains no terms or conditions that would conflict with the terms and conditions of the project's license. Determining whether two licenses have conflicting terms and conditions requires a provision by provision comparison of the two licenses.

That comparison must be analyzed separately in each direction. For example, as I shall describe later, a contributor license like the BSD license is compatible with the other project licenses in this book, including the GPL, but the converse is not true; contributions licensed under GPL cannot be used in BSD-licensed projects. Incompatibility may exist in both directions; GPL-licensed contributions cannot be used by the

Apache project and Apache-licensed contributions cannot be used by GPL projects. I will have much more to say about license compatibility in Chapter 10.

What happens if a project decides that it wants to use a contribution in a way that is incompatible with the terms of the contributor's license? The answer is obvious: The project is bound by the terms of the licenses under which it receives contributions. In general, if the contributor's license is incompatible with the project's open source license, then the project cannot use the contribution.

Open source projects are usually not the owners of the copyrights in the contributions to them, and they have no right to change those licensing terms on their own. Sometimes, to ensure that they have freedom to choose licensing terms, open source projects seek to own the copyrights in contributions made to them, or to enter into written agreement with contributors that expressly allows the projects to decide license terms for contributions. These contributor agreements take the form of copyright and patent assignments that actually transfer ownership of the intellectual property, or broad license grants much more comprehensive than the open source licenses in this book. License compatibility is not an issue for projects that are copyright and patent owners, because the contributors no longer have any right to refuse the projects' licensing decisions for contributions the contributors no longer own.

What happens, then, if an open source project faces an actual relicensing decision but it doesn't own the copyrights and patents in its contributions? For compatible relicensing, no additional license is necessary. But it must obtain the agreement of the contributors to any relicensing that is incompatible with the terms of the license it received from its contributors.

Who should have the right to make future licensing decisions about contributions, the project or the contributor? There is no single answer to this question in the open source community. In fields other than software, this issue has long been a fruitful source of litigation. Musicians and artists have often fought against their own publishers, to whom they once willingly assigned their copyrights, trying to regain those valuable rights for other markets. In recent years, contributors to newspaper articles fought against their own publishers for the rights to republish their articles in new online forums. These cases often turn on the interpretation of contributor agreements. Of course, had they been handled as copyright or patent assignments, no rights would remain and the musicians, artists, and newspaper writers would have been without recourse regardless of what decisions their publishers made.

I personally don't want to give up too much control to my publisher. When the words are mine, I want to own them. I will license them to everyone under an appropriate open source license, but I will not give them away to someone else who can then elect to take them private or license them in ways of which I don't approve. This is true no matter how much I like my publisher, and no matter how much I want to save my publisher from having to worry about future relicensing problems.

This is obviously just my own opinion about an issue of copyright policy. Each contributor of intellectual property to a project or to a publisher must decide for himself how many rights—and therefore how much control—to give away. Beyond this I will not advise and will merely proceed to explain the various kinds of open source licenses that projects adopt. If you intend to contribute to an open source project and it presents you with a contributor agreement different from an open source license, make sure you read it carefully and consult an attorney if you are unsure what you're being asked to give away.

What about Users?

I will begin in Chapter 4 to explain the broad categories of open source licenses—particularly academic and reciprocal licenses—that are available today. I follow that in Chapters 5 through 9 with detailed license descriptions of the major open source licenses.

Fortunately for *users* of open source software, none of the distinctions between academic and reciprocal licenses, or among the various project and company licenses described in this book, matter much. Individual *users* don't often have to concern themselves with the intricate conditions of these licenses, or warranties, or patent defenses, or other esoteric legal issues. Users of open source software typically do not create and distribute derivative works, so a reciprocity provision does not apply to them.

For these reasons, mere users of open source software can safely ignore the rest of this book. Open source software is completely free for users. All open source software, whether licensed under academic or reciprocal licenses, can be freely used by anyone, anywhere, for any purpose whatsoever. Copies of that software can be made without payment of additional royalties to the licensor and, for the most part, without concern about the specific license terms.

4

Taxonomy of Licenses

What Is a License?

I've used the word *license* quite loosely in the preceding chapters, waiting for an opportune time to explain that word from a legal perspective. In one sense, a license is a permission to do something. The government issues licenses, such as a license to drive a vehicle on the public right of way or a license to run a business, pursuant to laws regulating such activities. The government tells you that you may not drive a car or engage in business without an appropriate license. You are required to obey the traffic laws and the laws regulating businesses, although the license you bought has nothing to do with those obligations. If you exceed the speed limit or if you engage in a fraudulent business practice, you can be penalized even if you didn't bother to get an appropriate license.

An owner of a private property right can grant licenses to allow others to exercise property rights that otherwise would be exclusive to the property owner. For example, the owner of beachfront property can license a telescope club to pass onto the beach to witness a solar eclipse. (There are subtle differences between this kind of license and an easement that grants access to real property, about which nothing more will be said in this book.) Such licenses can be limited as to time. They may grant rights only to specific people or to the public as a whole.

In this book, the term *license* is used to describe the legal way a copyright and patent owner grants permission to others to use his intellectual property.

An *open source license* is the way a copyright and patent owner grants permission to others to use his intellectual property in such a way that *software freedom* is protected for all.

A *proprietary license* is the way a copyright or patent owner grants permission to others to use his intellectual property in a restricted way, through secrecy or other limitations, so that software freedom is not protected.

The word *proprietary* is often confused with the word *commercial*. But a *commercial license* – which is merely a term used to describe a license used in commerce – can be either open source or proprietary.

Licenses can be express or implied. An express license is typically a written document that is reviewed and agreed to by the owner of the licensed property (the *licensor*) and by the receiver of the license grant (the *licensee*). All of the licenses described in this book contain at least some express written terms and conditions.

A license may also be implied by the kind of license being granted, by the conduct of the licensor, or by the licensor's apparent refusal to exercise its exclusive rights to the licensed property. In one very important example, some open source licenses say nothing about a grant of patent license, leaving the patent license to implication.

Be careful about implied licenses. An implied license is necessarily vague and incomplete. The terms and conditions of an implied license may not be clear to either the licensor or the licensee. Reliance on an implied license is particularly risky when important property interests are at stake.

Bare Licenses

I now address a topic that is a kind of Heisenberg Uncertainty Principle of open source: Are open source licenses bare licenses or are they contracts? The answer to this question depends on how you look and what you're trying to measure. Open source licenses, it turns out, can be both bare licenses and contracts. Adding to the confusion, the parties to open source licenses are typically referred to as *licensor* and *licensee* regardless of whether the licenses are bare licenses or contracts.

Among the examples I cited in the previous section was one about drivers' licenses. A driver's license is issued by a government agency, but it does not constitute an agreement of any sort between the driver and the agency. There is no contract; the driver's license is merely a permission slip. The licensor has made no promises and neither has the licensee.

Private parties also can grant licenses. In the software licensing context this is what we mean:

> *Bare license: A grant by the holder of a copyright or patent to another of any of the rights embodied in the copyright or patent short of an assignment of all rights. (Merriam-Webster's Dictionary of Law 1996.)*

It is possible for a copyright owner to grant a license to copy, modify, and distribute software without signing a contract between the parties. The argument goes like this: Since those exclusive rights cannot be exercised without the permission of the copyright owner, a licensee must either obey the terms of the license or not exercise the rights. Anything else is copyright or patent infringement.

Here is how one open source license, the GPL, expresses this point:

> *You are not required to accept this License, since you have*
> *not signed it. However, nothing else grants you permission to*
> *modify or distribute the Program or its derivative works.*
> *These actions are prohibited by law if you do not accept this*
> *License. Therefore, by modifying or distributing the Pro-*
> *gram (or any work based on the Program), you indicate your*
> *acceptance of this License to do so, and all its terms and con-*
> *ditions for copying, distributing, or modifying the Program*
> *or works based on it. (GPL section 5.)*

This reference to *acceptance* in the GPL involves a concept from contract law. Quite simply, a contract cannot be formed unless there is both an offer (from the licensor) and acceptance (by a licensee). Licensees are not required to accept the GPL, and if they don't accept, a contract is not formed. But a bare license has been granted—a bare license that ceases to exist if the terms and conditions are not obeyed.

The law governing an open source license in the absence of a contract is the Copyright Act, Title 17, of the U.S. Code, the equivalent laws of other countries, and international copyright treaties. To the extent that patent rights are implicated, the law governing the license is the Patent Act, Title 35, of the U.S. Code, the equivalent laws of other countries, and international patent treaties.

Those laws forbid anyone from exercising the exclusive rights of a copyright or patent owner without a license. If such a person doesn't have a license, he is an infringer subject to substantial penalties. (See Chapter 12 for a discussion of open source litigation.)

One problem with treating open source licenses as bare licenses is that intellectual property law does not say much about how to interpret license terms. Attorneys and courts are familiar with licenses that are contracts and they regularly apply the well-developed law of contracts to handle issues of license interpretation. In the absence of contract law, there is no ready framework for license language interpretation.

This practical interpretation problem can take many forms. When a license like the GPL doesn't even demand acceptance, can a licensor assume that licensees have agreed to all of those terms? What about terms that are inconsistent with consumer protection laws such as certain warranty disclaimers? What about terms in a license that are inconsistent with the definitions of terms of art in copyright law, such as derivative work or distribution? If there is no express agreement by the parties to a common set of terms and conditions, can the licensor's interpretation of the terms and conditions be enforced against the licensee? Did the licensee accept the differing definitions?

There is no body of cases and statutes to help us answer those questions. In the absence of a contract, the terms and conditions of a bare license may be subject to varying court interpretations around the world. Some legal scholars even argue that terms and conditions of bare licenses like the GPL are completely unenforceable, although the legitimacy of the GPL has never been tested in any court. Neither have any other open source licenses. This vague uncertainty hovering over bare licenses like the GPL has not been much of an obstacle to the adoption of GPL-licensed software, but it is unpleasant for attorneys nonetheless.

Another practical problem with bare copyright licenses is that only the owners of copyrights and patents can enforce those copyrights and patents in court. The cause of action for a refusal to comply with the terms and conditions of a bare copyright or patent license is just infringement rather than also breach of contract. This causes open source distributors to concern themselves with "who owns the copyrights or patents," rather than "who licensed this software." (This topic is also discussed more fully in Chapter 12.)

A third problem with bare licenses is that they may be revocable by the licensor. Specifically, *a license not coupled with an interest may be revoked.* The term *interest* in this context usually means the payment of some royalty or license fee, but there are other more complicated ways to satisfy the interest requirement. For example, a licensee can demonstrate that he or she has paid some consideration–a contract law term not found in copyright or patent law–in order to avoid revocation. Or a licensee may claim that he or she relied on the software licensed under an open source license and now is dependent upon that software, but this contract law concept, called promissory estoppel, is both difficult to prove and unreliable in court tests. (The concepts of *consideration* and *promissory estoppel* are explained more fully in the next section.) Unless the courts allow us to apply these contract law principles to a license, we are faced with a bare license that is revocable.

Most of those issues about bare licenses have never been addressed directly in a court so lawyers have no good way to predict how they will ultimately be answered. In the absence of a court decision interpreting bare open source copyright licenses, distributors of software under such licenses should ask their attorneys whether they have adequate protection.

In my opinion, it is safer for a licensor and his licensees to enter into enforceable contracts. That usually doesn't require any changes to the license text; it only requires that the license be offered and accepted as a contract, and that there be an understanding between the parties about the consideration paid for the license.

Licenses as Contracts

Read in a different light, open source licenses contain promises, just like ordinary contracts. In effect, each licensor promises, subject to certain terms and conditions, not to interfere with licensees who copy, modify, distribute, make, use, and sell open source software embodying the licensor's intellectual property. Licensees rely on those promises when they adopt open source software to do useful things.

Many open source licenses are designed as contracts.

> *A contract is a promise or set of promises for breach of which the law gives a remedy, or the performance of which the law in some way recognizes as a duty. (Restatement, Second, Contracts § 3.)*

> *A promise is a manifestation of intent to act or refrain from acting in a specified way, so made as to justify a promisee in understanding that a commitment has been made. (Restatement, Second, Contracts § 2.)*

I'll discuss later in this book the specific promises made (express and implied) in open source licenses. In particular, there are software licenses called *unilateral contracts*, in which only the licensor makes promises, and other licenses called *bilateral contracts*, in which both parties make promises. Most open source licenses are unilateral in intent. (Even lawyers who draft licenses are sometimes confused by these concepts; you will occasionally find terms of art, such as "licensee agrees" promissory language appropriate for *bilateral* contracts, in otherwise *unilateral* contracts.) For now, it is important only to identify the differences between a bare license and a contract.

Contract law, unlike copyright and patent law, provides procedures and rules for license interpretation and enforcement. Contract law, in the published court decisions and in the statutes adopted by legislatures around the world, addresses almost every possible term or condition a lawyer could dream up for a contract. Contract law specifies how contracts are to be formed, how they are to be interpreted, how they are to be enforced, and the remedies for breach. In many situations, where a license is silent about a particular term or condition, contract law even provides default "fill-in" provisions.

Some suggest that since contract law varies around the world, open source contributors and distributors should rely exclusively on consistent copyright and patent law for their licenses. But the varieties of contract law are exaggerated, as are the similarities of copyright and patent law around the world. The global requirement for consistency of commercial transactions—a requirement of the capitalist market system—helps ensure that contracts are interpreted in much the same way around the world. Meanwhile copyright law is *not* consistent; the courts around the world, for example, don't agree on what constitutes a derivative work of software. That is why it is sometimes better for an open source contract to define the term *derivative work* than to have a bare license simply use that term of art as if it had a consistent meaning worldwide.

Unlike a bare license, a contract can be enforced by a licensor even if he doesn't own the underlying copyrights and patents. This means that a distributor of software can enforce his contract against his licensees without needing the approval of the copyright and patent owner(s) to do so. For open source software containing original software contributed by programmers worldwide, it can be particularly important for a distributor to be able to enforce his licenses even without owning the underlying patents or copyrights.

Finally, the generally accepted rule that *the contract is the law* encourages us to create complete licenses that state the terms and conditions as clearly as we want. We don't have to rely on vague interpretations of copyright or patent law since we can write the law-of-the-contract exactly as we want it to be enforced. For example, later in this book I will describe two recent open source licenses, the Academic Free License (AFL) and the Open Software License (OSL), that specify in contract form and in clear and precise terms the rules for open source licensing. Those licenses—one an academic license and the other a reciprocal license, but otherwise identical—are intended to be enforceable under both contract and copyright law.

The main difference between a bare license and a contract is in the way the relationship between licensor and licensee is formed. To create a contract, there must be an offer and acceptance, and there must be consideration. I will describe these three elements in turn. (In first-year contract law courses, these elements are often referred to as the *legs of a stool;* a contract is the seat of the stool; it will fall if any of the legs—offer, acceptance, or consideration–fails.)

None of these three elements is needed for a bare license.

Offer

An *offer* is fairly simple in the software licensing context.

> *An offer is a manifestation of willingness to enter into a bargain so made as to justify another person in understanding that his assent to that bargain is invited and will conclude it. (Restatement, Second, Contracts § 24.)*

In an open source license, the licensor offers to allow licensees to copy, modify, and distribute the licensed software for any purpose whatsoever in accordance with the Open Source Principles in Chapter 1.

The appropriate manifestation of willingness required for an offer can be (and often is) expressed by posting the software on some Internet portal like SourceForge or on a public website in such a way that all prospective licensees will be able to retrieve the software under the terms of the license. Open source distributors offer licenses to everyone.

Acceptance

The offer empowers the licensee to create a contract by his acceptance. The second step in forming a contract, then, is for the licensee to accept it. He must *intend* to accept it.

Traditionally, a signed written agreement is evidence of both offer and acceptance, but that is no longer practical with the mass marketing of software. The most typical way to obtain acceptance of a software license is to require licensees to express their assent in a positive way, such as by making a purchaser of boxed software open an inner package that boldly announces the presence of the license (known as *shrink-wrap*), or by making someone who downloads software click on an "I ACCEPT" button on a website (known as *click-wrap*). Many courts around the world now agree that clicking on "I ACCEPT" or tearing the shrink-wrap is ample evidence that the licensee accepted the contract.

The law doesn't require shrink-wrap or click-wrap. Indeed, for many forms of software distribution and installation, neither of those specific techniques is appropriate. Any acceptance procedure that ensures an explicit manifestation of assent is usually sufficient. Even that is difficult to accomplish when open source software is merely posted and distributed on the Internet. So it is important to understand the implications of not obtaining an *explicit manifestation of assent* up front. There are three alternative situations:

- Both parties can later affirm that they intended to form a contract and agree to abide by its terms and conditions. That subsequent stipulation suffices to prove acceptance. (The courts won't care as long as the parties agree among themselves.)

- The licensor wants out of the contract: In the case of a unilateral contract (such as almost all the open source licenses in this book) in which the licensor is the only one making promises, the subsequent testimony of the licensee that he intended to accept the contract and that he acted in reliance on it is usually sufficient evidence of acceptance even if the licensor now wants out of the contract.

- The licensee wants out of the contract: As long as the licensor wants to enforce the contract, the licensor has the burden of proving that a contract was formed. This situation demonstrates why licensors should demand an explicit manifestation of assent that they can introduce as evidence if necessary.

Consideration

The third requirement for contract formation, consideration, is often the most complicated.

(1) To constitute consideration, a performance or a return promise must be bargained for.

(2) A performance or return promise is bargained for if it is sought by the promisor in exchange for his promise and is given by the promisee in exchange for that promise.

(3) The performance may consist of (a) an act other than a promise, or (b) a forbearance, or (c) the creation, modification, or destruction of a legal relation. (Restatement, Second, Contracts, § 71.)

If the requirement of consideration is met, there is no additional requirement of (a) a gain, advantage, or benefit to the promisor or a loss, disadvantage, or detriment to the promisee; or (b) equivalence in the values exchanged; or (c) mutuality of obligation. (Restatement, Second, Contracts, § 79.)

Taken together, these two legal principles from the Restatement prevent the enforcement of a *gift*, which may have both offer and acceptance but lacks the element of consideration. Section 79 in particular makes it clear that the value of the consideration, while it can't be zero, doesn't need to be very large at all. Early legal scholars made the point that a peppercorn could be sufficient consideration for a contract.

To cut to the chase, I'll refer to the following Simple License:

The copyright owner of this software hereby licenses it to you for any purpose whatsoever.

This is, of course, a bare license. Like any bare license, it is enforceable by the copyright owner under copyright law and can be revoked by the licensor at any time.

Assume, now, that we want this Simple License to be treated as a contract so that it can be enforced under contract law and so that it cannot be revoked. Assume also that we have satisfied the procedural requirements for offer and acceptance. Where can we find consideration in the language of the Simple License?

Laws in some jurisdictions provide that specified types of promises are enforceable without consideration. This is usually restricted to certain commercial transactions and written contracts. While it is not common now, the growth of the open source software industry may eventually demand that, by statute, the grant of a written license to computer software in commercial settings creates an enforceable contract between licensor and licensee even in the absence of consideration. Without such a legal exception, however, we must find consideration or we don't have a contract.

Perhaps we can look deeper into the Simple License to find consideration, even though *consideration* isn't among the express words of the license. Consideration might be implied.

The licensor's detriment is an implied result of copyright law. The licensor has licensed the otherwise exclusive rights under copyright, and as to that licensor, forbearance to enforce those exclusive rights is detriment (e.g., consideration) enough.

What about consideration or detriment by the licensee?

The easiest way for the licensee to ensure that the Simple License can be enforced as a contract is if he pays a royalty or license fee for the software to be used, copied, modified, and distributed. It needn't be much, and perhaps a penny is sufficient, but there must be consideration by the licensee or there is no contract. (That is not contrary to the Open Source Principles; some open source software is sold in stores.) That demand for payment needn't be expressed in the Simple License itself, because although consideration is an element of contract formation, it is not necessarily a part of the contract itself. Consideration may be obtained by demanding a license fee before allowing download of open source software. Of course, licensors should avoid sham consideration—such as a penny—that might convince a court that a gift rather than a contract was intended.

Many customers obtain their open source software from established commercial enterprises either combined with hardware and services or as part of a comprehensive support package. Those associated agreements often establish the element of consideration that is required for treating the license itself as a contract.

But ultimately, the issue of price is irrelevant for most open source software. Most is available truly free of charge for those who want it. Not even a penny is demanded for its download. Where can we find consideration by a licensee in an open source license that otherwise promises the free use of software—at zero price—and allows copies and derivative works to be distributed without payment of royalties? (See Open Source Principles # 1, 2 and 3.)

This question becomes even more confusing when we realize that open source licenses are almost always written as unilateral contracts in which only the licensor has made promises. At no time has the licensee been requested to bind him- or herself to do anything, and even if the licensee starts to use the software that licensee is not bound to continue to do so. A court may find the necessary detriment to the licensee, and thus the necessary consideration, in the very act of using, copying, modifying, and distributing the software. This is the basis of the contract law doctrine of *promissory estoppel*, in which *detrimental reliance* becomes a substitute for consideration. The law of contracts describes it as follows:

> *A promise which the promisor should reasonably expect to induce action or forbearance on the part of the promisee or a third person and which does induce such action or forbearance is binding if injustice can be avoided only by enforcement of the promise. The remedy granted for breach may be limited as justice requires. (Restatement, Second, Contracts, § 90.)*

A court may find detrimental reliance by licensees who have accepted open source software for use in the infrastructure of the modern economy. It is inconceivable to me, for example, that licensors of Linux, or Apache, or any of the other major open source software packages, would be allowed to revoke their licenses for lack of consideration. But it remains to be seen whether promissory estoppel will generally serve as a substitute for consideration in open source licensing. It has never been tested in court.

Just because there is uncertainty about the element of consideration shouldn't lead us to ignore the other two elements of contract formation, offer and acceptance. A court is unlikely to find promissory estoppel when licensors haven't even made the effort to offer clear promises in the first place and to get them accepted.

If open source licenses are to be treated as contracts, all three elements of contract formation should be satisfied wherever possible.

Failure of Offer, Acceptance, or Consideration

Of all the licenses described in this book, only the GPL makes the explicit point that it wants nothing of *acceptance* or *consideration*:

> *You are not required to accept this License, since you have not signed it. (GPL section 5.)*

> *You must cause any work that you distribute or publish ... to be licensed as a whole <u>at no charge</u> to all third parties under the terms of this License. (Underline added; GPL section 2[b].)*

The GPL authors intend that it not be treated as a contract. I will say much more about this license and these two provisions in Chapter 6. For now, I simply point out that GPL licensors are in essentially the same situation as other open source licensors who cannot prove offer, acceptance, or consideration. There is no contract.

What is left? Even if the contract fails, a bare license remains, and that license can be enforced under copyright law—with all the limitations on such enforcement actions described earlier—or it can be revoked.

Here is how the Open Software License and the Academic Free License make this legal point:

> *Any use of the Original Work outside the scope of this License or after its termination shall be subject to the requirements and penalties of the U.S. Copyright Act, 17 U.S.C. § 101 et seq., the equivalent laws of other countries, and international treaty. This section shall survive the termination of this License. (OSL/AFL section 11.)*

Even if this provision isn't explicit in all open source licenses, that's probably the way the law will treat the situation anyway.

Also note that licensees have little to gain by denying the existence of a contract unless they're willing to have their licenses revoked, and licensors almost always want their contracts enforced. Litigation about contract formation issues probably won't arise in commercially relevant situations.

Patent Licenses

There is an entire breed of specialized licenses that are used for patents. Patent owners license their patent rights to other companies, authorizing the licensees to make, use, sell or offer for sale, or import products embodying the claims of the patent. Rarely are such patent licenses unlimited. Instead, we typically see limitations for specific fields of use (e.g., a semiconductor patent licensed only for making disk drive heads), for specific products (e.g., a browser patent licensed only for a particular operating system), or for specific markets and geographic regions (e.g., a telephone system patent licensed only for products sold in the European Community).

To be compatible with an open source license, a patent license necessary to make, use, or sell the software under license must not prevent the creation of derivative works or prohibit use anywhere in the world. (See Open Source Principles #1 and 3.)

Patent licenses often require payment of royalties to the patent owner. Such licenses may be incompatible with open source licenses if they require licensees or sublicensees to pay for the right to make and distribute copies or derivative works. (See Open Source Principles #2 and 3.) Some *paid-up* patent licenses, which require a single up-front payment for all patent rights, can be consistent with open source software. But it is difficult to find an angel to invest significant money in a paid-up patent license where those costs cannot be passed on to downstream licensees.

Large companies with extensive patent portfolios often negotiate cross-licenses with other companies. Each party to the license agrees to allow the other to make, use, sell or offer for sale, or import products embodying claims in the licensed portfolios. Such patent licenses are compatible with open source licenses as long as the software licensor has rights, under the cross-license, to allow downstream open source–compatible patent licensing.

It is difficult in a book like this to say much of value about stand-alone patent licenses. Software is not licensed that way because software is inevitably both copyrightable and patentable. A software license always has a copyright component. Where stand-alone patent licenses do become important to open source is in the context of open standards that are intended to be implemented in software. These specialized patent licenses for open standards are discussed in Chapter 13.

For now, I'm going to focus on the patent license grants contained within open source licenses themselves. Such licenses convey sufficient patent rights to make, use, sell or offer for sale, or import the specific software in ways consistent with the Open Source Principles. These patent licenses are *implied* in some open source licenses, *expressed* in others. Patent license terms differ subtly among open source licenses. I will point this out when I introduce each license.

Template Licenses

Since a software license is a specific contract between two parties, a specific licensor and a specific licensee, there are literally millions of such licenses in effect today. Fortunately, many of those licenses have very similar wording. Rather than negotiate one agreement at a time, many software companies use fill-in-the-blank agreements drafted by their attorneys, defining the licensor and licensee as, for example, Company X and Company Y, respectively, but otherwise the same. In such ways, large companies often license large proprietary software packages using standard terms and conditions. It would be a waste of time to redraft and negotiate every license agreement afresh.

For mass marketed software, software licenses are even more generalized, defining the licensor and licensee as Company X and Licensee, respectively, where *Licensee* is defined generally as "the person or company exercising rights under this license," or words to that effect.

Open source software licenses sometimes add yet another level of generality. They don't specifically name Company X as the licensor, instead defining *Licensor* as "the person or company granting rights under this license," or words to that effect. That can allow a single form of license to be used without modification for many licensors and many licensees. These generalized licenses are sometimes called *license templates*.

Often more than the names of the licensor and licensee are replaceable in the template. Other template fields can be the name of the software, the copyright notice, or even important matters such as jurisdiction and governing law.

At the end of the day, however, it is essential to tie together a specific piece of software, a specific licensor, and a specific licensee, because it is those three pieces of information that determine what license terms apply to the specific parties doing the licensing. A license template without the blanks filled in is not a complete license.

As I discuss various licenses in this book, I will identify the ways, if any, that they serve as license templates.

Types of Open Source Licenses

With as difficult a concept as *software freedom* to contend with, it is not surprising that many licenses have been proposed to implement it. As of this writing, over fifty approved open source licenses are listed aty *www.opensource.org*. Understanding those licenses would be impossible without a licensing taxonomy, a way of organizing those licenses into appropriate categories.

Licenses generally fall into these categories:

- *Academic licenses*, so named because such licenses were originally created by academic institutions to distribute their software to the public, allow the software to be used for any purpose whatsoever with no obligation on the part of the licensee to distribute the source code of derivative works. The Berkeley Software Distribution (BSD) license used by the University of California to distribute its software is the archetypal academic license. Academic licenses create a public commons of free software, and anyone can take such software for any purpose—including for creating proprietary collective and derivative works—without having to add anything back to that commons.

- *Reciprocal licenses* also allow software to be used for any purpose whatsoever, but they require the distributors of derivative works to distribute those works under the same license, including the requirement that the source code of those derivative works be published. The GPL license, written by Richard Stallman and Eben Moglen at the Free Software Foundation, is the archetypal reciprocal license. Anyone who creates and distributes a derivative work of a work licensed under a reciprocal license must, in turn, license that derivative work under the same license. Reciprocal licenses, like academic licenses, contribute software into a public commons of free software, but they mandate that derivative works also be placed in that same commons.

- *Standards licenses* are designed primarily for ensuring that industry standard software and documentation be available to all for implementation of standard products. These licenses sometimes require that any differences from the industry standard be published as a reference implementation so that the standard may evolve if necessary.

- *Content licenses* ensure that copyrightable subject matter other than software, such as music, art, film, literary works, and the like, be available to all for any purpose whatsoever. These licenses are discussed more fully on the Creative Commons website at *www.creativecommons.org*. While the Creative Commons goals are not directly related to *software freedom*, there are many similarities of objective. A few of the software licenses discussed in this book, in particular the Academic Free License (AFL) and the Open Software License (OSL), are appropriate for use with content as well as software, as will be explained in due course.

Over the last few years, many organizations and companies have embraced open source software. In the process, they have written many open source licenses that are subtle variants on the academic and reciprocal themes. Those licenses are submitted to Open Source Initiative for review of compatibility with the Open Source Definition and approval as an open source license. There are already over fifty OSI-approved open source licenses.

All of the licenses discussed in this book are published at the website run by Open Source Initiative, *www.opensource.org*. Only approved licenses are listed. Software distributed under any of those licenses is OSI Certified open source software.

Open Source Initiative created a certification mark for licensors to display on open source software. As long as an OSI-approved license is used for distribution of the software, such open source software can be marketed with this certification mark:

OSI certified

5

Academic Licenses

The BSD Gift of Freedom

The first open source license, the original BSD (Berkeley Software Distribution), was designed to permit the free use, modification, and distribution of certain University of California software without any return obligation whatsoever on the part of licensees.

The term *academic freedom* usually means the freedom of a (tenured) professor to speak openly without risking his or her job. This presumably results in a dynamic and diverse community of thought that enriches everyone's academic experience and results in the exploration of new ideas. But that isn't the type of academic freedom that open source deals with.

Academic open source licenses promote a slightly different kind of freedom, relating to the mission of an academic institution to promote education and scholarship. Teachers are encouraged to publish their ideas rather than hide them under a cloak of secrecy. Students are expected to take what they learn and apply it to their own work, creating new ideas in turn. In pursuing this type of academic freedom, universities often forgo an immediate profit motive and instead consider the bigger benefit to society of releasing their intellectual property to the public. Of course, not all universities practice this ideal all the time.

The University of California decided to use the BSD license to promote this latter type of academic freedom. It apparently concluded that some of its software would be more valuable if it were made freely available for all to copy, modify, and distribute than if the University were to keep it secret or to attempt to sell it privately.

Some suggest that the University could have accomplished this merely by waiving its copyright or dedicating its software to the public domain. Under the copyright law, though, there is no mechanism for waiving a copyright that merely *subsists*, and there is no accepted way to dedicate an *original work of authorship* to the public domain before the copyright term for that work expires. A license is the only recognized way to authorize others to undertake the authors' exclusive copyright rights.

In Chapter 4, I created a simple license to accomplish this goal:

> *Simple License: The copyright owner of this software hereby licenses it to you for any purpose whatsoever.*

(This isn't the BSD license. The grant in the BSD license is longer and more complex, but I'll get to that in a bit. I'm using this one-sentence Simple License for illustrative purposes only.)

The Simple License, if properly accepted, is a *unilateral contract* in which only the copyright owner has offered promises, in particular the promise to let you use the software as you see fit. The licensee has promised nothing but is nevertheless bound to the terms and conditions of the contract if he or she uses the software as licensed.

Such unilateral contracts are formed all the time in daily life, although we don't often think about their terms and conditions when we enter into them. That is because, for many commercial transactions, we leave it to the law to specify the implied terms of contracts that we enter. You can take comfort when you go to a store to buy a toaster that the store will return your money if the toaster is unsatisfactory, or will repair or replace the toaster if it doesn't work as advertised. The only way for a store to avoid its *implied* promises is to *expressly* disclaim them; it may sell you the toaster "AS IS" and "subject to all flaws."

Notice that you, the consumer, don't promise anything to the store in return. You can use the toaster however you want, or not use it at all. The store and you have a *contract* even though only the store has made promises—in this case implied ones—about efficacy and safety.

As with the purchase of a toaster, every other condition in the Simple License could be left to the legal defaults for software licenses—whatever those defaults are. Such a one-sentence license is fully compatible with the Open Source Principles, and in theory at least it could be approved by Open Source Initiative as a valid open source license.

What are the licensor's implied promises in this Simple License? The law prescribes that, at least in the case of a commercial or consumer transaction for *goods*, there are implied promises that the goods will perform as they were advertised to do. If software is *goods*, and if the software turns out to break computers or doesn't perform the way its documentation specifies, the licensor may be responsible to pay damages—even when the license is silent about it.

But software isn't *goods*. The law in many jurisdictions hasn't quite decided what it is. *Implied* promises for software contracts aren't well defined.

The University of California didn't want a dispute about whether software was *goods*. It merely wanted protection from implied promises, and it wanted to avoid having to pay damages if a user was injured in any way by the software. It protected itself with an *express* warranty disclaimer and an *express* liability disclaimer, about which more later. That added two sentences to what otherwise could have been a one-sentence license.

The University of California also wanted to impose a few *conditions* that would be required of every licensee. (Ignore for a moment the particulars of those conditions.) How can a *unilateral contract* impose conditions on licensees if all the promises are made by the licensor? The answer is that, under the law, a *condition* is not a *promise*. In the case of a unilateral contract like the BSD, the conditions must be satisfied by the licensee or it relieves the licensor of his promise to let you have the software.

The BSD license accomplished much more than simply giving a particular piece of software away. By encouraging the contribution of software into a public commons of software available to anyone, it created a growing benefit to the University of California and everyone else. As the theory goes, more and more people will contribute BSD-licensed software to the commons in response to, and as consideration for, earlier contributions. The huge amount of software now available under the BSD license (and similar academic licenses) has proven that this theory works in real life.

The BSD license even allows software to be taken from that public commons and used in proprietary applications. There is no obligation for the licensee to return anything to the commons. But despite the absence of such an obligation, the BSD "gift of freedom" is being repaid over and over by companies and individuals who see more value to them in giving software away under an academic license than in keeping it private.

BSD License as Template

The BSD license has been through several revisions. The current version discussed in this chapter has been redesigned to work as a *template* appropriate for software other than the original Berkeley Software Distribution. A copy of the current version of the BSD license is shown in the Appendices.

When a licensor says "I license my software under the BSD license," that licensor is not suggesting that he or she is or represents the University of California, or that the licensed software is or is derived from the original Berkeley Software Distribution. Instead, this sentence means only that the license is in the form of the BSD license, inserting the licensor's own name as the name of the licensor and an original copyright notice instead of the copyright notice for that other university's software.

If you use software that purports to be under the BSD license, look for the license itself somewhere in the source code of the software. The license should be complete, with all blanks filled in. That text is the authoritative version of *your* BSD license, not the version shown in the Appendices.

The BSD License Grant

Here is the actual BSD license grant:

> *Redistribution and use in source and binary forms, with or without modification, are permitted provided.... (BSD license.)*

I will describe the *provided...* clause (what is also called a *proviso*) soon, but first I need to describe just which of the

University of California's intellectual property rights were actually being licensed by the first BSD license.

Almost everyone believes that the redistribution and use clause of the BSD license was intended to include all of the exclusive intellectual property rights the University then owned for something called the "Berkeley Software Distribution." The fact that the BSD license does not expressly list those exclusive rights (e.g., copy, create derivative works, distribute, perform, display, make, use, sell, offer for sale, import) doesn't mean they intended any of those rights to be excluded from the license.

The term *redistribution* means *distribution again*. This necessarily includes the right to make copies, since one cannot distribute software again without making copies. And since the word *modification* later in the sentence implies *derivative work*, I assume that the license allows the copying and distribution of both the original and derivative works. The word *redistribution* in the BSD license appears to encompass all those copyright rights that must be granted to ensure software freedom. The BSD license passes the filter of the Open Source Principles.

The word *use*, on the other hand, is not found among the exclusive rights of *copyright* owners. The *use* of software can be affected by a *patent*, because under the law, a patent owner has the exclusive right to *make, use, and sell* any product in which the patent is embodied. But the University of California made no patent grant in the BSD license. Indeed, later in the license the University specifically used the phrase *this software is provided by the copyright holders and contributors*, suggesting by its absence that there are no patent holders or that those patent holders are not granting anything in this license.

In the absence of an explicit patent grant, but considering the word *use* in the license, can we assume that the BSD license impliedly grants enough of whatever patent rights the University of California then owned that a licensee may use the software as it was originally distributed by the University? Most licensees under the BSD assume it does on the theory that otherwise the copyright license would be of no value. What good, they say, is software that can be copied but not used?

Such a conclusion is not based on the law of licenses. Indeed, a *bare license of copyright* need not include a *bare license of patent* at all. It is only if the BSD is viewed as a contract that we can introduce contract law principles such as *reliance* or *reasonable expectations of the parties*. If software is licensed under the BSD without forming a contract between licensor and licensee, the extent of any patent grant is at best ambiguous.

As to whether an implied grant of patent rights extends to versions of the software *with modifications*, that's an even more complicated question. The BSD license is silent about a patent license for derivative works. So if a licensee improves the original Berkeley Software Distribution in a way that infringes a patent owned by the University of California, there is no easy way of knowing whether an implied BSD patent license includes a patent license for that improvement.

Since courts are likely to construe implied grants of license narrowly, a licensee should consider obtaining separately from the licensor an explicit grant of patent rights that might be needed for modified versions of BSD-licensed software.

Source and Binary Forms of Code

In the late 1980s, when the BSD license was new, software was written in source code and compiled into a binary form for execution. Those terms now have more complex practical meanings, with computer programs written in a variety of languages and executed by computers in many forms other than binary.

The phrase *source code* is assumed to mean the form of the software in which it was originally written by a human being. Used in this way in the BSD license, the phrase *source code* does not necessarily include any documentation about the program or even instructions on how to modify the source code.

Nothing in the BSD license actually requires the publication of the source code, either by the licensor of the original software or by the licensee of modified versions. Distribution in source form is merely *permitted*. However, any software someone might attempt to distribute under the BSD license without at least making source code available upon a licensee's request would, as a practical matter, merely be ignored by the open source community; it would find no projects willing to accept it.

Conditions under the BSD

The BSD license includes the following proviso that must be met for source code distributions:

> *Redistributions of source code must retain the above copyright notice, this list of conditions and the following disclaimer. (BSD license.)*

The phrase *above copyright notice* is somewhat misleading. Presumably the BSD license really refers to the actual copyright notice that is displayed on the software being distributed rather than the copyright notice shown above in the license, for otherwise this would be a meaningless requirement.

The phrase *this list of conditions* includes three items: the requirement for source code distributions quoted above and two other conditions. The second condition is:

> Redistributions in binary form must reproduce the above copyright notice, this list of conditions and the following disclaimer in the documentation and/or other materials provided with the distribution. (BSD license.)

The phrase *binary form* is assumed to mean something broader than what that term meant in 1989, what we now more commonly refer to as the *executable* form of the software. BSD-licensed software may be distributed in binary (executable) form alone, without source code.

I assume that the requirement to include *the above copyright notice* in binary distributions means the original copyright notice valid for the work itself rather than the copyright notice shown in the license. And since there is no actual requirement to provide *documentation and/or other materials* with the distribution, it isn't clear that the *above* copyright notice will ever actually be seen by users.

The third BSD license condition relates to the name of the licensor, either *University of California, Berkeley,* for the original Berkeley Software Distribution or, since the BSD license is a template, whatever the BSD licensor's name is:

> Neither the name of the <ORGANIZATION> nor the names of its contributors may be used to endorse or promote products derived from this software without specific prior written permission. (BSD license.)

The *name* of a company or individual is not a copyright or patent, but it is nevertheless an important property interest that is protected by law in many countries. It can—and from the perspective of the open source community of contributors *should*—be protected from association with other people's work or products. (Remember item 5 of the Open Source Definition in Chapter 1, although it is not included as a mandatory feature of open source licenses in the Open Source Principles.)

The BSD license explicitly prevents the name of the licensor or contributors from being used *to endorse or promote products.* This restriction clearly covers marketing activities. It probably doesn't cover otherwise naming the original licensor and contributors, as long as those names aren't used for product endorsement or promotion.

A more comprehensive requirement concerning advertising was present in the original BSD license:

> *All advertising materials mentioning features or use of this software must display the following acknowledgement: "This product includes software developed by the University of California, Berkeley, and its contributors." (Previous version of BSD license.)*

This condition was removed from the BSD license in 1999 after extensive public criticism of that requirement. Many people complained that it is one thing to prohibit the use of the licensor's and contributors' names for publicity purposes (i.e., the third condition already discussed), but it is quite another to require that a specific advertisement for the University be included in all advertising materials for the software or its derivative works. The concern was not merely for the University of California's one-sentence advertisement, but that other licensors using the BSD template could demand even more grandiloquent advertisements that create unacceptable burdens for subsequent creators of derivative works. Such advertising demands are no longer acceptable for open source licenses because they interfere with the freedom to create derivative works.

There are other forms of *reputation* interests of this type, such as property interests in trademarks, which are not mentioned in the BSD license. The BSD license refers only to *names* and doesn't explicitly say that a licensor's trademarks can't be used to endorse products. Even in the absence of a provision relating to trademarks, however, the law of unfair competition, at least in the United States, prevents a licensee from using a licensor's trademark on different but similar goods without the licensor's permission.

Warranty and Liability Disclaimer

The BSD license contains a *warranty and liability disclaimer*. It is reproduced here, but not in the all-capital-letters form of the original license text.

> *This software is provided by the copyright holders and contributors "AS IS" and ANY EXPRESS OR IMPLIED WARRANTIES, including, but not limited to, the implied warranties of merchantability and fitness for a particular purpose ARE DISCLAIMED. IN NO EVENT SHALL THE COPYRIGHT OWNER OR CONTRIBUTORS BE LIABLE for any direct, indirect, incidental, special, exemplary, or consequential damages (including, but not limited to, procurement of substitute goods or services; loss of use, data, or profits; or business interruption) however caused and on any theory of liability, whether in contract, strict liability, or tort (including negligence or otherwise) arising in any way out of the use of this software, even if advised of the possibility of such damage.*

The reason such provisions are often shown in all capital letters is that the law requires that these provisions be prominent so licensees will notice and read them. But capital letters are harder to read and are frequently ignored simply because of the printing. I much prefer to capitalize only very important words, such as the words *AS IS* in the above disclaimer, to highlight what is truly important.

The first sentence of the BSD disclaimer deals with warranties and the second sentence with liability. A disclaimer of warranty is independent of a disclaimer of liability. The BSD warranty disclaimer makes it clear that the licensor promises nothing about the software, and the liability disclaimer makes it clear that the licensor will not pay for any kind of damage, however caused.

A software warranty is a promise relating to such things as the quality, effectiveness, and reliability of software. Under the BSD license, there are no such promises. The licensor only promises to allow the user to practice the licensor's exclusive copyright (and perhaps patent) rights, nothing more.

Contract law and consumer protection laws provide for certain express and implied warranties. The BSD license intends to disclaim absolutely all of them. That is generally what the words *AS IS* means in contract law. Whatever faults or defects exist in the software as licensed, and whatever problems are later encountered while using the software, are not the licensor's concern.

The laws in some jurisdictions override warranty disclaimers in licenses and contracts. For example, in the United States certain warranty disclaimers for a consumer product are ineffective and will generally be ignored by the courts. Software by itself is not a consumer product under this law, but when software is combined into a consumer product such as a PDA or television recorder, the warranties of merchantability and fitness for a particular purpose cannot be disclaimed for that product regardless of what a license says, at least in the United States.

The second sentence of the BSD disclaimer deals with the liability of the licensor to pay damages actually incurred as a result of the use of the software.

The BSD license disclaims liability of any sort. This means that any damages caused by the software, whether to people, to computers, or to the licensee's business, are not going to be paid for by the licensor. Such liability disclaimers may not be legally effective in certain jurisdictions, particularly for consumer products. If a company distributes a consumer product that causes harm to people or property, the distributor may be liable regardless of what a license says.

It is unlikely that a court would extend liability in such a situation all the way up the chain of title to the contributor or distributor of general purpose software that happens to be included in a consumer product, but that is a factual situation that would need to be analyzed by an attorney at the appropriate time. The disclaimer language in the license, the characteristics of the software, and the existence of an agreed contract rather than just a bare license would be among the relevant facts that a judge would consider in determining whether a liability disclaimer is fair, under the circumstances, to an ordinary consumer who is injured by a software-based product.

The MIT License

The lawyers at the Massachusetts Institute of Technology (MIT) created their own version of the BSD license. They cleaned up some of the vague language of the BSD license and made their version simpler to read and understand. A copy of the current version of the MIT license is shown in the Appendices.

The license grant of the MIT license reads as follows:

*Permission is hereby granted, free of charge, to any person ob-
taining a copy of this software and associated documentation
files (the "Software"), to deal in the Software without restriction, including without limitation the rights to use, copy,
modify, merge, publish, distribute, sublicense, and/or sell
copies of the Software, and to permit persons to whom the
Software is furnished to do so, subject to the following conditions.... (MIT license first paragraph.)*

This improves on the BSD license by specifically mentioning all of the exclusive rights under copyright law and almost
all of the exclusive rights under patent law (e.g., "make" is
omitted, but that is probably unnecessary given the other
verbs in that sentence). No longer are we limited by the BSD's
reference to *redistribution and use*. On the other hand, the new
phrase *deal in the software* has no precise legal meaning. In
light of the longer list of rights in the MIT license grant, it
appears not to limit copyright or patent rights in any way.

Like the BSD license that preceded it, the scope of the
patent grant in the MIT license is implicit rather than explicit.
This means that a licensee cannot be sure that the *implied*
patent rights granted by MIT are broad enough to cover derivative works.

The grant in the MIT license extends not just to the software itself but to its *associated documentation files*. It is not clear
whether MIT is offering here to provide all documentation in
its possession concerning the software or only certain files that
are associated in some way with the software.

The phrase *free of charge* means that the licensor (MIT in
this case) will not charge a royalty or license fee. But the word
sell among the list of rights granted means that downstream
licensees are not restricted in any way from charging their cus-

tomers royalties or license fees for modified versions of the software.

The MIT license also serves as a license template. It is so short a license that only the copyright notice needs to be changed to fill in the template. Unfortunately, the phrase *this software and associated documentation files* doesn't clearly identify which software the license applies to. The only way to correlate particular software with a particular copy of the MIT license is to physically find the license text in the source code of the software.

The Right to Sublicense

The MIT license also grants the right to sublicense, a word missing entirely from the BSD license grant. Sublicensing is an important concept in open source licensing.

Referring back to the chain of title explanation earlier in Chapter 2, I described how contributions from many people can be combined into collective and derivative works, and how those works can in turn be used by others to create still more collective and derivative works. That is the very premise and promise of open source development. The ever lengthening chain of title is reflective of the robust creative energies of community development. A major open source software program may have a long chain of title by the time it arrives on your computer.

From whom does the person at the end of the chain of title get a license to use, copy, modify, and distribute the software? Does the user receive a set of licenses, one from each of the original authors of each of the contributions all the way along the chain, or is there a single license from the immediate predecessor on which the user can rely?

If a license *is not sublicensable*, then only the owner of the original work can grant licenses. For each nonsublicensable component of a collective or derivative work, each prospective licensee must obtain a license to that component directly from its owner. In principle this requires tracing the entire chain of title, obtaining copies of each copyright or patent license up the chain, but in practice it means nothing so complicated. Leaders of nonsublicensable open source projects take steps to ensure that licenses to components will be available for the asking, but they don't actually expect everyone to ask. The project team merely announces that licenses are available and points to the open source code, with its copyright, patent, and other attribution notices there for all to read, for information about where to get those licenses. If you want to make sure you have a license to each component, they in effect say, go get it yourself; but considering the low risk, most licensees don't bother. This is a reasonable solution for most open source software, but as a legal matter it is risky not to confirm that all licenses up the chain are actually available.

On the other hand, if a license *is sublicensable*, then any distributor has the right to grant a license to the software, including its component parts, directly to third parties. For each sublicensable work that is a component of a collective or derivative work, each prospective licensee obtains a license directly from the owner of the collective or derivative work. Leaders of sublicensable open source projects take steps to ensure that licenses to components are consistent with their own licensing terms and are sublicensable. They then extend sublicenses to their customers sufficient to allow those customers to exercise their rights under the open source licenses.

Note that the license terms for a sublicense must be consistent with—not necessarily the same as—the original license terms. A sublicensor cannot sublicense more rights than have been granted by the original author. The sublicensors needn't use the identical words as in the earlier license they received, but they cannot override terms and conditions that are mandated by that license.

This subject will be addressed again in Chapter 10 when I discuss how open source projects should in-license contributions and how they can relicense their collective and derivative works when new and better licenses become available despite being bound by the licenses of their contributors.

The fact that the MIT license is sublicensable is an advantage for anyone who wants to distribute copies or derivative works of MIT-licensed works. A distributor can provide to his customers all the rights needed to the entire work without expecting those customers to follow the chain of title to its beginning.

The Warranty of Noninfringement

Another important aspect of the MIT license is its disclaimer of the *warranty of noninfringement*. This concept is entirely missing from the BSD license. Here's how the MIT license says it (converted from uppercase letters):

> *The software is provided "AS IS", without warranty of any kind, express or implied, including but not limited to the warranties of merchantability, fitness for a particular purpose and noninfringement. (MIT license third paragraph.)*

You can *infringe* someone's intellectual property by exercising any of the exclusive rights of the owner of that intellectual property—copyright or patent—without a license to do so. If you copy, modify, or distribute copyrighted software without a license, or if you make, use, sell or offer for sale, or import a patented invention without a license, you are an *infringer*.

Infringement can happen accidentally, but infringers can be penalized even if the infringement is not intentional. If software that you use infringes someone's intellectual property and you have no license to do so, a court may assess damages and order you to stop the infringement, no matter how costly or disruptive that may be to your business.

Infringement may not be the fault of the licensor who distributed the software to you. A patent owned by some third party of whom neither of you were aware may suddenly be asserted against all users of the software, including you and your distributor, and suddenly you can find yourself accused of patent infringement. As for copyrights, to your own and to your software distributor's surprise, some third party may assert that somewhere in the chain of title to the software someone made a mistake or committed a fraud, turning what everyone thought were legitimately licensed copies into infringing copies.

Warranting against infringement is an impossible burden to impose upon an open source licensor who is, after all, giving software away for free. No open source license provides a warranty of infringement. Neither, for that matter, do most proprietary software licensors, because the uncertainty and potential cost of infringement are far too expensive a risk to take. Even those few software companies that do provide a warranty of infringement typically limit their liability to the purchase price of the software; this is a trivial amount considering the potential costs of infringement.

Even for open source licenses that don't mention the warranty of noninfringement, the "AS IS" phrase should warn you that a meaningful warranty of noninfringement is simply not available. Where it is critical to your business that you avoid infringement risk, you must accept the burden to perform your own diligent analysis of the chain of title, or purchase your own insurance policy to protect you. It is foolish to look to typical software licenses—and certainly to open source software licenses—to eliminate your risk of copyright or patent infringement.

The Apache License

Of the two most widely known and successful open source projects, Linux and Apache, only the latter is licensed under an academic license. That means—as is true for any software licensed under an academic license—that Apache software may be used by anyone, anywhere, for any purpose, including for inclusion in proprietary derivative works, without any obligation to disclose source code.

A copy of the current version of the Apache license is shown in the Appendices.

The first difference between the current Apache license and the BSD license is the following provision:

> *The end-user documentation included with the redistribution, if any, must include the following acknowledgment: "This product includes software developed by the Apache Software Foundation (www.apache.org/)." Alternately, this acknowledgment may appear in the software itself, if and wherever such third-party acknowledgments normally appear. (Apache License section 3.)*

This provision differs significantly from the rescinded advertising clause of the original BSD license. (As a reminder, here's how that provision read: "All advertising materials mentioning features or use of this software must display the following acknowledgment: This product includes software developed by the University of California, Berkeley and its contributors.") The Apache license only requires an acknowledgment in "end-user documentation" or "in the software itself," not in "all advertising materials." The Apache license does not specify the prominence that must be given to that acknowledgment. The Apache license is consistent with the Open Source Principles because it does not interfere with the freedom to modify or create derivative works of open source software.

Protecting Trademarks

The most important feature of the Apache license that distinguishes it from the BSD and MIT licenses is that it specifically protects the Apache trademark. This is an acknowledg-ment that trademarks are important assets of open source projects.

Here's what the license says:

> *The names "Apache" and "Apache Software Foundation" must not be used to endorse or promote products derived from this software without prior written permission. For written permission, please contact apache@apache.org. (Apache License section 4.)*

> *Products derived from this software may not be called "Apache", nor may "Apache" appear in their name, without prior written permission of the Apache Software Foundation. (Apache License section 5.)*

On the surface, this is similar to the BSD provision preventing the University of California name from being used "to endorse or promote products." But the Apache license goes even further when it states that a derivative work may not use "Apache" as part of its name.

Trademarks are brand names of products. You will recall that a *trademark* is a word, name, symbol, or design used to identify a company's products and to distinguish those products from the competition. Trademarks are a form of intellectual property.

Open source software poses some difficult marketing problems. The licenses under which such products are distributed require the distribution of source code and permit the creation and distribution of derivative works. It is difficult for a distributor of such products to compete on price alone, because almost any knowledgeable company can undercut the price by simply copying the original software.

Trademarks can be particularly useful in this kind of environment. A company can demonstrate that its software is of high quality, reliable, efficient, feature-rich, and user-friendly. It can promise continual enhancements, product support, user groups, and other goodwill activities. Then over time, through those marketing efforts, that company's customers will begin to associate its trademarks with that software. New or repeat customers will pay for software they perceive to be worth the price even though there may be cheaper competitive products. Customers will select products whose trademarks they identify.

It would not be fair to allow a licensee who receives free software to also receive a license to the valuable trademarks of his licensor. The Apache license makes it clear that the Apache trademark isn't licensed along with the software.

The Apache Contributor License Agreement

The Apache Software Foundation (ASF) has recently begun to require its contributors to submit a signed Contributor License Agreement. This agreement is copied in the Appendices.

The Apache Contributor License Agreement is intended to convey to ASF all necessary rights to the contributor's intellectual property so that ASF can do what it wishes with those Contributions. The agreement itself asserts that the goal of the Contributor License Agreement is to protect the Contributor:

This license is for your protection as a Contributor of software to the Foundation and does not change your right to use your own contributions for any other purpose. (Apache Contributor License Agreement, initial paragraph.)

In fact, the main purpose of the Apache Contributor License Agreement is to protect ASF in two important ways:

1. It allows ASF to license its collective and derivative works including the *Contribution* under any license it chooses. That gives the ASF flexibility regarding relicensing. (Relicensing is discussed more fully in Chapter 10.) The Apache Contributor License Agreement does not constrain ASF's licensing options for collective and derivative works in any way.

2. It allows ASF to assert that each *Contribution* is actually owned by its *Contributors*, and that third party licenses and restrictions known to the *Contributors* have been divulged. This will make it possible for future Apache licenses to convey a *warranty of provenance*. (That term is described in Chapter 9; the OSL and AFL licenses contain an express *warranty of provenance*.)

Contributor agreements such as the Apache Contributor License Agreement are *licenses*, in both name and effect. They convey copyright and patent rights, as do all the other open source licenses described in this book. But these contributor agreements are not submitted to Open Source Initiative for its review and approval, and so there is no established process for verifying that those agreements are compatible with the Open Source Principles.

This book is also not the place to do that analysis. I will suggest, however, that this contributor agreement, in use by the Apache Software Foundation, is truly open source, based upon my own reading of its terms. Whether that is true for the contributor agreements demanded by other projects remains an open question. Contributors should seek their own legal advice before signing such contributor agreements.

Contributor agreements are relatively new to open source software projects, but they are not new to other industries. Musicians, journalists, photographers, and other contributors of intellectual property have often been asked to sign contracts with their publishers under which they grant broad intellectual property rights. Through the passage of time, some of those works have dramatically increased in value, and the publishers have sometimes failed to share their profits.

While that is not a likely result when the publisher is a nonprofit open source project such as the Apache Software Foundation, not all open source projects are (or will remain) benign; not all projects serve the public interest. Each contributor should decide for himself or herself whether to sign a contributor agreement.

Nor is a contributor agreement always necessary. If an open source contribution is submitted under a *compatible* open source license, no other contributor agreement is necessary. Chapter 10 discusses open source license compatibility.

The Artistic License

The Artistic License was the first open source license to protect the rights of software authors to attribution and integrity. In the U.S. Copyright Act, those protections apply, as a matter of right, for authors of works of visual art. The law provides that:

*... The author of a work of visual art (1) shall have the right
(A) to claim authorship of that work and (B) to prevent the
use of his or her name as the author of any work of visual
art which he or she did not create; (2) shall have the right
to prevent the use of his or her name as the author of the
work of visual art in the event of a distortion, mutilation,
or other modification of the work which would be prejudi-
cial to his or her honor or reputation.... (17 U.S.C.
§ 106A.)*

Software is not a work of visual art, however, so it is not
subject to this provision of the law. But a license expresses the
law of the contract, and in the case of the Artistic License, the
law of *this* contract protects software authors' rights to attribution and integrity. It does what the copyright law doesn't do—
protect the rights of software artists.

The ways in which the Artistic License does this are interesting and effective, albeit legally confusing. But before I deal
with this, I need to comment on the structure of that
license—a preamble about preambles.

License Preambles

The Artistic License is the first of the academic licenses to
consider its message important enough to warrant a license
preamble. A copy of the current version of the Artistic License
is shown in the Appendices. Its preamble starts as follows:

*The intent of this document is to state the conditions under
which a Package may be copied, such that the Copyright
Holder maintains some semblance of artistic control over the
development of the package, while giving the users of the
package the right to use and distribute the Package in a
more-or-less customary fashion, plus the right to make reasonable modifications. (Artistic License preamble.)*

Preambles to open source licenses are occasionally written in strident political or philosophical terms (although the preamble to *this* Artistic License is not stridently political), intended to convince others of the rightness of the licensor's position rather than to inform licensees of the rules they are to follow. Many lawyers believe license preambles are a bad place to make a political or philosophical statement. There are two reasons for that:

1. Licenses establish terms and conditions governing the relationship between two parties, in our case a licensor and a licensee. The preamble is not a term or condition. It is merely a statement. Therefore, it has no positive legal effect and it is not binding on a court. As such, it is surplusage.

2. The preamble may subtly conflict with the actual rules, or may be stronger or more conciliatory than the actual license provisions. There is no absolute rule that tells a judge that, in the event of a conflict between the preamble and the license terms, the license terms prevail. How a court will rule in the event of an actual conflict between the license and the preamble is difficult to predict.

While preambles and other philosophical arguments should not be used to qualify or modify the terms of software licenses, the points they make are important to some licensors. The software artists who wrote the Artistic License (and, as I will soon describe, the free software activists who wrote the GPL) spent a lot of time crafting their preambles. Those preambles should be read as general statements of the licensor's intent rather than as legally binding terms and conditions.

When Amateurs Write Licenses

The same programmers who cringe when a lawyer attempts to write high-quality software feel no qualms about writing their own open source licenses. Their goal, it appears, is to craft something that sounds like a license, to define a form of software freedom with reasonable terms and conditions, and then wait for the community to adopt the license and distribute software under it. This technique sometimes works. Some members of the open source community are more concerned with making a philosophical statement, getting free software distributed to the world, and letting license enforcement take care of itself somehow in the future. That can be a commendable goal, but from a lawyer's perspective, it is amateurish and risky.

The Artistic License is one such amateur license. It is a license that a lawyer would have difficulty explaining and that a judge would probably not be able to understand. I will incautiously invoke the wrath of the authors of that license by candidly expressing my concerns about it. In this, I don't mean to be harsh to them personally; I'm really trying to make a point about the art of license drafting. I know what those authors were trying to say, and I support their goals of artistic attribution and integrity, but I believe they made a legal mess of it.

Here are a few examples from the definitions in the Artistic License:

> *"Package" refers to the collection of files distributed by the Copyright Holder, and derivatives of that collection of files created through textual modification. (Artistic License definitions.)*

This definition of *Package* assumes that a licensor is distributing only one collection of files; assumes that the phrase *collection of files* has a clear meaning; confuses the terms *derivative works* and *collective works* by referring to *derivatives of that col-*

lection; and then describes the process by which derivative works are created as involving something called *textual modification* (what other kinds of modifications are possible?).

> *"Standard Version" refers to such a Package if it has not been modified, or has been modified in accordance with the wishes of the Copyright Holder. (Artistic License definitions.)*

The law has little to do with *wishes*. The law of contracts has nothing to do with enforcing the *wishes* of a party, or even determining what those wishes are. Precatory language about *wishes* creates what in law are called *illusory rights and obligations*; such language is unenforceable.

> *"You" is you, if you're thinking about copying or distributing this Package. (Artistic License definitions.)*

The law has little to do with what people *think*. A person does not become a licensee of intellectual property merely by *thinking* about it.

> *"Reasonable copying fee" is whatever you can justify on the basis of media cost, duplication charges, time of people involved, and so on. (You will not be required to justify it to the Copyright Holder, but only to the computing community at large as a market that must bear the fee.) (Artistic License definitions.)*

The courts don't care about matters that the parties to the license admit is not important enough to *justify* to the copyright owner. The only point of this definition of *reasonable copying fee* is for the authors to describe a law of economics, namely that the marketplace determines whether a price is reasonable. It has no legal significance whatsoever.

At various places the Artistic License refers to the *public domain*. (The *public domain* was explained earlier in Chapter 2 when I discussed the duration of copyright and patent.) The

use of that term in the Artistic License is misleading. For
example:

> *You may apply bug fixes, portability fixes and other modi-*
> *fications derived from the Public Domain or from the*
> *Copyright Holder. A Package modified in such a way shall*
> *still be considered the Standard Version. (Artistic License*
> *section 1.)*

What the authors of this license may have meant was that
modifications derived *from other open source works*, because
there is so little software actually available in the *public
domain*. It is not clear how works licensed under different
licenses will interact legally with works licensed under the
Artistic License. I will discuss the complex issue of license
compatibility later in this book.

I understand that the authors of the Artistic License wanted
to retain some control over subsequent derivative and collective works. In this, they subtly cross the line that distinguishes
academic and reciprocal licenses. An academic license, remember, imposes no burdens or obligations on the creator and distributor of collective and derivative works. However, the
Artistic License imposes burdens and obligations that require
the licensee "to place ... modifications in the public domain or
otherwise make them freely available" (§ 3[a]) and "to rename
any non-standard executables" (§ 3[c]). It requires distributors
of executable versions of the licensed software to "accompany
the distribution with the machine-readable source of the package with ... modifications" (§ 4[b]) and to "document clearly
the differences" between the standard version and the modified version (§ 4[c]). There is one other option, to "make other
distribution arrangements with the Copyright Holder"
(§§ 3[d] and 4[d]). All of these requirements can be avoided,
however:

You may distribute this Package in aggregate with other (possibly commercial) programs as part of a larger (possibly commercial) software distribution provided that you do not advertise this Package as a product of your own. (Artistic License section 5.)

Given the confusing language in the Artistic License, I suggest that the best way to deal with it is to treat it as an academic license granting broad freedom to copy, modify, distribute, make, use, and sell the original software. If you distribute copies or derivative works of software licensed under the Academic License, you are obligated to attribute the original software to the original author, and to make it clear to your licensees that you—and not the original author—are responsible for your derivative works. Because of the ambiguity, in legal terms, of the terms *aggregate* and *larger*, this is an easy out. With the broad exception provided in this section 5, it appears, the other strictures in the Artistic License can be easily avoided simply by being careful not to advertise the software as a product of your own.

Big Picture of Academic Licenses

As you have seen, academic open source licenses are typically short and to-the-point. Often less than a page in length, academic licenses intend to grant to everyone all the copyrights and patent rights needed to exercise software freedom. There are few conditions in such licenses. A licensee, at most, needs to accept the absence of warranty or liability and to acknowledge the contributions of the original authors.

The brevity of most academic licenses is encouraging to users but somewhat perplexing to attorneys. Before open source licenses, it was not unusual to see multi-page licenses, with lots of terms and conditions that clearly defined the expectations of the parties. But with open source academic licenses, licensors have no expectations for what happens with their works. In a form of generosity not typical for major software companies, those licensors are entirely comfortable giving up any vestiges of control over what happens to their works after they are released to the world.

A different kind of academic license, the Academic Free License, handles the academic open source bargain in a more comprehensive way. I will defer commenting on that license until Chapter 9, after I describe the GPL and other reciprocal licenses in the next few chapters.

Apache License Version 2.0

While I was finishing the final edits for this book, the board of directors of the Apache Software Foundation approved version 2.0 of the Apache License. I debated with myself whether to insert a review of that license here. I was reminded of a cat chasing its tail. If I delay the publication of this book for every new license that comes along, I'll never finish.

The Apache License version 2.0 is a much more robust open source license than the other academic licenses already discussed in this chapter. It deserves careful analysis, perhaps a chapter all its own like the GPL, MPL, CPL, and OSL/AFL licenses in the chapters that follow this one. It is a very good open source license, a dramatic improvement over its predecessor. I decided that, rather than try to catch that Apache License for this book, I will use it only as an object lesson: Open source licensing is part of a dynamic, fast-moving world. New licenses and licensing strategies are introduced constantly. Companies that intend to play seriously in the open source marketplace will want to dedicate some effort to remaining current. This book unfortunately doesn't have all the answers.

6

Reciprocity and the GPL

The GPL Bargain

The world of software was transformed by the GNU General Public License. The word *GNU* in the license name is a play on words by the license author, Richard Stallman. "The name GNU was chosen following a hacker tradition," he says, "as a recursive acronym for 'GNU's Not Unix.'" Throughout the world, the license is mostly referred to simply as the *GPL*. (The GPL is reprinted in the Appendices.)

The GPL has been enormously influential in creating a large public commons of software that is freely available to everyone worldwide. As the GPL advocates might describe it in political tones, they have prevented much software from being captured by proprietary software interests and converted into restricted private property for personal gain. The GPL is both praised and reviled for that accomplishment.

The bargain created by the GPL can be paraphrased simply as follows: You may have this free software on condition that any derivative works that you create from it and distribute must be licensed to all under the same license.

Here's how the GPL actually says it:

You must cause any work that you distribute or publish, that
in whole or in part contains or is derived from the Program
or any part thereof, to be licensed as a whole at no charge
to all third parties under the terms of this License. (GPL,
Section 2.)

This is the most powerful idea in the GPL and the one that has aroused the most passion in its adherents and its detractors.

Adherents of the GPL suggest that this provision protects free software. It guarantees that all derivative works of GPL-licensed software will also be GPL-licensed software. Licensees cannot selfishly remove their improvements from the public commons. Derivative work software will always be free and open. The result is a dynamic and ever growing collection of GPL-licensed software that can be reused and improved.

Detractors say that this provision creates an island of software from which only GPL-licensed software can escape. The rest of the world cannot share the benefits of the source code of GPL-licensed software unless they are willing to travel to that island and commit to using the GPL license for their works.

Some of these GPL detractors are licensors of *proprietary* software. Their complaints are hypocritical. They too have created islands of software from which nothing can escape.

The only principled complaint about the GPL comes from those who license their software under *academic* open source licenses. Such software can be incorporated into GPL-licensed software but the converse is not true. In one sense, academic licenses are for *generous donors* of software, and the GPL and other reciprocal licenses are for *generous sharers* of software. Because of the GPL we have two—not just one—public commons of free software.

This book is not the place to resolve this ongoing debate. It is enough to say that licensors are free to decide what licensing model suits them best and whether or how to give away rights. Licensees may accept or reject software under the terms of the license, but they don't get to set their own terms. That's what copyright law allows, and the GPL uses that law effectively and brilliantly for its avowed purpose of fostering the creation of free software available to all under a single license.

Copyleft and Reciprocity

Partly to emphasize the role of copyright law to protect the freedom of GPL-licensed software and partly to create a catchy term to highlight their focus on software freedom, the authors of the GPL coined the term *copyleft* to describe its license bargain. It is both a play on the word *copyright* and an acknowledgment that it promoted a radical (i.e., *left-wing*, perhaps) departure from traditional software licensing models. The role of a *copyleft* software license is to grow the public commons of software rather than allow each owner's *copyright* to pull from that commons.

The Free Software Foundation also describes *copyleft* as a rule that, when redistributing a program, one cannot add restrictions to deny other people the central software freedoms. The word *restriction* is very vague in a licensing context; almost any of the terms and conditions in a license can be described as a restriction of some sort. This limitation on restrictions in the definition of copyleft causes some attorneys, including me, heartburn. We contend it would be helpful to add some restrictions to open source licenses that the GPL's authors didn't think of when they wrote their license. For example, provisions for defense against patent infringement lawsuits or to protect the licensor's trademarks can be very useful; both provisions are missing from the GPL.

In practice, the Free Software Foundation's restriction on adding restrictions has had the effect of allowing them to veto any restriction they find unacceptable—even those that are improvements over the GPL. Their avoidance of restrictions has delayed the adoption of new and useful licensing concepts for open source software. This topic will be addressed again when I discuss license compatibility in Chapter 10.

I find the word *reciprocity* to be less alarming and more descriptive than the word *copyleft*. I particularly like that word because it does not carry with it the reference to *restrictions* espoused by the Free Software Foundation.

> *Reciprocity means a mutual or cooperative interchange of favors or privileges. Something is reciprocal when it is performed, experienced, or felt by both sides. (The American Heritage Dictionary of the English Language, 4th edition.)*

The GPL license is reciprocal, because it is "performed, experienced, or felt" by both sides—the licensor and the licensees both use the GPL.

For these reasons, I refer to *reciprocity* rather than *copyleft*. The term *copyleft*, of course, needn't disappear. It still has great rhetorical value. It is a useful word to toss back at those who mistakenly complain that the GPL destroys copyrights; the GPL requires copyright law to create a copyleft bargain. But I do not find the term useful and I won't use that word again in this book.

Reciprocity provisions are now quite common in open source licenses; the GPL is merely the first and most influential proponent of that particular software bargain. The reciprocity obligations of other open source licenses are subtly different. I shall explore those differences when the individual licenses are discussed. But first, I must explore the policy objectives of the GPL, as much as possible in its authors' own words.

Policy Objectives

Traditional software licenses serve business needs. Their objective is usually to maximize profit from licensing of the software. The GPL has an entirely different policy objective. It seeks to maximize the amount of free software available in the public commons.

The authors of the GPL point out that placing software into the public commons under an academic open source license doesn't always serve that important purpose. Any licensee under an academic open source license can take that free software, create derivative works from it, and then distribute those derivative works under a proprietary license. The resulting software is not free. The Free Software Foundation politely characterizes these licensees as "uncooperative people."

> *They can make changes, many or few, and distribute the result as a proprietary product. People who receive the program in that modified form do not have the freedom that the original author gave them; the middleman has stripped it away. (From www.fsf.org.)*

The GPL seeks to prevent that situation by imposing a reciprocity obligation on all such middlemen. Licensees must use the GPL as their license if they distribute modified versions of the software. Any resulting derivative works will also be free software.

The GPL also seeks to prevent a software problem that was common in the early 1990s and continues to this day. Many software vendors believe that the only path to profit is through the creation of unique proprietary versions of standard soft-

ware. This leads to software incompatibility, ultimately lock-
ing customers into specific vendors, reducing meaningful
choices for consumers, and creating roadblocks to software
sharing. The story of UNIX is replete with examples of that.
(Eric Raymond's book, *The Art of UNIX Programming*, paints
a turbulent history of the various proprietary forks of the
UNIX operating system.)

By the time Linux was released under the GPL, there were
many versions of UNIX available from many vendors, many
of them incompatible with each other. Now, under the GPL,
there can be many versions of Linux, but the improvements in
any of them can be incorporated back into the rest of them as
market forces dictate. There are no longer licensing obstacles
to taking the best components of Linux software available anywhere and incorporating them back into anyone else's version
of Linux. Compatibility can be created at will by any licensee
of Linux. That is guaranteed by the GPL.

A third policy point of the GPL is that free software is an
ethical objective, distinct from the practical objective of making the source code of software available to licensees. Free software, they say, is a good in itself.

> *Whatever approach you use, it helps to have determination and
> adopt an ethical perspective, as we do in the Free Software Move-
> ment. To treat the public ethically, the software should be free—as
> in freedom—for the whole public. (See www.fsf.org.)*

Because this is a book about the law of licensing rather than
ethics, I will only make two comments about this. First, contract and copyright law doesn't generally deal with the ethical
concerns of private parties; courts are expected to interpret the
plain language of their license agreements in accordance with
legal principles only. Second, whether you agree or disagree

with the ethics of a licensor, accepting software under a license binds you to the terms of that license; you need only concern yourself with doing what you agreed to, not with whatever gods or demons the licensor prays to.

The Preamble to the GPL

Richard Stallman and Eben Moglen, the authors of the GPL, write eloquently in the GPL's preamble about their primary objective in creating the license:

> *The licenses for most software are designed to take away your freedom to share and change it. By contrast, the GNU General Public License is intended to guarantee your freedom to share and change free software—to make sure the software is free for all its users. (GPL Preamble.)*

Eloquence, by the way, and discussions of public policy, are extremely rare in licenses; attorneys will recall no other such example from their law school courses in technology licensing. That is one feature that stands out about the GPL. It was the obvious intention of the authors of the GPL to arouse licensors and licensees to a higher purpose than the mere distribution of software. Strong and convincing language was called for. It is thus perhaps not surprising that some of the harshest critics of the GPL, and many of its most fervent admirers, point to the preamble to that license when engaging each other in political debate about free software.

The preamble, of course, is not an operative part of the GPL license. It is not among its *terms and conditions*. There is nothing in its words that must be obeyed. It is merely a helpful preface so that you can better understand the GPL in its context.

The preamble proceeds to define *free software*:

*When we speak of free software, we are referring to freedom,
not price. Our General Public Licenses are designed to make
sure that you have the freedom to distribute copies of free software (and charge for this service if you wish), that you receive
source code or can get it if you want it, that you can change
the software or use pieces of it in new free programs; and that
you know you can do these things. (GPL Preamble.)*

You will note that this is a shorthand definition of software
freedom, shorter even than the definition on the Free Software
Foundation website quoted in the first chapter of this book.
This paragraph from the license is not the authoritative definition of free software. Unfortunately, arguments about precisely
what *free software* means have engaged the open source community and perplexed the public for some time now. This
additional definition in the preamble to the GPL doesn't help.

The next paragraph foretells the reciprocity bargain of the
GPL:

*To protect your rights, we need to make restrictions that for-
bid anyone to deny you these rights or to ask you to surrender
the rights. These restrictions translate to certain responsibilities for you if you distribute copies of the software, or if you
modify it. (GPL Preamble.)*

This paragraph is particularly interesting. It subtly trans-
forms what had previously been a focus on *freedom* to a statement about *rights*. It suggests to me a number of questions
that have no easy answers, at least within the four corners of
the GPL license or its preamble: How does a freedom become
a right? Whose rights are being protected by the GPL, and
from whom? Who is trying to deny you those rights, and who
has the authority to forbid them from doing it? Can someone
make you surrender a right simply by asking? Do the GPL
restrictions effectively protect you from those awful prospects?

Why do you have to incur responsibilities to protect your own rights?

The fact that these questions have no ready answers points out once again why preambles are bad in licenses. Preambles are not helpful, and they potentially confuse. They are too brief and too ambiguous to guide in the interpretation of the license. And to the extent that they raise discomforting questions for potential licensors and licensees—and their attorneys—they discourage the adoption of the license.

Fortunately, the GPL preamble has no legal significance and is not going to matter if the license is ever litigated in court. But it is still worth reading and analyzing to understand the license authors' achievements and possible misconceptions.

For example, the first sentence of the next paragraph of the GPL preamble is technically incorrect and the rest of that paragraph is misleading:

> *If you distribute copies of such a program, whether gratis or for a fee, you must give the recipients all the rights that you have. You must make sure that they, too, receive or can get the source code. And you must show them these terms so they know their rights. (GPL Preamble.)*

The problem with that first sentence is with the word *all* in the phrase *all the rights that you have*. Neither the free software guidelines nor the open source definition require a licensor to grant *all* his rights; he retains, for example, the right to grant licenses to his own software under different terms than the GPL, and the right to refuse to issue new licenses. Technically, a copyright owner retains all his or her rights and merely grants licenses to others in accordance with certain terms and conditions. The phrase *give the recipients all the rights that you have* is unnecessarily frightening and is not true.

I think what that first sentence intends to say is that, when you sublicense a GPL-licensed work, you must pass along the software under its original license without adding further restrictions. Only in that context does the rest of that paragraph make sense: You received source code when you received the GPL-licensed work, and so you must provide source code when you sublicense it. And to make sure that your sublicensees know that they have the rights to copy, modify and distribute the software and the right to the source code, you must provide them with a copy of the GPL license text, just as you were provided with this copy of the license.

The next paragraphs of the preamble anticipate that the GPL will give licensees "legal permission to copy, distribute, and/or modify the software"; will not provide a warranty; will protect the reputations of the original authors; and will deal effectively with the threat of patents. The actual license terms for this, of course, are not these in the preamble, but those that follow later in the license, under the heading "TERMS AND CONDITIONS FOR COPYING, DISTRIBUTION AND MODIFICATION."

GPL as Template

The GPL devised an elegant solution to the problem of associating a generic software license with specific software. Instead of placing the name of the software in the license (as is usually and inconveniently done with proprietary and many other open source software licenses), it requires that a notice be placed in the software by the copyright holder saying, "it may be distributed under the terms of this General Public License." Where this notice is to be placed is not specified, but at the end of the GPL, in a separate nonbinding section entitled "How to Apply These Terms to Your New Programs," the

GPL suggests that the notice should be at the start of each source file.

The GPL is thus a template license, applicable to software by any author who chooses to use it. All a licensor has to do to use it is to include a notice in his or her source code saying, in effect, "I'm licensing this software to you under the GPL." But which GPL? There was at least one earlier version and there are promises of another version to come. How can a licensor indicate which version of the GPL applies to the licensed software? Here's how the GPL handles that situation:

> *If the Program specifies a version number of this License which applies to it and "any later version", you have the option of following the terms and conditions either of that version or of any later version published by the Free Software Foundation. If the Program does not specify a version number of this License, you may choose any version ever published by the Free Software Foundation. (GPL section 9.)*

Some licensors object to giving anyone, including the Free Software Foundation, the opportunity to change the licensing rules for his or her own software after the software has already been distributed under a specific license. Those licensors, then, should be explicit in the notices they place in the software, being careful to identify that they are "licensing this software to you under the GPL version 2" if that is specifically what they intend.

The GPL Applies to Programs

Rather than use the generic term *software*, the GPL instead defines the term *Program* as *a program or other work*. We generally understand that a *program* (with lower case *p*) is computer software, but the phrase *other work* is left undefined.

The GPL, in section 0, then defines the phrase *work based on the Program* as either a *Program* or a *derivative work under copyright law*. (Careful readers will remember that, under copyright law a *derivative work* is a work based upon one or more preexisting works.... 17 U.S.C. § 101.) This definition is repeated in a different way in section 1 of the GPL, which says that a *work based on the Program* is formed by modifying the original Program. (Remember that a modification is one of the specific kinds of derivative works mentioned in the copyright law.) Thus far, the GPL is entirely consistent with copyright law definitions, and so it applies to Programs and to derivative works of those Programs.

Unfortunately, the section 0 definition of *work based on the Program* is then broadened beyond what is generally considered in the copyright law to be a derivative work:

> *...that is to say, a work containing the Program or a portion of it, either verbatim or with modifications and/or translated into another language. (GPL section 0.)*

Is a work based on the Program really the same as a work containing the Program or a portion of it?

I have already explained the fundamental difference in copyright law between a *collective work* and a *derivative work*. You will recall generally that the former is a collection of independent works and the latter is a work based upon one or more preexisting works. A work containing another work is a *collective work*. A work based on another work is a *derivative work*. Merging those concepts in the GPL would leave no distinction between a derivative and collective work, an absurd result considering the importance of those two defined terms in copyright law.

The issue is critical for another reason. It is the basis for a long-running dispute about the reach of the GPL to separate unmodified programs that merely link to each other but that are collected into one program for convenience. If, through linking to a program that is included in a collective work, one creates a *derivative work*, how widely does the *reciprocity* obligation of the GPL reach?

Linking to GPL Software

It is appropriate to look within the four corners of the GPL itself for guidance on this question about program linking.

The word *link* actually occurs only once in the official GPL, way at the end in the last paragraph of a nonbinding section called "How to Apply These Terms to Your New Programs." This paragraph deals with a different license, the LGPL, which I will describe in due course.

There are other provisions of the GPL that refer to *work based on the Program*. Here is the first possibly helpful reference:

> *...Output from the Program is covered only if its contents constitute a work based on the Program (independent of having been made by running the Program). Whether that is true depends on what the Program does. (GPL section 0.)*

This provision deals with the special case of a Program that generates other programs that contain either verbatim or modified/translated versions of itself. Such an esoteric example of program interdependence is best ignored in a general book like this about open source licensing. It is not likely to be encountered in typical open source applications.

The GPL, in section 2, then requires us to analyze the software based not upon how it is *linked* but upon how it is *distributed*. Because it will be helpful to parse this provision carefully, I quote each sentence separately.

> *These requirements apply to the modified work as a whole.*

If identifiable sections of that work are not derived from the Program, and can be reasonably considered independent and separate works in themselves, then this License, and its terms, do not apply to those sections when you distribute them as separate works.

But when you distribute the same sections as part of a whole which is a work based on the Program, the distribution of the whole must be on the terms of this License, whose permissions for other licensees extend to the entire whole, and thus to each and every part regardless of who wrote it. (GPL section 2.)

According to the first sentence, the entire GPL applies to a "modified work as a whole." Under the copyright law, such a "modified work" is a derivative work. (17 U.S.C. § 101.) So far, there is no hint that linking makes a difference.

The second sentence refers to portions of the work that "are not derived from the Program"—that is, are not derivative works. This necessarily means works that have their own copyrights, their own copyright owners, and potentially their own licenses. So the second sentence is true regardless of whether the independent and separate works are linked in some way to the GPL software. Such works remain "independent and separate works," at least "when you distribute them as separate works," and the GPL cannot possibly apply to them without their copyright owner's consent.

The third sentence refers to those "independent and separate works" when they are distributed "as part of a whole." Once again, we are reminded that the GPL applies to the whole work. But how are we to understand its reference to "the same sections as part of a whole which is a work based on the Program" and later "to each and every part regardless of who wrote it"? Is this a reference to the Copyright Act?

> *The copyright in a compilation or derivative work extends
> only to the material contributed by the author of such work,
> as distinguished from the preexisting material employed in
> the work, and does not imply any exclusive right in the pre-
> existing material. (17 U.S.C. § 103.)*

All that the third sentence of GPL section 2 could possibly
mean under the copyright law is that, for a work to be made
available under the GPL, its preexisting component parts must
be available to all subsequent licensees. The licenses to those
components must permit that combination. That much is
necessarily true for any software containing components
licensed by others. The law makes it clear that the GPL can't
affect the licenses to those preexisting component parts.
Again, linking doesn't matter.

The GPL then expresses its intent this way:

> *The intent is to exercise the right to control the distribution
> of derivative or collective works based on the Program. (GPL
> section 2.)*

That may be the intent, but is that what the GPL actually
does? This is a critical example of imprecise phrasing. Who
gets "to exercise the right to control" distribution? Certainly
the owner of a collective or derivative work gets "to exercise
the right to control" those works, and the owner of each contribution gets "to exercise the right to control" his or her contribution. (17 U.S.C. § 103[b].)

Does the phrase *based on the program* refer to both derivative and collective works? That isn't technically correct, at least
under the U.S. Copyright Act, because a derivative work is a
work based on one or more preexisting works, but a collective
work is not. (17 U.S.C. § 101.) There is still no meaningful
clue about linkage.

This entire GPL provision in section 2 relating to distribution of the *whole work* is technically trivial to avoid. Some open source projects, trying to stay on the "safe" side of this GPL provision, advise their customers to separately download and install required non-GPL software merely to avoid "distribution as part of a whole." Thus the distinction drawn by this part of GPL section 2 has become an inconvenience rather than a meaningful requirement.

Finally the GPL directly addresses the distribution of collective works, noting that the GPL does not apply to them:

> ...*In addition, mere aggregation of another work not based on the Program with the Program (or with a work based on the Program) on a volume of a storage or distribution medium does not bring the other work under the scope of this License. (GPL section 2.)*

This sentence seems to mean that only *derivative* works are covered by the GPL reciprocity provision, and that "mere aggregation" of separate works onto common media (or common computer memory?) does not require reciprocity, even if those mere aggregations are distributed in one unit (i.e., "as part of the whole").

We are left with uncertainty—and instructions to contact the author of the Program for guidance:

> *If you wish to incorporate parts of the Program into other free programs whose distribution conditions are different, write to the author to ask for permission. (GPL section 10.)*

Some authors have indeed provided that guidance. Linus Torvalds, for example, has set a policy that software that is merely combined with Linux is not subject to the GPL regardless of how that software is linked and distributed.

Copyright Law and Linking

Why do I spend so much time dealing with issues of software linking? Does this topic really matter to anyone but open source zealots?

Consider the metaphor of the World Wide Web, a huge collection of individually written web pages that anyone can access and display just by linking. Those pages are individually copyrighted works, made available to all by their authors, generally for free (i.e., at zero price). Under the copyright law, you do not create a derivative work of someone's web page by linking to it, nor is it a derivative work of your web page if it links to you.

At most, such linkages create collective works. A web page, for example, that contains links to articles about open source may present those links in an original, copyrightable way. That list of links is a copyrightable *original work of authorship*, and the links operate to create a *collective work*. But the original articles remain the copyrightable works of their own authors.

Not that we can't envision using the Internet to create derivative works of web pages. You can find a web page you like and make changes to it, using the modified version as your own. You can translate a web page from one language to another. You can provide editorial revisions, annotate the web pages, or elaborate upon them. You can then link to your new versions. In doing so, you create *derivative works*. But it is not the linking that made the difference.

I do not want to discourage the creation of *collective works*. To do so would be inconsistent with the goals of free and open source software, just as it would be inconsistent with the goals of a free and open World Wide Web. Are the GPL's *Programs* so different from other copyrightable works that they deserve a narrower range of freedom?

One could, of course, ask the authors of the GPL how to interpret their license provisions, and they have indeed spoken out about this topic on their website, *www.fsf.org*, and in other public venues. But it is legally unnecessary to know what the drafter of a license—usually just an attorney with no stake in the matter—meant to say. That is why I can legally ignore the advisory notice that is published with the GPL after its terms and conditions have ended:

> *This General Public License does not permit incorporating your program into proprietary programs. (See "How to Apply These Terms to Your New Programs.")*

Under the law, only the common understanding of a licensor and his licensees matters, as reflected in the written terms and conditions of the license agreement between them. It is Linus Torvalds, and the thousands of other licensors under the GPL, who have standing under the law to assert their interpretations of the GPL, not the Free Software Foundation (except for that software for which *they* own the copyrights). And it is a judge who would ultimately decide such an issue if it reaches that level of conflict.

One final warning: If there is an ambiguity or uncertainty of interpretation in a license, the license will generally be interpreted *against* the licensor regardless of what the license drafter meant to say. It is up to the authors of the GPL to make their license clear, not up to licensees to seek outside guidance to interpret it. I explore that issue further in Chapter 12.

I won't give legal advice of a general nature to the readers of this book. So you can take with a grain of salt my belief that these interrelated sections of the GPL quoted earlier will ultimately be read by the courts to mean that *derivative works* are subject to the GPL's reciprocity provision, but *collective works* are not. And as I shall argue again more fully in the discussion of derivative works litigation in Chapter 12, the legal analysis of what constitutes a derivative work simply doesn't depend upon the style or mechanism of inter-program linking.

This, by the way, is also the only interpretation that is consistent with item 5 of the Open Source Principles listed in Chapter 1, that allows licensees freely to combine open source and other software.

The LGPL Alternative

Originally called the *Library GPL*, this special version of the GPL directly addresses the linking question. It is now called the *Lesser General Public License*, or *LGPL* for short. Advisory text at the end of the published GPL license (but not one of its terms and conditions) encourages the use of the LGPL for certain applications:

> *If your program is a subroutine library, you may consider it more useful to permit linking proprietary applications with the library. If this is what you want to do, use the GNU Lesser General Public License instead of this License. (GPL, "How to Apply These Terms to Your New Programs" following GPL Terms and Conditions.)*

The LGPL is an important, widely used open source license in its own right. The complete text of the terms and conditions of that license, leaving out the extraneous preamble and postscripts, is shown in the Appendices.

The LGPL is for the distribution of software libraries.

> *A "library" means a collection of software functions and/or data prepared so as to be conveniently linked with application programs ... to form executables. (LGPL section 0.)*

This definition suggests that a *library* is designed with a goal in mind: It is "to be conveniently linked with application programs to form executables." The important characteristics of a library are not the form of linkage used by the members of that collection, nor the specific functions and/or data that are prepared. The LGPL is, after all, a general purpose license intended for adoption by software in many technological forms.

Here is how that same definition might be rephrased in copyright law terms: A "Library" is an original work of authorship that is intended to be incorporated into other works through some form of linkage.

The LGPL then grants a license for the Library to be used in its intended way:

> *The act of running a program using the Library is not restricted.... (LGPL section 0.)*

The LGPL repeats this same point a second time:

> *A program that contains no derivative of any portion of the Library, but is designed to work with the Library by being compiled or linked with it, is called a "work that uses the Library". Such a work, in isolation, is not a derivative work of the Library, and therefore falls outside the scope of this License. (LGPL section 5.)*

Both license grants are consistent with copyright law, of course, and nobody could reasonably suggest that mere invocation of a Library, however the linkage takes place, is a *derivative work*.

Modifications of a *Library* itself, of course, are derivative works, subject to the LGPL's reciprocity provision, just as modifications to any *Program* are subject to the GPL's reciprocity provision when you distribute those modifications:

> *You must cause the whole of the work to be licensed at no charge to all third parties under the terms of this License. (LGPL section 2[c].)*

Two other requirements from LGPL section 2, however, are not so clear:

> *The modified work must itself be a software library. (LGPL section 2[a].)*

Is this a definition or a requirement? How is it to be satisfied by a diligent licensee? And later:

> *If a facility in the modified Library refers to a function or a table of data to be supplied by an application program that uses the facility, other than as an argument passed when the facility is invoked, then you must make a good faith effort to ensure that, in the event an application does not supply such function or table, the facility still operates, and performs whatever part of its purpose remains meaningful. (For example, a function in a library to compute square roots has a purpose that is entirely well-defined independent of the application. Therefore, Subsection 2[d] requires that any application-supplied function or table used by this function must be optional: if the application does not supply it, the square root function must still compute square roots.) (LGPL section 2[d].)*

And still later:

> *If such an object file uses only numerical parameters, data structure layouts and accessors, and small macros and small inline functions (ten lines or less in length), then the use of the object file is unrestricted, regardless of whether it is legally a derivative work. (Executables containing this object code plus portions of the Library will still fall under Section 6.)*
>
> *Otherwise, if the work is a derivative of the Library, you may distribute the object code for the work under the terms of Section 6. Any executables containing that work also fall under Section 6, whether or not they are linked directly with the Library itself. (LGPL section 5.)*

These sections of the LGPL are an impenetrable maze of technological babble. They should not be in a general-purpose software license. The LGPL even concedes that "the threshold for this to be true is not precisely defined by law." (LGPL section 5.) A licensee under these provisions won't have a clue how extensive his or her *good faith efforts* must be when creating a *derivative work* in accordance with sections 2(d) and 5 of the LGPL.

In any event, a careful comparison of the text of the GPL and LGPL licenses (far too detailed and specific to attempt here) reveals that, if the process of adding or deleting library functions creates a *derivative work* of the Library, then the LGPL functions identically to the GPL.

The LGPL concedes that the GPL is a better, more appropriate license, and it allows any licensees to convert to the GPL at their option:

> *You may opt to apply the terms of the ordinary GNU General Public License instead of this License to a given copy of the Library. To do this, you must alter all the notices that refer to this License, so that they refer to the ordinary GNU General Public License, version 2, instead of to this License. (If a newer version than version 2 of the ordinary GNU General Public License has appeared, then you can specify that version instead if you wish.) Do not make any other change in these notices.*

> *Once this change is made in a given copy, it is irreversible for that copy, so the ordinary GNU General Public License applies to all subsequent copies and derivative works made from that copy.*

> *This option is useful when you wish to copy part of the code of the Library into a program that is not a library. (LGPL section 3.)*

The LGPL, therefore, is an anomaly—a hybrid license intended to address a complex issue about program linking and derivative works. It doesn't solve that problem but merely directs us back to the main event, the GPL license itself.

GPL Grant of License

The first place in its terms and conditions that the GPL mentions its license grant is in the negative:

> *Activities other than copying, distribution and modification are not covered by this License; they are outside its scope. (GPL section 0.)*

Thus are the first three exclusive rights of a copyright owner from 17 U.S.C. § 106 introduced. (Refer to the discussion of the exclusive rights of copyright owners in Chapter 2.) The license grant is stated in an affirmative way later in the GPL:

> *You may copy and distribute verbatim copies of the Program's source code as you receive it, in any medium, provided.... (GPL section 1.)*

> *You may modify your copy or copies of the Program or any portion of it, thus forming a work based on the Program, and copy and distribute such modifications or work under the terms of Section 1 above, provided.... (GPL section 2.)*

> *You may copy and distribute the Program (or a work based on it, under Section 2) in object code or executable form under the terms of Sections 1 and 2 above provided.... (GPL section 3.)*

These, plus the source code grant discussed in the next section, are the required grants to comply with the Open Source Principles listed in Chapter 1.

You may have noted that the GPL does not grant *all* the rights under copyright; missing are licenses to perform the work or to display the work publicly. For most software, that's not important.

There are more interesting things than that missing from the GPL's license grant. The first and most important is a patent grant. The GPL does not expressly grant rights to make, use, sell or offer for sale, or import software that embodies the licensor's patents. This omission is important for a bare license like the GPL, because nothing in the law requires the licensor of copyrights to also license his patents. Bare patent licenses are not implied.

The GPL attempts to solve this problem by including the following condition:

> *If a patent license would not permit royalty-free redistribu-*
> *tion of the Program by all those who receive copies directly or*
> *indirectly through you, then the only way you could satisfy*
> *both it and this License would be to refrain entirely from dis-*
> *tribution of the Program. (GPL section 7.)*

In other words, a licensor cannot distribute software under the GPL while simultaneously demanding royalties for his patents. His act of distributing the software implies a royalty-free license.

As to the scope of such an implied patent license, can we assume that it extends to the creation of derivative works since the GPL contemplates that licensees will create derivative works? That is possible, but there's nothing in the law of bare licenses that requires that result. Any company intending to create and distribute derivative works under the GPL ought to obtain separately the patent licenses it needs.

The second item that is missing is a statement of what other intellectual property rights, if any, are intentionally excluded from the license grant. For example, suppose a GPL-licensed program bears a trademark and that trademark is printed out by the program in some initial welcome message. Does a licensee under the GPL have the right to apply that trademark to his or her own derivative works? Must the licensee remove the trademark from executable versions of this derivative work? The GPL is silent on that point.

The GPL is also silent about the scope and duration of the licenses it does grant. One can assume that the license is *worldwide*, consistent with the open source definition. One can also assume that the license is *perpetual,* since there is no mechanism for terminating the license as long as the licensee complies with the terms of the license:

> *You may not copy, modify, sublicense, or distribute the Program except as expressly provided under this License. Any attempt otherwise to copy, modify, sublicense or distribute the Program is void, and will automatically terminate your rights under this License. However, parties who have received copies, or rights, from you under this License will not have their licenses terminated so long as such parties remain in full compliance. (GPL section 4.)*

This GPL section 4, with its negative wording, is also the only place that references the right to *sublicense*. One might assume from the way GPL section 4 is worded that the right to sublicense was intended in sections 1 (right to copy), 2 (right to modify) and 3 (right to distribute) as well. However, section 6 implies that there are no sublicenses but instead a direct license from each up-stream contributor:

*Each time you redistribute the Program (or any work based
on the Program), the recipient automatically receives a license from the original licensor to copy, distribute or modify
the Program subject to these terms and conditions.... (GPL
section 6.)*

As to sublicensing, then, the GPL is ambiguous. I refer you
to the discussion in Chapter 5 of sublicensing in the MIT
license. Sublicensing rights can be very important to open
source distributors for dealing properly with the chain of title
to contributions. In practice, most software projects ignore the
issue completely and assume that, for GPL software, only the
most recent license in the chain of title matters. They assume
that GPL licensed software is sublicenseable, but the GPL isn't
clear about that.

Access to Source Code

The GPL allows licensees to copy and distribute the source
code:

*You may copy and distribute verbatim copies of the
Program's source code as you receive it, in any medium,
provided.... (GPL section 1.)*

Source code is defined as follows:

*The source code for a work means the preferred form of the
work for making modifications to it. For an executable
work, complete source code means all the source code for all
modules it contains, plus any associated interface definition
files, plus the scripts used to control compilation and installation of the executable. (GPL section 3.)*

This is a broad definition and its intent is obviously to
ensure that usable source code is available for licensed software. Deliberate obfuscation of the source code (as has been

rumored to have been done by some GPL licensors) is potentially actionable as bad faith.

The GPL then offers a curious *special exception* for software that is normally distributed with the operating system on which the Program runs:

> *However, as a special exception, the source code distributed need not include anything that is normally distributed (in either source or binary form) with the major components (compiler, kernel, and so on) of the operating system on which the executable runs, unless that component itself accompanies the executable. (GPL section 3.)*

The licensor of the operating system, and not the licensor of the Program, is the only one who can elect to publish his or her own source code. The GPL cannot possibly grant that permission or provide an exception relating to it. As was discussed at length in the previous section, the fact that software is merely distributed with the Program doesn't bring it under the GPL. This "special exception" is irrelevant if one accepts that only derivative works, and not collective works, are brought under the GPL.

As one of the conditions for distributing a Program or a derivative work of the Program in object code form, the licensor must also commit to the following:

> *a) Accompany it with the complete corresponding machine-readable source code, which must be distributed under the terms of Sections 1 and 2 above on a medium customarily used for software interchange; or,*
>
> *b) Accompany it with a written offer, valid for at least three years, to give any third party, for a charge no more than your cost of physically performing source distribution, a complete machine-readable copy of the corresponding source code, to*

be distributed under the terms of Sections 1 and 2 above on
a medium customarily used for software interchange; or,

c) Accompany it with the information you received as to the
offer to distribute corresponding source code. (This alterna-
tive is allowed only for noncommercial distribution and only
if you received the program in object code or executable form
with such an offer, in accord with Subsection b above.)
(GPL section 3.)

A licensor under the GPL is expected to distribute or make available the source code for software he or she writes. That is what items a) and b) of GPL section 3 require. But what is the licensor's obligation regarding the source code of GPL-licensed software that he or she merely distributes, perhaps as a component of a GPL-licensed collective or derivative work? Must the licensor undertake to distribute the source code to all the contributions of the entire collective work, including components he or she didn't write? Item c) would appear to solve this problem, but only for *noncommercial distribution*. I believe that, in practice, most distributors under the GPL provide source code for their entire collective works, not just the portions they themselves write, regardless of this limitation to *noncommercial* licensors.

The GPL also gives licensors the option to distribute source code through the Internet, although it acknowledges that licensees *are not* compelled (i.e., they *cannot be* compelled) to accept the source code if they don't want it:

If distribution of executable or object code is made by offering
access to copy from a designated place, then offering equiva-
lent access to copy the source code from the same place counts
as distribution of the source code, even though third parties

are not compelled to copy the source along with the object code. (GPL section 3.)

This provision relates only to software that is downloaded, and is needed only because items a-c) of GPL section 3 relate to distribution on a physical medium. Almost all open source software is now distributed electronically on the Internet. A more modern open source license would probably condense these complex source code rules in the GPL into a few brief sentences to require that the licensor make source code available online.

The GPL is thus consistent with the source code requirements of the Open Source Principles listed in Chapter 1.

"At No Charge"

There are three words in the GPL's reciprocity provision that I saved until now. Here's how the GPL reads:

You must cause any work that you distribute or publish, that in whole or in part contains or is derived from the Program or any part thereof, to be licensed as a whole at no charge to all third parties under the terms of this License. (GPL section 2.)

The GPL, unlike most other licenses, requires that derivative works be licensed as a whole *at no charge* to third parties under the terms of this License.

The open source principles listed in Chapter 1 allow reciprocity conditions, under which a licensor can insist that licensees operate on the exact same playing field as the licensor does. The GPL licensors distributed their software for free, and they insist that their licensee's derivative works also be *zero price, as a reciprocal condition for being allowed to create derivative works in the first place.*

Earlier in the license, however, the GPL left a big escape hatch for those who want to recover their costs of distributing software. It provides:

> *You may charge a fee for the physical act of transferring a copy, and you may at your option offer warranty protection in exchange for a fee. (GPL section 1.)*

Anyone familiar with business accounting will recognize that it is relatively simple to allocate costs to the "physical act of transferring a copy" when it is really a cost of getting copies ready to be transferred.

Regardless of this loophole, the laws of economics dictate that customers will only pay for value received. If they are free to make copies without paying anyone royalties for those copies, then the price that distributors can charge for copies of original software or derivative works will soon approach the marginal cost of production and distribution regardless of whether the GPL mandates a zero price.

There is also a problem that may prevent enforcement of the GPL's *at no charge* provision. It may be an illegal restraint of trade in some countries. Ordinarily, companies are allowed to set their own prices, and it is improper for a GPL licensor to constrain that in any way.

Most other reciprocal licenses do not require that derivative works be distributed at zero price. Their reciprocity obligation extends simply to requiring that the source code be published and that derivative works be distributed *under the terms of this License*. The price of the derivative work software is left for market forces to determine.

Other Obligations in the GPL

The GPL doesn't grant unconditional licenses. Those who copy and distribute verbatim copies of a Program are required to:

...Conspicuously and appropriately publish on each copy an appropriate copyright notice and disclaimer of warranty; keep intact all the notices that refer to this License and to the absence of any warranty; and give any other recipients of the Program a copy of this License along with the Program. (GPL section 1.)

Those who create and distribute derivative works are also required to:

a) Cause the modified files to carry prominent notices stating that you changed the files and the date of any change. (GPL section 2)

c) If the modified program normally reads commands interactively when run, you must cause it, when started running for such interactive use in the most ordinary way, to print or display an announcement including an appropriate copyright notice and a notice that there is no warranty (or else, saying that you provide a warranty) and that users may redistribute the program under these conditions, and telling the user how to view a copy of this License. (Exception: if the Program itself is interactive but does not normally print such an announcement, your work based on the Program is not required to print an announcement.) (GPL section 2.)

These provisions protect the integrity and reputation of the original authors and ensure that subsequent licensees know that the GPL applies to that software.

The GPL and Patents

Nobody is quite sure what effect software and business method patents will have on open source software. That is because patent problems often arise from unexpected quarters. A person nobody heard of may claim that software infringes his or her patent. Suddenly software embodying that patent cannot be made, used, or sold absent a license from the patent owner—unless, of course, the patent can be designed around and similar functionality accomplished in a different way.

It may thus happen that open source software that was previously free is no longer so. But that conclusion is here just a vague abstraction. Which software and which patent, and what effect on software freedom, is a mystery until it actually happens.

The GPL deals with such potential patent claims in a philosophically consistent way. If and when a valid patent claim by a third party prevents a GPL licensor from making, using, or selling the software, such software will no longer be *free* (in the GPL's sense of that word) and the software can no longer be distributed under the GPL. Here is the provision:

> *If, as a consequence of a court judgment or allegation of patent infringement..., conditions are imposed on you (whether by court order, agreement or otherwise) that contradict the conditions of this License, they do not excuse you from the conditions of this License. If you cannot distribute so as to satisfy simultaneously your obligations under this License and any other pertinent obligations, then as a consequence you may not distribute the Program at all....*
> *(GPL section 7.)*

This leaves undefined just what "pertinent obligations" one might incur as a "consequence of court judgment," and leaves to later analysis what "obligations under this License" might be contradicted by the court judgment. The provision clearly means, though, that it will take more than the threat of patent infringement to invoke this provision. An actual patent dispute has to be alleged and either litigated or settled.

At the end of section 7, the GPL describes this patent provision not as a new provision but as "a consequence of the rest of this License." And so it is important to ask whether this form of self-imposed restriction on licensing in the face of a third party patent claim is an inevitable consequence of open source licensing in general or something unique to the GPL. It is particularly instructive that only the GPL has this provision, and that many other important open source licenses have very different patent defense provisions that don't require subsequent licensees to forgo their rights to create and distribute derivative works.

The only obligations a licensee accepts under the GPL are (1) the reciprocity obligation and (2) obligations regarding the integrity of the original authors. It is difficult to see how a court judgment regarding a patent would prevent either of these two obligations from continuing to be met.

I will describe in more detail in a later chapter on open source litigation that there are really only two significant consequences of civil litigation about a software license: an *injunction* or an *economic penalty*. As to injunction, whatever the injunction you must obey it; if a court orders you to stop making, using, or selling a patented invention, you must do so. As to economic penalties, if a court orders you to start paying royalties or to pay royalties for past infringement, you must do so. (You agree to accept those risks; the GPL's warranty provision, similar to those in most other open source licenses, provides no warranty of noninfringement.) The risk from patent infringement is the same whether you use the GPL, any other open source license, or indeed any proprietary license.

If a court order requires that you stop distributing derivative works unless you pay a license fee to a patent holder, you may elect to stop distributing derivative works or to pay the fee. The *at no charge* language of the GPL's reciprocity provision may prevent you from recovering that cost, but by itself it doesn't prevent you from continuing distribution if you're willing to do so at your own cost.

Patents are a local problem. Patents are awarded nationally; what is patented in one country may be free to use in other countries. The GPL acknowledges this by allowing licensors to continue to license their works in the geographical regions where the patents don't apply:

> *If the distribution and/or use of the Program is restricted in certain countries either by patents or by copyrighted interfaces, the original copyright holder who places the Program under this License may add an explicit geographical distribution limitation excluding those countries, so that distribution is permitted only in or among countries not thus excluded.... (GPL section 8.)*

Accepting the GPL

Under contract law, a contract is not properly formed unless the parties to the contract manifest their assent to being bound by it. Such assent is traditionally manifested by signatures on a license agreement, a technique that is not appropriate for mass-marketed software distributed at retail stores or over the Internet.

For software downloaded from the Internet, distributors generally require a *click-wrap* form of assent. Before they can download the software, prospective licensees are presented with the license and are given a chance to "Click to Agree." Only those who manifest their assent by clicking are allowed to download the software. Courts have also blessed this procedure under contract law.

For retail store purchases, distributors often use *shrink-wrap* agreements. A license is placed in the package along with the software. By careful packaging (usually in a shrink-wrap plastic), licensors can ensure that prospective licensees have an opportunity to review the license agreement before they gain access to the copy of the software they have purchased. By proceeding to open the software, licensees are presumed to have seen and agreed to the license. Opening the inner software package is deemed to be an appropriate manifestation of assent. Licensees who don't assent to the license have the opportunity to return the copy of software, unopened, for a full refund of their purchase price. Courts have generally blessed this procedure as satisfying the *manifestation of assent* requirements of contract law.

Some software implements a *click-wrap* procedure that occurs as the copy of software is actually installed on a computer rather than when it is purchased. Regardless of when the assent is requested, any purchaser of a copy who does not assent must be given an opportunity to return the copy for a full refund.

Courts don't generally care whether prospective licensees actually read the license agreements as long as there is a reasonable opportunity to do so, and as long as their intent to assent is manifested.

Of course, since most consumers don't actually read license agreements, and since most license agreements are complicated legal documents with largely unintelligible legal language, courts will also protect consumers from being surprised by unfair or unexpected provisions, even if they have manifested their assent. For now, I assume that most people reading this book accept that open source licenses—and the Open Source Principles upon which they are based—are fair.

The GPL relies on an entirely different set of legal principles, based on copyright law rather than contract law, to ensure that the license terms are accepted. It does not require—indeed its authors seek to prevent attempts to obtain—a manifestation of assent to GPL license terms. The GPL license acceptance provision reads as follows:

> *You are not required to accept this License, since you have not signed it. However, nothing else grants you permission to modify or distribute the Program or its derivative works. These actions are prohibited by law if you do not accept this License. Therefore, by modifying or distributing the Program (or any work based on the Program), you indicate your acceptance of this License to do so, and all its terms and conditions for copying, distributing or modifying the Program or works based on it. (GPL section 5.)*

Copyright law says that an author has exclusive rights to make copies of, to modify, or to distribute copyrighted software. Nobody can make a copy without a license from the author to do so. The mere exercise of someone else's exclusive rights without a license is an illegal *copyright infringement*. It is not necessary to prove that a defendant intended to infringe.

If you modify and distribute software without a license, the GPL suggests, you are presumed to know that your actions are illegal and, even if you don't know that you're breaking the law, the copyright law still makes you a copyright infringer. Don't do it, or you will expose yourself to potentially substantial penalties under the copyright law. (Possible penalties for copyright infringement include injunctions, the impounding and destruction of infringing articles, actual damages and profits, statutory damages, costs, and attorneys' fees.)

While this GPL reliance entirely on copyright law for license enforcement is legally sound, it has two shortcomings.

1. Only a copyright owner, not a distributor under a nonexclusive license, has standing to sue to enforce the GPL copyright license. On the other hand, if a contract is formed through a manifestation of assent, then contract law allows the distributor to enforce a license even if he or she doesn't own the copyrights in the underlying works. This means that if you use the GPL to distribute software but you don't own the copyrights to parts of that software, you can't sue under copyright law to protect those parts from infringement even if they were copied from *your* distribution. If you can prove that the licensee assented to a contract, however, you can protect your version of the entire work, and its component parts, against license violations.

2. At least in the United States, copyright disputes are heard only in federal court. Contract claims, on the other hand, can be heard in state and local courts, or in federal court if the amount in dispute is large enough and if the parties are not in the same state. If you use the GPL, you are limiting your litigation options to federal court.

If you are an open source licensor, I encourage you to obtain a proper manifestation of assent to your open source software licenses so that your enforcement options match your business strategies. If you want the option to pursue contract litigation and obtain contract law remedies, you probably don't want to use the GPL.

All open source licenses rely, at heart, upon the copyright law, as the GPL says in its section 5. But then, once a license is granted, that license may be interpreted under contract law provisions. Open source licenses should be clean, well-written contracts, or they may not be enforced by the courts.

This is the direction taken by all the licenses in the rest of this book. The GPL is the only license whose authors insist that it be treated as a bare copyright license but not a contract.

7

The Mozilla Public License (MPL)

The Mozilla Story

In the late 1990s, Netscape was facing a serious problem. Its browser, the Netscape Communicator, was rapidly losing market share to Microsoft's Internet Explorer, and it was difficult for them to define a competitive business case to justify ongoing development and licensing of their proprietary browser. Rather than simply shut down development, however, Netscape decided to turn it into an open source project and to license their software to the public under an open source license. But which license?

Netscape resisted using an academic license because, in the company's opinion, such licenses don't go far enough to return certain modified code back to the community. (This history is discussed in much more detail at *www.mozilla.org*.) They realized that academic licenses allow "middlemen" to remove improvements from the free software commons—and they didn't want that to happen.

They also resisted using the GPL for four important business and legal reasons. First, they believed that the GPL was incompatible with certain obligations they had under other licenses for software they had previously incorporated into their browser. Second, they weren't sure if the GPL was consistent with cryptographic code regulated by U.S. law. Third, they weren't sure what their reciprocity obligations would be under the GPL for other Netscape products (particularly servers), and they wanted to be sure that other software of theirs could remain proprietary. And fourth, they were concerned that other companies would decline their software if the GPL were used.

Netscape even considered using the LGPL because that license seemed to narrow the risk that software that merely interacted with their browser would come under the reciprocity provision. But it too was rejected.

A Netscape executive and attorney, Mitchell Baker, who understood both the structure of Netscape software and the legal requirements, wrote a new open source license to address these problems. The resulting Mozilla Public License (the MPL), has been the model for most of the important commercial open source licenses that followed. Next to the BSD and the GPL, the MPL is the most influential open source license. Baker went on to become the *Chief Lizard Wrangler* of the Mozilla open source project.

The MPL is a serious license. I will direct much less criticism to the structure and terms of the MPL in this book than to the other licenses I've already written about, because the MPL is a high-quality, professional legal accomplishment in a commercial setting.

One of the challenges to writing about licensing in a book not specifically written for licensing professionals is to make a very dull subject interesting. For those readers who are skilled computer programmers, compare my challenge to that of an engineer who wants to explain C++ programming or the TCP/IP stack to the public.

How do I explain an open source license like the MPL deeply enough to make my description accurate without quoting pages of legal provisions and explaining how courts will interpret them? The most recent version (1.1) of the MPL is copied in the Appendices. Obviously I don't have to reprint each section seriatim and translate it into colloquial English, nor parse each sentence so that you can recognize a derivative work or a collective work when you see it.

So instead what I will do is paint a broad picture. I'll describe how the MPL and similar licenses from many other commercial companies are structured. I'll highlight things you and your attorney should look for in such licenses when accepting software under them, and what you need to consider when you modify those licenses for use in distributing your own software.

The MPL Reciprocity Bargain

Although the MPL is a much longer license than the others I've discussed, when you get beyond the complex words, its reciprocity provisions can be paraphrased very simply as follows: *If you create and distribute a Modification to one of the files containing Original Code or previous Modifications, or create and distribute a new file containing Original Code or previous Modifications, those files must be released as Modifications under the same MPL license.*

Your newly released files become *Modifications* for future licensees. One can recognize in this recursive definition how a chain of title is created to ever-more-modified derivative works, with each Contributor adding to the chain. But here, unlike with previous licenses, the MPL deals with *files containing derivative works* rather than *derivative works* more broadly.

This calls for precise definitions, which the MPL provides. Here are four of them:

*"Contributor" means each entity that creates or contributes
to the creation of Modifications. (MPL section 1.1.)*

*"Covered Code" means the Original Code or Modifications
or the combination of the Original Code and Modifications,
in each case including portions thereof. (MPL section 1.3.)*

*"Modifications" means any addition to or deletion from the
substance or structure of either the Original Code or any previous Modifications. When Covered Code is released as a series of files, a Modification is:*

*A. Any addition to or deletion from the contents of a file con-
taining Original Code or previous Modifications.*

*B. Any new file that contains any part of the Original Code
or previous Modifications. (MPL section 1.9.)*

*"Original Code" means Source Code of computer software
code which is described in the Source Code notice required
by Exhibit A as Original Code, and which, at the time of its
release under this License is not already Covered Code governed by this License. (MPL section 1.10.)*

Such definitions are extremely important in software
licenses. You have already seen how words in simple academic
licenses, and even some words in the venerable GPL, are confusing and subject to misinterpretation. Words without definition are ambiguous; there is no reliable way to predict how the
parties—or a court—might interpret a license without clear
definitions when performance under it is called for or ques-
tioned.

One way to deal with that problem is to rely on *terms of art,*
words that will be understood by the parties and by courts
because they are defined in the legal lexicon or by statute. That
is why I have been so adamant in this book about using the
terms *collective works* and *derivative works* precisely. Those
terms are defined by statute for all lawyers to understand

(although few really do), and if we use them consistently we'll at least all mean the same thing. We can also use court decisions from similar cases to help us predict how the courts will interpret certain terms of art in our own licenses.

Commercial open source licenses like the MPL, in addition to using legal terms of art precisely, often rely on their own definitions of terms. (The GPL did that for the term *Program*.) Those *definitions* must be read carefully because, in license interpretation and enforcement, they often take precedence over the *terms of art*. For example, the four definitions I quoted from the MPL above distinguish carefully between *Covered Code* and *Original Code*; the latter is included in the former. Note that the term *Modifications* is defined in light of *Original Code* in its first sentence and *Covered Code* in its second sentence. We must parse very carefully to know our reciprocity obligations under such licenses.

Contributors and Modifications

I described in the first chapters of this book how open source development is a continuous process. Contributors and distributors enhance and improve software at each step by creating collective and derivative works. That explanation was necessary because the BSD and earlier licenses weren't explicit about it. Collaborative open source development progressed under those licenses without the licenses mentioning the process at all.

The MPL defines this process much more precisely in sections 2 and 3. Open source development starts with *Original Code* supplied by an *Initial Developer* (in the first instance Netscape Corporation, although the MPL is a *template license*) who licenses all relevant open source rights to *You*. *You* make *Modifications* and become a *Contributor*. As a *Contributor, You* are required by the reciprocity terms of the MPL to license all relevant open source rights for *Your Modifications* to everyone under the MPL, and to provide *Source Code*. *You* also received, by that recursive MPL license, a license to all the *Modifications* made by earlier *Contributors*. (Notice the MPL-defined terms are the italicized nouns with capital letters throughout this paragraph.)

Once again, because of the MPL's definitions, this continuous enhancement process applies not to derivative works as a whole but separately to each *file* containing *Modifications*. (The word *file* is not defined in the MPL. This word is a *term of art* from the computer field; we must rely on experts to tell a court what that word means; I'm confident, though, that every reader of this book has a clear idea what the word *file* means and would recognize a *modified file* even without an MPL definition for it.)

The license grant under the MPL was structured so as to apply more narrowly than the GPL and other previous licenses. It licenses *files* to be modified, not *programs* to be turned into *derivative works*. This has one major consequence for those who create *Larger Works*, works that combine Covered Code with code not governed by the terms of the MPL License. Under copyright law, such *Larger Works* might be *derivative works*, depending upon the nature of the *combination* of software being created; but under the MPL's definitions, a *Larger Work* has more limited implications:

> *You may create a Larger Work by combining Covered Code with other code not governed by the terms of this License and distribute the Larger Work as a single product. In such a case, You must make sure the requirements of this License are fulfilled for the Covered Code. (MPL section 3.7.)*

You are only obligated to apply the MPL's license restrictions to *files* containing *Original Code* or *Modifications*. The rest of the files—your own files—are not affected by the reciprocity obligation, even if you have created a derivative work by adding your own files.

Any licensee intending to create *Larger Works* would be wise to consult an attorney to decide whether such a work is considered a *Modification* that must be contributed back under the MPL, or whether there are any other license obligations still to honor for the *Covered Code*.

In a way, the MPL is a kind of compromise between the academic and reciprocal license models. Reciprocity under the MPL is defined narrowly so as to encourage the use of open source software as building blocks to create *Larger Works*. (Those *Larger Works* may even be derivative works under copyright law; that doesn't matter.) Those *Larger Works* may be open or proprietary; with respect to them, the MPL acts like an academic license. But the individual building blocks are licensed with reciprocity obligations. If you distribute improvements to those building blocks, you must license those improvements under the MPL as open source software.

The MPL and Patents

The MPL also deals with patents much more thoroughly than any preceding open source license.

To review, a patent is a grant under power of law of the right to exclude others from making, using, selling, offering to sell, or importing certain specifically claimed inventions. The claims in a patent can be licensed to others. The MPL actually defines *Patent Claims* more precisely as "including, without limitation, method, process, and apparatus claims in any patent Licensable by grantor." (MPL section 1.10.1.) This is consistent with the types of utility patents actually granted by the U.S. Patent and Trademark Office. Fortunately, these technical distinctions among types of claims won't be important for us here.

First, the *Initial Developer* grants a patent license:

> ...*Under Patents Claims infringed by the making, using or selling of Original Code, to make, have made, use, practice, sell, and offer for sale, and/or otherwise dispose of the Original Code (or portions thereof). (MPL section 2.1[b].)*
>
> *Notwithstanding Section 2.1(b) above, no patent license is granted: 1) for code that You delete from the Original Code; 2) separate from the Original Code; or 3) for infringements caused by: i) the modification of the Original Code or ii) the combination of the Original Code with other software or devices. (MPL section 2.1[d].)*

These complex provisions draw important lines around patented intellectual property. They are the first explicit patent grant we've yet seen in open source licenses. The licenses I described earlier in this book contain at most implied patent grants. (If a license, like the GPL, is a *bare license*, then there may be no implied patent grant at all.) Implied patent grants are, at best, ambiguous.

Under the express provisions of the MPL, an *Initial Developer* licenses his or her patent claims to licensees of a specific embodiment of software, the *Original Code*, without limiting the *Initial Developer's* right to exclude others from making, using, or selling other embodiments in other software.

Patent Claims are potentially valuable even if the Initial Developer doesn't realize initially how his or her inventions will later be applied. The developer may discover that his or her claims cover very different applications from what was originally conceived, or such claims may cover applications that combine technology contributed (or kept proprietary) by others. Thus, Patent Claims infringed by the making, using or selling of Original Code may find applications broader than just making, using, or selling the Original Code.

For example, a patent claim for a cut/paste function licensed under the MPL for use in specific Original Code that does word processing ("WP version 1") may have other valuable applications, such as in an email or graphics program. Consider an open source licensor, an Initial Developer, who distributes WP version 1. That licensor owns a patent that contains three valuable claims, which I will paraphrase very incompletely (and unprofessionally, were I actually writing patent claims) as follows:

(1) Software to perform a cut/paste function.

(2) The software of claim 1 for a word processor.

(3) The software of claim 1 for an email program.

The *Initial Developer* (i.e., the patent owner and MPL licensor) grants enough patent rights so licensees can make, use, or sell WP version 1, the *Original Code*. (See MPL section 2.1[b].) Licensees under the MPL thus obtain limited licenses to the *Initial Developer's* broad claim 1 and the narrower claim 2. (Claim 1 is broader than claim 2 because claim 2 only applies to word processors, but claim 1 applies to any cut/paste application.)

- Does the MPL patent license allow licensees to create and distribute a derivative word processor, WP version 2, which includes a cut/paste function? Probably not. The MPL patent license covers the *Original Code* only, *or portions thereof.*

(MPL section 2.1[b].) We'd have to examine WP version 2 to make sure that it contains at least the portions of *Original Code* that perform the cut/paste functions. If the cut/paste software in the *Original Code* is modified, the *Initial Developer*'s patent license doesn't cover it. (MPL section 2.1[d].)

- Can a licensee perform cut/paste functions in different word processors obtained from other licensors? Not if that software infringes the original licensor's broad claim 1 or narrower claim 2. The MPL patent license doesn't cover software separate from the *Original Code*. (MPL section 2.1[d].)

- Can a licensee perform cut/paste functions in email programs? No. The MPL patent license excludes claims that aren't infringed by making, using, or selling the *Original Code*. (MPL section 2.1[b].) The *Initial Developer*'s narrow claim 3 is excluded under the MPL license because an email claim is not infringed by the original word processing program.

- Can a licensee perform cut/paste functions in graphics programs? Not without a separate license to the *Initial Developer*'s broad claim 1. Notice that, in this example, the *Initial Developer* doesn't have a claim specifically covering graphics programs, but the cut/paste claim 1 is broad enough to apply to such new applications. Suppose that a *Contributor* invents a new graphics application for *Initial Developer*'s claim 1. Nothing prevents anyone from patenting separately an *improvement* on someone else's patent claim; he or she simply can't *practice* his or her improvement without a license to the broader claim. Two companies might thus create patent claims worth cross-licensing with each other, one a broad claim covering cut/paste, and the other a narrower claim covering cut/paste in graphics programs. Note that neither patent owner is required by the MPL to license his or her patent claims (the *Initial Developer's* claim 1 or the *Contributor's* graphics claim) to each other for open source or proprietary graphics programs.

In other words, the original MPL patent license applies only to claims 1 and 2, and only to a specific *Original Work* and to certain types of authorized *Modifications*.

As for a *Contributor*, this is that subsequent licensor's reciprocal patent license:

...Under Patent Claims infringed by the making, using, or selling of Modifications made by that Contributor either alone and/or in combination with its Contributor Version (or portions of such combination), to make, use, sell, offer for sale, have made, and/or otherwise dispose of: 1) Modifications made by that Contributor (or portions thereof); and 2) the combination of Modifications made by that Contributor with its Contributor Version (or portions of such combination). (MPL section 2.2[b].)

Notwithstanding Section 2.2(b) above, no patent license is granted: 1) for any code that Contributor has deleted from the Contributor Version; 2) separate from the Contributor Version; 3) for infringements caused by: i) third party modifications of Contributor Version or ii) the combination of

*Modifications made by that Contributor with other software
(except as part of the Contributor Version) or other devices;
or 4) under Patent Claims infringed by Covered Code in the
absence of Modifications made by that Contributor. (MPL
section 2.2[d].)*

*"Contributor Version" means the combination of the Origi-
nal Code, prior Modifications used by a Contributor, and
the Modifications made by that particular Contributor.
(MPL section 1.2.)*

These provisions deal with *Modifications* submitted by *Contributors* who are licensees of the *Original Work*. Each *Contributor* grants a reciprocal license for his or her own patents to
allow *Modifications* to be made, used, or sold either alone or in
combination with the *Original Work*. So if a *Contributor*
invents cut/paste software that works for graphics, or an
entirely different invention (such as a new way of processing
fonts), and includes it in his or her *Contribution*, that claim is
reciprocally licensed to the *Initial Developer,* to all other *Contributors*, and to all subsequent *licensees*, under terms similar to
the complex ones I've just described.

Furthermore, these provisions don't mean that the *Contributor* can automatically obtain a license to the *Initial Developer's*
claim 3 simply by creating a *Modification* that adds an email
function; the *Initial Developer,* who has the right to license
that patent claim, has specifically excluded it. (See MPL section 2.1[d].)

If you intend to become a *Contributor,* you may need an
additional patent license from the *Initial Developer* or an earlier
Contributor before you can make, use, or sell your *Modification*.

The MPL makes this explicit but, under the patent laws, the
same issue exists under all the open source licenses, with their
potential implied patent license grants, previously discussed in
this book. Anyone planning to create improvements to open

source software must obtain licenses to any patent claims necessary to make, use, or sell those improvements. A patent grant from the licensor that would cover improvements is not implicit or explicit in any of the licenses I've discussed so far.

I like to think of such implied or explicit patent license restrictions as *field of use* restrictions; they limit the patent, sometimes in subtle ways, to use in specific fields or applications. How should we deal with *field of use* restrictions in open source licenses, where the copyright license provides unlimited freedom for licensees to create *derivative works* but the patent license does not?

The Free Software Guidelines, the Open Source Definition, and the Open Source Principles from Chapter 1 provide no guidance. They do not mention patents at all. The fundamental activities that open source deals with are copying, modification, and distribution. That's copyright law. What about patent rights: making, using, selling and offering for sale, and importing?

I believe the following is the only answer consistent with open source principles and with existing open source licenses:

> *An open source license must grant enough patent rights to allow the licensee to make, use, sell, offer for sale, or import the open source work as distributed by its licensor. Any additional license rights for derivative works or other uses are at the option of the licensor.*

The first sentence, identifying the minimum scope of a patent grant in an open source license, probably describes how a court would decide anyway in the absence of an express patent grant in the license—at least for a *contract* although not for a *bare license*—because a right to copy software is usually meaningless without a right to make and use, and the right to distribute is meaningless without the right to sell.

The second sentence describes an option for increasing the scope of the patent grant and so doesn't belong in a mandatory Open Source Principle.

I ultimately decided to leave this patent principle out of the Open Source Principles entirely because several important already-approved open source licenses don't say anything at all about the scope of the patent grant. Otherwise we might have to declare some existing open source licenses incompatible with this patent principle, further confusing people about what *open source* really means.

Defending Against Patents

The MPL grants a limited license to the *Initial Developer's* and *Contributors'* patents. But what is the MPL's response if a third party asserts its patents against an *Initial Developer* or *Contributor?*

The MPL handles this in various ways. First, the *Initial Developer* or any *Contributor* who learns about such a third party patent claim has an obligation to inform all subsequent licensees:

> *If Contributor has knowledge that a license under a third party's intellectual property rights is required to exercise the rights granted by such Contributor under Sections 2.1 or 2.2, Contributor must include a text file with the Source Code distribution titled "LEGAL" which describes the claim and the party making the claim in sufficient detail that a recipient will know whom to contact. If Contributor obtains such knowledge after the Modification is made available as described in Section 3.2, Contributor shall promptly modify the LEGAL file in all copies Contributor makes available thereafter and shall take other steps (such as notifying appro-*

priate mailing lists or newsgroups) reasonably calculated to inform those who received the Covered Code that new knowledge has been obtained. (MPL section 3.4[a].)

A far more dramatic response is authorized by the MPL if someone actually files a patent infringement lawsuit against the *Initial Developer* or a *Contributor* (both of whom are now called a *Participant* and whose code is now called a *Contributor Version*). The provision is generally referred to as a *patent defense*; it can be found among the MPL's termination provisions in section 8.

The MPL's patent defense provision can be summarized this way: Participant will license you his or her Contributor Version—with the right to make free copies, prepare derivative works, and distribute—as long as you don't sue for patent infringement. But if you sue the Participant claiming that the Contributor Version itself infringes your patent, all copyright and patent licenses to you under the MPL for the Contributor Version are terminated. And, if you sue the Participant for any other patent infringement unrelated to the Contributor Version, all patent licenses to you under the MPL for any software are terminated.

The success of a *patent defense* depends on the perceived value of the *Contributor Version* to the third party patent owner. For important and valuable open source software, it may be more painful to the patent owner to forgo use of the software than to forgo some potential patent royalties. It at least forces a potential patent litigant to think carefully before he or she sues a Participant for infringement. Patent litigation is no longer risk-free.

Here's how the patent defense provision actually reads in the MPL:

> *If You initiate litigation by asserting a patent infringement claim ... against Participant ... alleging that:*
>
> *(a) such Participant's Contributor Version directly or indirectly infringes any patent, then any and all rights granted ... under Sections 2.1 and/or 2.2 of this License shall ... terminate prospectively....*
>
> *(b) any software, hardware, or device, other than such Participant's Contributor Version, directly or indirectly infringes any patent, then any rights granted to You by such Participant under Sections 2.1(b) and 2.2(b) are revoked.... (MPL section 8.2.)*

This is the first *patent defense* provision we have encountered in an open source license, and it has proven to be quite controversial and yet widely copied. There are several interesting variations on patent defense in other open source licenses; I will discuss some of these variations later.

Other Important MPL License Provisions

As I said, the MPL is the first of the industrial-strength open source licenses. It deals with issues that are typically the province of licensing and legal professionals. But because several of these are critically important to license enforcement, I introduce them here.

U.S. Government Rights

The MPL contains what must seem like cryptic instructions regarding U.S. government users of the *Covered Code*:

> *The Covered Code is a "commercial item," as that term is defined in 48 C.F.R. 2.101 (Oct. 1995), consisting of "commercial computer software" and "commercial computer software documentation," as such terms are used in 48 C.F.R. 12.212*

> *(Sept. 1995). Consistent with 48 C.F.R. 12.212 and 48*
> *C.F.R. 227.7202-1 through 227.7202-4 (June 1995), all*
> *U.S. Government End Users acquire Covered Code with only*
> *those rights set forth herein. (MPL section 10.)*

The Code of Federal Regulations (C.F.R.) documents U.S. government policies and Chapter 48 of the C.F.R. contains Federal Acquisition Regulations. The relevant rules relating to patents, data, and copyrights are:

> *Commercial computer software or commercial computer*
> *software documentation shall be acquired under licenses cus-*
> *tomarily provided to the public to the extent such licenses are*
> *consistent with Federal law and otherwise satisfy the Gov-*
> *ernment's needs. (48 C.F.R. 12.212.)*

> *Offerors and contractors shall not be required to ... relin-*
> *quish control to, or otherwise provide, the Government rights*
> *to use, modify, reproduce, release, perform, display, or dis-*
> *close commercial computer software or commercial computer*
> *software documentation. (48 C.F.R. 227.7202-1.)*

> *The Government shall have only the rights specified in the li-*
> *cense under which the commercial computer software or*
> *commercial computer software documentation was ob-*
> *tained. (48 C.F.R. 227.7202-3.)*

> *A specific contract clause governing the Government's rights*
> *in commercial computer software or commercial computer*
> *software documentation is not prescribed. As required by*
> *227.7202-3, the Government's rights to use, modify, repro-*
> *duce, release, perform, display, or disclose computer software*
> *or computer software documentation shall be identified in a*
> *license agreement. (48 C.F.R. 227.7202-4.)*

Considering the broad scope of any open source license, under which the Government's rights—and everybody's rights—to use, modify, reproduce, release, perform, display, or disclose computer software is unquestioned, it is hard to imagine why open source licenses would need a U.S. Government Rights provision like the one in the MPL. The United States government—just like everybody else—is being given a license to free software. What more or less do they need?

Representations

> Contributor represents that, except as disclosed pursuant to Section 3.4(a) above, Contributor believes that Contributor's Modifications are Contributor's original creation(s) and/or Contributor has sufficient rights to grant the rights conveyed by this License. (MPL section 3.4[c].)

The MPL is the first license to assure licensees that *Modifications* are original to the *Contributors* who submit them or are being distributed under the authority of the original author.

This concept will appear as a *Warranty of Provenance* in the OSL/AFL licenses described in Chapter 9.

Jurisdiction and Venue

In the event of a dispute about the MPL, California law applies. As specified in the license, any litigation will take place in the federal courts of the Northern District of California, with venue in Santa Clara, California. (MPL section 11.)

I will discuss jurisdiction and venue, as well as governing law, in Chapter 12.

Attorneys' Fees and Costs

In the event of a dispute about the MPL, the losing party in court must pay *reasonable* attorneys' fees and costs. (MPL section 11.) What is *reasonable* is left to a court to decide.

Software Is Not Goods

I noted very early in this book that it is important to distinguish personal property rights in the copy of the software acquired in a store, and property rights in the intellectual property embodied in the software. Software licensed under the MPL is specifically intended *not* to be subject to laws intended for the sale and distribution of goods in international commerce.

> *The application of the United Nations Convention on Contracts for the International Sale of Goods is expressly excluded. (MPL section 11.)*

The most important reason for this provision is to ensure that international laws concerning implied warranties won't apply to this software. As the MPL and other open source licenses remind everyone, the software is provided on an "AS-IS" basis. (MPL section 7.)

This provision may not be enforceable in all jurisdictions.

Multiple-Licensed Code

I haven't yet explained why many open source licensors find it useful to license their software under more than one license. That topic will come in Chapter 11 when I discuss dual licensing models.

The MPL makes it clear, however, that the *Initial Developer* may designate its software as being available under multiple licenses, and may specify which license, besides the MPL, is allowed. (Frequently the second license is the GPL.) Note that a *Contributor* under the MPL cannot, independently, elect to use a different license for his or her *Modifications*. Only the Initial Developer makes that choice. This point will be discussed in Chapter 10 when I address the problem of *relicensing* open source software.

Other Corporate Licenses

Open source software has been adopted by many of the world's largest software companies. While most have adopted one or another of the licenses already discussed in this book (either the GPL or one of the academic licenses), some of them also now distribute their own open source software under their own corporate licenses. Open Source Initiative now lists licenses from a number of major companies including Apple, Lucent, IBM, Intel, Nokia, Real Networks, Ricoh, Sun, and Sybase. (See *www.opensource.org.*)

Each of those licenses puts a spin on one or another licensing technique already described in this book. Examining each of them in turn would be unproductive. Every one of those licenses satisfies the Open Source Principles listed in Chapter 1, although they sometimes do it in unusual ways.

The specific provisions of each license matters, particularly if you intend to create and distribute derivative works. If you use open source software from those companies under their licenses, I suggest that you consult an attorney to make sure you honor your obligations.

For the most part, those licenses are intended for use by the company that placed its name on it. None of them is an effective template that can be used by licensors generally.

There are three important exceptions. The first, the Common Public License (CPL) written by attorneys at IBM, is described in Chapter 8. Two other template licenses which I wrote, the Open Software License (OSL) and the Academic Free License (AFL), are described in Chapter 9.

8

The Common Public License (CPL)

CPL as a Template

IBM has long participated in the open source community. Its involvement along with other major software companies in the Linux project, the Apache project, and many other open source activities is well known. IBM also has its own commercial open source license, the IBM Public License, one of many vendor-specific licenses approved by Open Source Initiative.

But IBM also wanted a license that was available for other companies to use, companies who were distributing open source software that might be useful for IBM and others to use or sell with no ambiguous license provisions hanging over them.

IBM's attorneys designed the Common Public License (CPL) to be a template license. Here's how the template works: The CPL applies to "the accompanying program." (CPL first paragraph.) This introduces an interesting problem: How does a license *accompany* a program?

One way is to include a license as a *shrink-wrap* or *click-wrap* license that must be acknowledged before installation or first use. As I've described, the physical process of accessing the software requires a *manifestation of assent* and is evidence that

161

the *accompanying* license was available to be read. But after that assent, don't the license and the software go their separate ways, one to be installed and the other to be thrown away? Is there any convenient way for someone who receives a copy of the software to remember what license applies to it?

The CPL has no specific answer, although it requires that a copy of the license *be included* with each copy of the Program. (CPL section 3.)

The technique described in the GPL, to include a licensing statement in the source code of the Program, is obviously the most convenient. Such licensing statements can be placed immediately following the copyright notice. This technique is consistent with the word *accompany* in the CPL.

Presumably that licensing notice will remain with the source code as long as the copyright notice does:

> *Contributors may not remove or alter any copyright notices contained within the Program. (CPL section 3.)*

A Digression about Well-Written Licenses

The first open source licenses, the BSD and GPL, were written almost fifteen years ago. That was the time of UNIX. We used slow-speed modem data connections back then, before the high-speed Internet was available worldwide. Personal computers were much more primitive beasts.

Just as these fifteen years have witnessed improvements in software, so too have they produced improvements to software licenses. Attorneys are no longer struggling with unknown concepts when dealing with open source, and so, as the licenses described in this book demonstrate, competent attorneys are writing very good open source licenses.

The CPL is a very good one because it precisely describes a reasonable reciprocal bargain that promotes *free software*. It has seven brief sections (totaling only nine pages in the Appendices to this book) in which it defines terms, grants the appropriate licenses, states the reciprocity obligations, and then deals with the commercial and legal realities of:

> *...The laws of the State of New York and the intellectual property laws of the United States of America. (CPL section 7.)*

The CPL is fully compatible with the Free Software Guidelines, the Open Source Definition, and the Open Source Principles listed in Chapter 1.

Although this license may not be appropriate for everyone (see Chapter 10) it exemplifies the important qualities of a well-written open source license. Notice that important words are not used in the CPL without a definition (with two interesting exceptions). Notice that the CPL can be used as a template between any *Contributor* and any *Recipient*. Notice that the words *shall* and *must* and *may not* always mean something mandatory, and the word *may* is always permissive.

Some amateurs believe they can write open source licenses. They should first read a good license like the CPL and ask themselves if they can do as well.

Grant of Copyright and Patent Licenses

The CPL grants all the rights necessary for open source software:

> *...Each Contributor hereby grants Recipient a non-exclusive, worldwide, royalty-free copyright license to reproduce, prepare derivative works of, publicly display, publicly perform, distribute and sublicense the Contribution of such Contributor, if any, and such derivative works, in source code and object code form. (CPL section 2[a].)*

It also grants a patent license compatible with open source:

> ...*Each Contributor hereby grants Recipient a non-exclusive, worldwide, royalty-free patent license under Licensed Patents to make, use, sell, offer to sell, import and otherwise transfer the Contribution of such Contributor, if any, in source code and object code form. (CPL section 2[b].)*

The patent license in the CPL is limited in much the same was as it is in the MPL. Both licenses *exclude combinations of the licensed software with other software or hardware.* The MPL's language is much more complicated, involving a positive statement and an exclusion. (See MPL sections 2.2[b] and 2.2[d].) The CPL states essentially the same limitation much more clearly in three sentences:

> *This patent license shall apply to the combination of the Contribution and the Program if, at the time the Contribution is added by the Contributor, such addition of the Contribution causes such combination to be covered by the Licensed Patents. The patent license shall not apply to any other combinations which include the Contribution. No hardware per se is licensed hereunder. (CPL section 2[b].)*

Its clarity of language is one of the main advantages of the CPL over the MPL. But this provision still isn't very clear, is it? Just what do such limited patent licenses really mean? For the CPL, I must first define three terms:

> *"Contribution" means ... changes to the Program, and ... additions to the Program. (CPL section 1.)*

> *"Licensed Patents" mean patent claims licensable by a Contributor which are necessarily infringed by the use or sale of its Contribution alone or when combined with the Program. (CPL section 1.)*

"Program" means the Contributions distributed in accordance with this Agreement. (CPL section 1.)

Consider a *Contributor* who wants to add or change something in the *Program*. Assume that this new feature or function, the *Contribution* by itself, *necessarily infringes* the claims of one or more of *Contributor's* patents. One would expect *Contributor* to license those patent claims or his or her *Contribution* could not be used. Those patent claims are *Licensed Patents*.

But *Contributor* intends something more. He or she wants to combine a *Contribution* with the *Program* as it was received. Assume that this *combination (Contribution-plus-Program) necessarily infringes* the claims of one or more of the *Contributor's* patents. One would expect *Contributor* to license those patent claims also or the *Contributor's Contribution* could not be used in combination with the *Program* as it was received. Those patent claims are also *Licensed Patents*.

The first *Licensed Patents*—those relating to the *Contribution* alone—are always licensed by the *Contributor* to make, use, and sell the *Contribution*.

The second Licensed Patents—those relating to the *Contribution-plus-Program*—are not licensed by the Contributor for use with *Contribution-plus-Program* unless, at the time the *Contribution* is added by the *Contributor*, the combination of the *Contribution* and the *Program* as it was received necessarily infringed.

This confusing provision has the interesting effect of excluding from the patent license, for example, a license to *Contributor's* pending patent applications if they hadn't been issued at the time the *Contribution* was added. Such an exclusion would not be allowed for a patent license under the open source–compatible W3C patent policy described in Chapter 13.

The *Licensed Patents* are not licensed for any *other combinations* which include the *Contribution*. This means the following are not licensed:

- Combinations of the *Contribution* with software other than the *Program*.

- Combinations of the *Contribution* with later versions of the *Program* unless the *Licensed Patents* were necessary for the current version of the *Program*.

- Entirely new software that embodies any of the *Licensed Patents*, even if those new programs perform the same functions as the original *Program* or *Contribution*.

Those seem to be fairly broad limitations. When described this way, are they consistent with the open source principles in Chapter 1? Why would such limitations be needed?

To understand that one must view patents from the perspective of an international company with the largest patent portfolio in the world. IBM is prepared to license some of its patents for use in an open source *Program*. Other companies and individuals will also be *Contributors*, and they too may have patents to license. The CPL guarantees that IBM and all others will (in effect) cross-license necessary patent rights to make, use, and sell the *Program including Contributions*. The entire community, including IBM and the other *Contributors*, will benefit from enhanced versions of this open source software.

But what might IBM's competitors do with IBM's patent licenses? Will they find new applications for those patents outside of the *Contribution*? Will those competitors combine *Contributions* with other software in new and different ways IBM never thought of before?

Is IBM prepared to license all those potential uses? No. IBM wants to limit its license to those specific uses and combinations that it contemplated at the time of its initial *Contribution*.

The MPL and the CPL, and most of the other corporate licenses listed at *www.opensource.org*, contain this kind of restrictive patent license. A licensee creating derivative works from such software—and remember, the Open Source Principles guarantee that freedom—may not exceed the scope of the initial patent license. The *freedom to create derivative works* is not absolute.

This is true under any of the open source licenses in this book—including those licenses with implied patent grants. In some situations, it may be necessary to return to the *Contributor* and request an additional patent license in order to make, use, sell or offer to sell, or import a derivative work. Any licensee of open source software who intends to create and distribute derivative works should ensure that he or she has the necessary patent licenses to do so.

Patent licenses are particularly important for companies that make, use, or sell industry standard software. The importance of broad patent rights for such software is discussed in Chapter 13.

Reciprocity under the CPL

The CPL contains a reciprocity obligation much like the one in the GPL. Software licensed under the CPL can be used

to create a derivative work (e.g., *Program*) which can then be
distributed by a *Contributor* under its own license agreement.
But that other license agreement is required to be very like the
CPL:

> *A Contributor may choose to distribute the Program in ob-*
> *ject code form under its own license agreement, provided*
> *that:*
>
> *a) it complies with the terms and conditions of this Agree-*
> *ment; and*
>
> *b) its license agreement:*
>
> *... iv) states that source code for the Program is available*
> *from such Contributor, and informs licensees how to obtain*
> *it in a reasonable manner on or through a medium custom-*
> *arily used for software exchange. (CPL section 3.)*

Of course, this only pertains to derivative works distributed
in *object code form*. For derivative works distributed in source
code form, the CPL is more restrictive:

> *When the Program is made available in source code form:*
>
> *a) it must be made available under this Agreement; and*
>
> *b) a copy of this Agreement must be included with each copy*
> *of the Program. (CPL section 3.)*

Most derivative works of CPL-licensed software are distributed under the CPL itself, not some other license made to
comply with it.

Exception to Reciprocity

There is a very important explicit exception to the CPL's
reciprocity obligation:

> *Contributions do not include additions to the Program*
> *which: (i) are separate modules of software distributed in*

conjunction with the Program under their own license agreement, and (ii) are not derivative works of the Program. (CPL section 1.)

Does this have the same effect as the GPL? Instead of the ambiguous language of the GPL and LGPL that causes so much uncertainty about linking, the CPL offers two simple tests for exclusion from reciprocity. Both must be true:

1. The *Contribution* must be a *separate module of software*. The term *separate module of software* is not defined in the CPL. (Neither, you will recall, was the word *file* defined in the MPL.) As with other important concepts in any technical field, *separate module of software* is a term of art in the field of computer engineering that will be defined by experts when a judge or jury needs to do so during litigation. I'm sure most readers of this book will find the concept of a *separate module of software* fairly self-evident and will know what steps to take to ensure that engineers avoid creating *Contributions* that are subject to reciprocity.

2. A *Contribution* must not be a *derivative work*. This explicit statement in the CPL, of course, is the same conclusion I drew when I discussed linking in the GPL and LGPL. Does avoiding reciprocity always boil down to avoiding the creation of a derivative work?

Anyone can get around the *reciprocity* obligation of the CPL by both (1) creating a *separate module of software* and (2) making sure that *separate module of software* isn't a *derivative work*.

As I will describe in Chapter 9, the OSL and AFL licenses do not include the first element of this exclusion from reciprocity. The MPL's concept of *files* and the CPL's concept of *separate module of software* are not included in the OSL and AFL. All one must do to avoid reciprocity is to avoid creating a derivative work.

Of course, that is not nearly so simple a change as I make it seem. I defer until Chapter 12 the technical discussion about how courts determine whether derivative works have been created.

Patent Defense

The CPL license terminates automatically under two situations as of the date that a *Recipient* initiates certain kinds of patent litigation.

Many commercial open source licenses contain this kind of patent defense clause. A company such as IBM, with its vast portfolio of patents, wants to be able to terminate patent licenses when it is sued for patent infringement. That *defensive* use of patents is an important part of such companies' patent strategies.

This is the first situation:

> *...If Recipient institutes patent litigation against a Contributor with respect to a patent applicable to software (including a cross-claim or counterclaim in a lawsuit), then any patent licenses granted by that Contributor to such Recipient under this Agreement shall terminate as of the date such litigation is filed. (CPL section 7.)*

This termination provision applies to "litigation against a Contributor" and "a patent applicable to software," regardless of whether it is applicable to the software licensed under the CPL.

This is the second situation:

> *...If Recipient institutes patent litigation against any entity (including a cross-claim or counterclaim in a lawsuit) alleging that the Program itself (excluding combinations of the Program with other software or hardware) infringes such Recipient's patent(s), then such Recipient's rights granted under Section 2(b) shall terminate as of the date such litigation is filed. (CPL section 7.)*

This termination provision applies to litigation against "any entity" and "a patent applicable to the Program" only.

The first provision terminates "any patent licenses granted by that Contributor to such Recipient under this Agreement." The second provision terminates "rights granted under Section 2(b)." Curiously, there are no patent licenses granted by the CPL other than those in its section 2(b). I don't understand why the two termination provisions are worded differently in this way.

Notice also that the termination provisions apply to the patent license only; the copyright license remains. So if there are no patents that the Contributor actually licensed (i.e., the intellectual property in the software is merely copyrightable, not patentable), the termination provision doesn't apply. The CPL license provides no patent defense benefits to a licensor without patents.

Some companies do not want to in-license software under this kind of patent termination provision. Their concern is with the first half of section 7, which applies to infringement litigation "with respect to a patent applicable to software." This is the scenario they don't like: Suppose Company A licenses its software under the CPL to Company B. Company B then accuses Company A of infringing an entirely different software patent unrelated to the licensed software. Company B's license to the software terminates.

Should Company B have accepted Company A's software in the first place? Should it ever accept the risk of relying on open source software under the CPL if by doing so it may make the rest of its software patents unenforceable against Company A?

Some companies refuse to accept such license conditions. Open source projects need to decide whether such license conditions will frighten away too many prospective licensees. This may also present an opportunity for open source projects to use dual licensing, where they can offer a lower risk license alternative to such risk-averse companies—at a price. (See the discussion of dual licensing in Chapter 11.)

By the way, this situation can occur under the MPL as well. Under the defensive termination provisions in both the MPL and CPL, the licensor's patent licenses terminate if the licensee sues the licensor for patent infringement. Under both MPL and CPL, a licensee may eventually have to choose between continuing the license and suing for patent infringement.

Is that really such an unreasonable bargain? In return for accepting valuable free software from Company A, Company B must accept that its software patents are effectively unenforceable against Company A. But the software is free! Why should it not come at a price? Why isn't *reciprocity of patent licenses* a reasonable bargain?

One further comment: The OSL and AFL licenses described in the next chapter take license termination for patent infringement one step further than the MPL and CPL. In those licenses, both the *copyright and patent* licenses terminate, not just the patent licenses. Some believe that such enhanced reciprocity is justified, specifically for open source projects that don't own patents.

Defend and Indemnify

The CPL is the first major open source license to announce certain special responsibilities of licensees who are commercial distributors. It is the only place where the CPL uses the word *should*, implying that it has a philosophical or practical business objective in mind:

> *Commercial distributors of software may accept certain responsibilities with respect to end users, business partners and the like. While this license is intended to facilitate the commercial use of the Program, the Contributor who includes the Program in a commercial product offering should do so in a manner which does not create potential liability for other Contributors. (CPL section 4.)*

What, by the way, is a "commercial product offering"? Almost certainly it is a product that one can obtain at a store or online. Does the term apply to software distributed alone, or to software that is a part of some physical commercial product? Does it require that an offer for the product be made to the public as a whole, or merely to other *Contributors* in the context of an open source development project? Does the term apply where a distributor offers software to the public at *zero price*? Does it apply when the price merely covers the costs of distribution? The CPL is silent on those questions. This is an important undefined term in the CPL. I assume this ambiguity was intentional.

The CPL seeks to protect other Contributors from the acts of a Commercial Contributor. It does this through an agreement to defend and indemnify:

If a Contributor includes the Program in a commercial product offering, such Contributor ("Commercial Contributor") hereby agrees to defend and indemnify every other Contributor ("Indemnified Contributor") against any losses, damages and costs (collectively "Losses") arising from claims, lawsuits and other legal actions brought by a third party against the Indemnified Contributor to the extent caused by the acts or omissions of such Commercial Contributor in connection with its distribution of the Program in a commercial product offering. (CPL section 4.)

This provision is important in the context of consumer protection, which is mandated in various ways by all civilized countries. The laws acknowledge that products introduced into the stream of commerce sometimes harm people, their property or their businesses. In many jurisdictions, any company responsible for introducing a product into the stream of commerce is potentially liable to pay for *Losses* caused to consumers by that product.

Under the laws of some countries, this potential liability often cannot be disclaimed regardless of what a license says. Disclaimers of liability such as the one in the CPL and other licenses simply don't apply in a commercial–consumer situation in many countries. (See CPL section 5; MPL section 9; GPL section 12; OSL/AFL section 8.) Liability disclaimers are contrary to law and voidable in some situations by injured consumers.

So who then potentially pays when consumers sue? First, an individual plaintiff may sue a company for actual *Losses* incurred. More seriously perhaps, class action lawsuits may also be filed for individually small *Losses* to large numbers of similarly placed consumers; a defendant may pay the combined *Losses* of all members of the class. Defendant companies with deep pockets are particularly vulnerable to consumer lawsuits and to large jury verdicts for injured consumers.

Second, in the United States and in some other countries, each party in a lawsuit is generally responsible to pay its own attorneys' fees and litigation costs. This is not cheap. Merely defending such lawsuits occasionally bankrupts defendants, leaving little or no money to pay for *Losses*. Consider, for example, the cost of litigation relating to asbestos and silicone breast implants.

Also consider this example outside of the software field. When Firestone tires began to fail on Ford automobiles, injured plaintiffs sued both companies. It became the court's problem to determine degree of liability, if any, of each of the defendants, and then perhaps to allocate the damages accordingly. Legal procedures for analyzing degree of liability and for allocating damages vary widely around the world. Potentially, both Ford and Firestone would pay the judgments assessed against them individually, and each would pay its own attorneys' fees and costs.

But if Firestone had an obligation to *defend and indemnify* Ford, then it would be entirely Firestone's money on the line. Firestone would pay all judgments, and Firestone would pay all attorneys' fees and costs.

Broadly speaking, under the CPL, a *Commercial Contributor* must *defend and indemnify* every other *Contributor*. To the extent that IBM (and any other *initial Contributor*) allows others to be its *Commercial Contributors*, it is those other companies that will bear the burden to *defend and indemnify*.

This, of course, states the CPL's rule incompletely. The obligation to defend and indemnify applies only to the extent the Losses were caused by "the acts or omissions of such Commercial Contributor." This means that a Commercial Contributor may still prove it is not directly at fault. But because of its acceptance of an obligation to defend and indemnify, it cannot rely on the other companies to step in to protect it.

The CPL obligation to *defend and indemnify* does not apply to "Losses relating to any actual or alleged intellectual property infringement." (CPL section 4.) This is consistent with the CPL's warranty disclaimer, which disclaims the warranty of noninfringement. (CPL section 5.)

The obligation to *defend* can be very costly for a company that is a Commercial Contributor to open source software. Paying damages for an injured consumer can require a deep reach into the bank account. An obligation to defend and indemnify every other Contributor can be particularly painful where a Commercial Contributor must pay for particularly complicated or expensive consumer injuries. Commercial Contributors need to assess their exposure carefully under the CPL before distributing software under that license.

As for individual Contributors who are not directly distributing a "commercial product offering" (whatever that term really means), the *defend and indemnify* provision doesn't apply to them.

Ownership of the CPL License

I previously wrote about ownership of *software being licensed,* but I should also comment on ownership of the *license* itself. We must also distinguish between ownership of copyrightable intellectual property that is the license and ownership of a copy of that license.

When a *Contributor* licenses software to a *Recipient* under the CPL, a new copy of the license is created binding the parties to the terms of their agreement. IBM, the author of the CPL and the owner of the copyright in that work, expressly authorizes everyone to make such copies of the license but reserves the right to create derivative works of the license:

> *Everyone is permitted to copy and distribute copies of this Agreement, but in order to avoid inconsistency the Agreement is copyrighted and may only be modified in the following manner. (CPL section 7.)*

The right to create derivative works of the CPL is retained by an Agreement Steward, initially IBM. Because copyright law protects the CPL license itself, you can be confident that the version of the CPL you are offered by a prospective licensor is one that the Agreement Steward has blessed.

The CPL describes what happens if the Agreement Steward publishes a new version of the CPL:

> *The Program (including Contributions) may always be distributed subject to the version of the Agreement under which it was received. In addition, after a new version of the Agreement is published, Contributor may elect to distribute the Program (including its Contributions) under the new version. (CPL section 7.)*

Notice that a "Contributor may elect" to use the new CPL but is not required to do so.

For these reasons it is important to keep track of software not just in terms of which license you used, but which versions of the license. Proper record keeping is essential to managing open source licensing so you can know your rights and obligations.

9

The OSL and the AFL

Academic or Reciprocal?

The academic and reciprocal licenses described in this book so far have been very different from each other. This is at least in part because the two major categories of licenses—academic (BSD, MIT, Apache, etc.) and reciprocal (GPL, MPL, CPL, etc.)—have very different roots in the open source community, and they developed from different core philosophical beliefs about software freedom.

Proponents of academic licenses demand the freedom to incorporate open source software into any kinds of works, including proprietary works. Proponents of reciprocal licenses believe that freedom lies in a large public commons of software that grows through the contribution of derivative works back to the commons.

Because of their very different ancestry, good licensing concepts seldom crossed the license category boundaries. Academic licenses remained brief and vague like the BSD, while reciprocal licenses grew to include provisions relating to patents, source code publication, and protection of contributors' integrity. But times are changing. Efforts are now underway within some open source projects to relicense their software under more robust academic licenses, but that process is slow.

179

(I discuss relicensing in Chapter 10.) For example, the Apache project has just approved a new version of its license—thus inevitably rendering partly obsolete my discussion of the older Apache license in Chapter 5. The new Apache license is much closer in language and structure to the CPL, although it does not include reciprocity obligations.

Another reason that open source licenses vary so much is that licensing often reflects corporate intellectual property policies of licensors—and those policies vary widely. As open source licenses began to deal with patents and other forms of intellectual property and with the complex commercial laws that relate to software, they evolved into complicated legal documents with their own special rules about what licensees owe back to the public commons. As their corporate authors began to deal with important intellectual policy issues that the GPL left out, reciprocal licenses began to resemble the traditional license agreements that were used for proprietary software.

I have written two licenses that cross that academic/reciprocal divide. These licenses reflect one core set of provisions applicable to both academic and reciprocal open source licensing. Only in a few specific places do the licenses differ, and those few places relate solely to the reciprocity obligation.

The Open Software License (OSL) is a reciprocal license. The Academic Free License (AFL) is the exact same license without the reciprocity provisions. Because these two licenses are direct and short—less than eight pages in the Appendices—there is some prospect that licensors and licensees will actually read and understand the licenses rather than just click "I ACCEPT" when the open source license is presented for approval.

Both the OSL and AFL are *unilateral contracts*. That means that the licensor is the only one making *promises*, although the license also establishes certain *conditions* that must be met by all licensees. As with all unilateral contracts, licensees must satisfy the conditions—including the reciprocity condition—in order for them to enforce the promise by the licensor that permits them to exercise otherwise exclusive copyright and patent rights.

I will describe these two licenses in this chapter differently than I did for earlier licenses. I will explain each license section in turn, noting the four places where the AFL differs from the OSL because of the reciprocity provision. But then I will also describe how each section compares to provisions in the other licenses. This chapter, then, can be read as a summary of open source license provisions in all the licenses in this book.

Every license described in this book guarantees the five Open Source Principles that I listed in Chapter 1—but they do it in different ways. You will immediately recognize as I compare licenses in this chapter that the differences among licenses are often subtle. Some licenses rely on the definition of *derivative work*; others add or subtract from that concept for reciprocity purposes. Some licenses contain express patent grants, others do not; every express patent license contains a field of use restriction of some sort.

This chapter is for comparison purposes. I will leave to the next chapter the important issues of choosing an appropriate open source license among the alternatives available to you.

Initial Paragraph of OSL/AFL

OSL	AFL
This Open Software License (the "License") applies to any original work of authorship (the "Original Work") whose owner (the "Licensor") has placed the following notice immediately following the copyright notice for the Original Work: Licensed under the Open Software License version 2.0	This Academic Free License (the "License") applies to any original work of authorship (the "Original Work") whose owner (the "Licensor") has placed the following notice immediately following the copyright notice for the Original Work: Licensed under the Academic Free License version 2.0

This is how the OSL/AFL serve as templates. To distribute an "Original Work" under one of these licenses, merely place the appropriate licensing notice after the copyright notice for that work. Although the law doesn't require a copyright notice, this OSL/AFL requirement serves as a friendly reminder that placing a copyright notice on your writings is always a good idea.

This provision gives the license a name and defines the owner ("Licensor") of intellectual property broadly described as an "original work of authorship." You will recognize that term of art from copyright law:

> *Copyright protection subsists ... in original works of authorship fixed in any tangible medium of expression....*
> *(17 U.S.C. § 102.)*

The use of that copyright term of art and the later explicit references to the copyright law (see OSL/AFL sections 9 and 11) suggest that these licenses are intended to be interpreted in light of copyright law and terminology.

The OSL/AFL are also intended to be useful for documentation, pictures, art works, music, and other copyrightable works that often accompany software. Therefore you will not see the words *software* or *program* or other words that might limit the reach of this license except in the name of the OSL license itself and in section 10 (referring specifically to "a patent applicable to software" and "combinations of the Original Work with other software").

The OSL and AFL are not just open source *software* licenses. They are open *content* licenses.

Comparison to Other Licenses

Some open source template licenses (BSD, MPL) require a licensor to modify the words of the license or to append an exhibit to the license in order to associate the license with particular open source software. (MPL sections 1.10, 3.5, 5, and 6.3 and Exhibit A.)

The GPL contains a notice provision similar to the OSL/AFL. A licensor places a notice in his or her *Program*, but the GPL does not specify where the notice is to be placed. (GPL section 0.)

The CPL is a license between a *Contributor* and a *Recipient*. The license applies to the "accompanying program." (CPL first paragraph.) How that program *accompanies* the license is not specified.

1. Grant of Copyright License

OSL	AFL
Licensor hereby grants You a world-wide, royalty-free, non-exclusive, perpetual, sublicensable license to do the following:	Licensor hereby grants You a world-wide, royalty-free, non-exclusive, perpetual, sublicensable license to do the following:
a) to reproduce the Original Work in copies;	a) to reproduce the Original Work in copies;
b) to prepare derivative works ("Derivative Works") based upon the Original Work;	b) to prepare derivative works ("Derivative Works") based upon the Original Work;
c) to distribute copies of the Original Work and Derivative Works to the public, <u>with the proviso that copies of Original Work or Derivative Works that You distribute shall be licensed under the Open Software License</u>;	c) to distribute copies of the Original Work and Derivative Works to the public;
d) to perform the Original Work publicly; and	d) to perform the Original Work publicly; and
e) to display the Original Work publicly.	e) to display the Original Work publicly.

This first section of the OSL/AFL is the all-important open source license grant under copyright law. The license satisfies Open Source Principles # 2 and 3.

The underlined words in section 1(c) are in the OSL but not the AFL. This is the reciprocity provision that distinguishes academic and reciprocal open source licenses.

This section identifies the licensee as *You*. See OSL/AFL section 14 for the definition of that word.

The OSL/AFL grant to *You* a license for all five of the exclusive rights in copyrighted works from U.S. copyright law—copy, create derivative works, distribute, perform, and display. (17 U.S.C. § 106.) There are no exclusive rights under the copyright law withheld by the Licensor.

In case there might be any doubt, the term *Derivative Works* is defined to be *derivative works*. This obviously doesn't answer the question, "What is a derivative work of software?" (I'll discuss that problem further in Chapter 12.) But what it does accomplish is to bring into the OSL/AFL licenses the term of art, *derivative work*, as that term is defined in copyright law (17 U.S.C. § 101).

The underlined proviso in section 1(c) of the OSL, absent from the AFL, is a clear statement of reciprocity that applies broadly to "copies of Original Work or Derivative Works." Such works may be distributed, but only under the same OSL license. *You* can *sublicense* your rights under the copyright owner's license to others, but only under the same license as you received the work.

Because it has no reciprocity provision, the AFL allows *You* to *sublicense* your rights under any license you please.

The OSL/AFL copyright license is:

- *World-wide*—No territory is excluded. Of course, there is no such thing as a common law of copyright or contract that applies world-wide, and all nations have the authority to make their own laws to govern intellectual property licenses undertaken within their jurisdiction. For example, export control laws prevent some software from being exported to certain other countries regardless of the license. Also, at least in theory, a country somewhere could forbid this license entirely. The relationship between local laws and the law of the contract is addressed further by section 11 of the OSL/AFL.

- *Royalty-free*—The license is at *zero price*. This does not restrict any licensee from setting his or her own prices for copies and derivative works. Any such restrictions on licensees setting their own prices would be an unfair business practice in many countries.

- *Non-exclusive*—There may be other licensees besides *You*.

- *Perpetual*—As far as we know, nothing in the universe really is forever. These licenses are perpetual only in the sense that the *Licensor* promises not to terminate them—except perhaps under the termination provisions in sections 9 and 10. Note also that, in the United States and other countries, a license to an *Original Work* (other than a work for hire) is terminable under certain circumstances regardless of what the license says. (17 U.S.C. § 203.)

- *Sublicensable*—The term *sublicensable* means that *You* can pass these rights on to anyone else you want. This simplifies the process by which open source software containing many contributions can be distributed without requiring each downstream licensee to go back to the original authors of contributions for licenses.

Comparison to Other Licenses

The BSD and Apache licenses permit "redistribution and use." (BSD license first paragraph; Apache license first paragraph.) Everyone assumes this means all the exclusive rights under copyright law, but those licenses aren't explicit. The BSD and Apache licenses are not sublicensable.

The MIT license permits everyone to "deal in the Software without restriction," including "without limitation" many of the same rights as listed in the OSL/AFL. (MIT license first paragraph.) Everyone assumes this means all the exclusive rights under copyright law. The MIT license is sublicensable.

The Artistic License grants permission to "make and give away verbatim copies; apply bug fixes...; modify your copy ... in any way...;" and "distribute...." (Artistic License sections 1 through 4.) Everyone assumes this means all the exclusive rights under copyright law. The Artistic License is not sublicensable.

The GPL ignores all activities other than "copying, distribution and modification," and then grants a license to "copy and distribute" and "modify ... and distribute." (GPL sections 0, 1, and 2.) The only reference to sublicensing rights in the GPL is ambiguous. (GPL section 4.) In practice the GPL is worldwide, royalty-free and nonexclusive. The GPL's "at no charge" requirement for derivative works (GPL section 2[b]) is not found in the OSL/AFL; indeed, the GPL's "at no charge" provision may be an illegal restraint of trade in certain countries.

The MPL copyright grant is explicitly "world-wide, royalty-free, non-exclusive" and "sublicensable." It includes all the exclusive rights under copyright law. (MPL sections 2.1 and 2.2.)

The CPL copyright grant is explicitly "worldwide, royalty-free, non-exclusive" and "sublicensable." It includes all the exclusive rights under copyright law. (CPL section 2.)

The OSL/AFL reciprocity provision applies to "derivative works." By comparison, the MPL applies only to modified "files," and the CPL applies only to "additions to the Program which ... are separate modules of software." The GPL's reciprocity provision is ambiguous and the LGPL confuses it even further with its references to "linking," as I described at length in Chapter 6. These subtle but important differences can have significant effects on the licensing requirements for derivative works. Be sure to consult an attorney if you are at all uncertain about the import of open source license reciprocity obligations.

2. Grant of Patent License

Both OSL and AFL

Licensor hereby grants You a world-wide, royalty-free, non-exclusive, perpetual, sublicensable license, under patent claims owned or controlled by the Licensor that are embodied in the Original Work as furnished by the Licensor, to make, use, sell and offer for sale the Original Work and Derivative Works.

The OSL/AFL patent license grants "world-wide, royalty-free, non-exclusive, perpetual sublicensable" rights coextensive with the copyright license grant.

The license grant to "make, use, sell and offer for sale" is intended to encompass the patent owner's rights under the patent laws to practice the claimed invention. (35 U.S.C.

§ 154.) Unfortunately, this patent grant neglects to mention the right to import.

The patent license applies only to a specific set of the Licensor's patent claims, namely those that are "embodied in the Original Work as furnished by the Licensor." It is not a license to the *Licensor's* entire patent portfolio.

Those licensed patent claims are available for both the Original Work and Derivative Works. This is not a license to embody those patent claims in independent works.

Comparison to Other Licenses

Of the other licenses discussed in this book, only the MPL and CPL grant an express patent license. For the other licenses, we can only assume that there is an implied license to make, use, sell or offer for sale, or import the original licensed software—at least as long as they are *contracts* and not *bare licenses*.

The MPL grants a patent license only for the *Original Code* and the *Contributions*. No patent license is expressly granted for *derivative works* as such, and so depending on the specific patent claims and the specific software under the license, the MPL patent license may not extend to derivative works. (MPL sections 2.1[b], 2.1[d], 2.2[b], 2.2[d].)

The CPL's patent license applies only to each *Contribution*, but only if the patent license covered the work at the time the *Contribution* was added. Otherwise, *derivative works* may not be covered. (CPL section 1 definition of *Licensed Patents* and section 2[b].)

3. Grant of Source Code License

Both OSL and AFL

The term "Source Code" means the preferred form of the Original Work for making modifications to it and all available documentation describing how to modify the Original Work. Licensor hereby agrees to provide a machine-readable copy of the Source Code of the Original Work along with each copy of the Original Work that Licensor distributes. Licensor reserves the right to satisfy this obligation by placing a machine-readable copy of the Source Code in an information repository reasonably calculated to permit inexpensive and convenient access by You for as long as Licensor continues to distribute the Original Work, and by publishing the address of that information repository in a notice immediately following the copyright notice that applies to the Original Work.

Because the OSL and AFL are *unilateral contracts*, only the licensor makes promises. One of those promises is an explicit one to provide source code for any software he or she distributes under the license.

This section defines source code and guarantees its availability for the licensed software. Again, this provision is a commitment for the licensor, not the licensee, to disclose source code. Licensees must provide source code for their *derivative works* only if they are subject to the *reciprocity* obligation.

Source code in the OSL/AFL includes "documentation describing how to modify the Original Work." This goes beyond most other open source licenses to prevent the intentional obscuring of the source code. If the licensor has documentation about how to modify the work, it must be made available.

This documentation requirement does not include documentation on how to use the software. It only applies to documentation on how to modify the software.

These licenses provide two ways to satisfy the source code obligation. Either the licensor can include source code along with the executable software he or she distributes, or the licensor can provide an online copy that licensees can access.

Comparison to Other Licenses

Most of the licenses described in this book do not contain explicit source code requirements. The BSD, MIT, and Apache licenses, for example, permit licensors to distribute source code but do not require it.

The Artistic license requires the licensee to make source code available, but the license provides alternatives that would allow a licensee to avoid that obligation under certain circumstances.

The GPL requires licensees to provide source code for derivative works they distribute. (GPL section 3.) The definition of *source code* in the GPL does not include any documentation.

Under the MPL, licensees must provide source code for files containing derivative works they distribute. (MPL section 3.2.) That requirement can be satisfied by making the source code available online. *Source code* is defined to include "associated interface definition files, scripts used to control compilation and installation," and "source code differential comparison." The MPL expressly allows *source code* to be in compressed or archival form. (MPL section 1.11.)

Under the CPL, each *Contributor* grants the *Recipient* a license to the work "in source code and object code form." (CPL section 2[a].) The term *source code* is not defined. Contributors under the CPL must "inform licensees how to obtain it in a reasonable manner on or through a medium customarily used for software exchange." (CPL section 3.)

4. Exclusions from License Grant

Both OSL and AFL

Neither the names of Licensor, nor the names of any contributors to the Original Work, nor any of their trademarks or service marks, may be used to endorse or promote products derived from this Original Work without express prior written permission of the Licensor. Nothing in this License shall be deemed to grant any rights to trademarks, copyrights, patents, trade secrets or any other intellectual property of Licensor except as expressly stated herein. No patent license is granted to make, use, sell or offer to sell embodiments of any patent claims other than the licensed claims defined in Section 2. No right is granted to the trademarks of Licensor even if such marks are included in the Original Work. Nothing in this License shall be interpreted to prohibit Licensor from licensing under different terms from this License any Original Work that Licensor otherwise would have a right to license.

This OSL and AFL provision is intended primarily to make explicit what most other licenses don't say: There are some rights that the original owner will not license. By doing this explicitly, there will be no uncertainty by either party about implied licenses to intellectual property.

This provision prohibits the use by any licensee of the name and trademarks of the licensor. This section later makes it clear that, even if the licensor's trademarks are present in the software, there is no license to those trademarks for derivative works. In other words, the author of a derivative work may actually have to remove references to the licensor's trademarks from his or her derivative works.

Second, the OSL/AFL exclude *all* implied copyright and patent licenses; only express licenses are granted, limited by the words of the express grants. (See OSL/AFL sections 1 and 2.)

Finally, the OSL/AFL make it clear that the licensor reserves the right to license original works under other licenses besides this one.

Comparison to Other Licenses

None of the other licenses described in this book contain a specific section excluding certain rights from the license grants. This does not mean that those licenses *include* the licenses that are excluded by the OSL/AFL, but only that the exclusion is left to implication.

The BSD license excludes the right to use the name of the licensor or any contributors "to endorse or promote products" derived from the software.

The Apache license excludes the right to use *Apache* or *Apache Software Foundation* in derivative works "to endorse or promote products." (Apache license sections 4 and 5.)

The Artistic License excludes the right to use the name of the *Copyright Holder* in derivative works to endorse or promote products. (Artistic license section 8.)

The GPL contains no explicit statement of exclusion from license grant.

The MPL grants intellectual property rights from the Initial Developer and Contributor, but excludes trademark rights. (MPL sections 2.1[a] and 2.2[a].) It also requires every licensee to rename derivative works of the license itself and to remove references to the Mozilla and Netscape trademarks.

The CPL contains no explicit statement of exclusion from license grant.

5. External Deployment

OSL	AFL
The term "External Deployment" means the use or distribution of the Original Work or Derivative Works in any way such that the Original Work or Derivative Works may be used by anyone other than You, whether the Original Work or Derivative Works are distributed to those persons or made available as an application intended for use over a computer network. As an express condition for the grants of license hereunder, You agree that any External Deployment by You of a Derivative Work shall be deemed a distribution and shall be licensed to all under the terms of this License, as prescribed in section 1(c) herein.	(This section is deleted in its entirety.)

Because the AFL does not include the section 1(c) reciprocity provision, there is no need for it to include an expanded definition of distribution. Under the AFL, distribution of software does not result in any additional obligations.

The reciprocity provision of the OSL requires licensees to use the OSL for "copies of the Original Work or Derivative Works that you distribute." (OSL section 1[c].) The word *distribute* was not defined there, although it certainly includes such activities as selling or giving copies of software away to others.

The Internet and high-speed data connections have made it possible now for companies to make software available to third parties for execution even though it is not physically distributed to them. This section 5 of the OSL makes it clear that these activities are, for purposes of OSL license interpretation, to be treated as a *distribution*.

This expanded definition of *distribution* is to prevent companies from escaping the reciprocity obligation by avoiding a physical distribution while still allowing third parties to use the software over a network.

Consider, for example, open source software that is a component of an electronic mail system. Under typical reciprocity provisions (such as are found in the GPL, MPL, and CPL licenses), there is no distribution unless third parties actually receive copies of derivative works of that software to run on their computers. Mere use of that email system software over a network is not a distribution.

Under section 5 of the OSL, if a derivative work of an OSL-licensed component is used for an electronic mail system that has third party users, that derivative work must be licensed under the OSL. It is subject to the reciprocity obligation.

Comparison to Other Licenses

The section 5 definition of *external deployment* is a modified version of a provision originally found in the Real Networks Public Source License. That license reads:

> *"Externally Deploy"* means to Deploy the Covered Code in any way that may be accessed or used by anyone other than You, used to provide any services to anyone other than You, or used in any way to deliver any content to anyone other than You, whether the Covered Code is distributed to those parties, made available as an application intended for use

*over a computer network, or used to provide services or oth-
erwise deliver content to anyone other than You. (Real Networks Public Source License section 1.7.)*

This definition is far broader than the one in the OSL. In
particular, it includes as an *external deployment* the use of the
software "to deliver any content to anyone other than You." If a
derivative works of a Real Networks–licensed component is
used for an email system that delivers mail (i.e., *content*) to third
parties, that derivative work is subject to the Real Networks reciprocity provision even if third parties don't actually use the
email system. The OSL/AFL are much narrower in effect.

None of the academic licenses described in this book deal at
all with restrictions or conditions on distribution. For that reason, as in the AFL, a definition of *external deployment* is
unnecessary.

None of the reciprocal licenses described in this book (the
GPL, MPL, and the CPL) contain a similar definition of *external deployment*. Under those licenses, only the distribution of a
physical or electronic copy would invoke the reciprocity obligation.

6. Attribution Rights

Both OSL and AFL

You must retain, in the Source Code of any Derivative Works that You
create, all copyright, patent or trademark notices from the Source Code
of the Original Work, as well as any notices of licensing and any
descriptive text identified therein as an "Attribution Notice." You must
cause the Source Code for any Derivative Works that You create to carry
a prominent Attribution Notice reasonably calculated to inform
recipients that You have modified the Original Work.

Section 6 of the OSL/AFL is intended to protect the reputations of contributors and distributors as their Original Works are copied, modified, and distributed by downstream licensees.

Note that this provision deals with the *Source Code* of the *Original Work* or *Derivative Works*. It does not affect executable versions of the software in any way.

The first sentence prevents licensees from removing any notices in the *Source Code* that would reasonably serve to identify the *Original Work*. Such notices include "copyright, patent or trademark notices" (such as the copyright notice on this book); "licensing notices" (such as the licensing notice described in the first paragraph of the AFL/OSL licenses); and "any descriptive text identified therein as an Attribution Notice."

The second sentence prevents licensees from implying that the original licensor is responsible for their *Derivative Works*. Licensees must place notices in the *Source Code* of their *Derivative Works* that would reasonably serve to notify recipients that the *Original Work* has been changed.

Comparison to Other Licenses

This provision of the OSL/AFL is intended to accomplish what the Artistic License sought without the confusing other terms and conditions of that license. (See the discussion in Chapter 5 about the Artistic License.)

The advertising clause that the University of California removed from the BSD license was a much more onerous version of the first sentence of the OSL/AFL *attribution rights* provision. That provision read:

All advertising materials mentioning features or use of this software must display the following acknowledgement: This product includes software developed by the University of California, Berkeley and its contributors. (BSD license provision now deleted.)

That BSD advertising clause affected "all advertising materials," but the OSL/AFL only affects the Source Code.

7. Warranty of Provenance and Disclaimer of Warranty

Both OSL and AFL

Licensor warrants that the copyright in and to the Original Work and the patent rights granted herein by Licensor are owned by the Licensor or are sublicensed to You under the terms of this License with the permission of the contributor(s) of those copyrights and patent rights. Except as expressly stated in the immediately preceding sentence, the Original Work is provided under this License on an "AS IS" BASIS and WITHOUT WARRANTY, either express or implied, including, without limitation, the warranties of NON-INFRINGEMENT, MERCHANTABILITY or FITNESS FOR A PARTICULAR PURPOSE. THE ENTIRE RISK AS TO THE QUALITY OF THE ORIGINAL WORK IS WITH YOU. This DISCLAIMER OF WARRANTY constitutes an essential part of this License. No license to Original Work is granted hereunder except under this disclaimer.

A warranty is a promise that a proposition of fact is true. The licensor intends that the licensee rely on that promise, and under contract law may be required to compensate licensees for any loss if the fact warranted proves untrue.

The first sentence of section 7 is a warranty of provenance.

The word *provenance* (from the French *provenir*, "to originate") is used in the art and antiques world to refer to an object's history and ownership. Knowing the provenance of an art object is equivalent to knowing the chain of title to a piece of land. When used in the context of open source software, it indicates that the chain of title to the intellectual property in the software is known. (Refer to the discussion on chain of title to copyrights and patents in Chapter 2.)

The OSL/AFL provide a warranty of provenance to reassure customers that the origins and ownership of the intellectual property in the licensed open source software are known and legitimate. A licensor is in an ideal position to know the origins of his or her software and therefore to make such a warranty:

1. The licensor may have written the software him- or herself and, as the author of an *original work of authorship*, is the owner of the copyright in that software. A warranty of provenance is obviously justified in this situation.

2. The licensor may have received a written assignment of copyright from the original author. (In the United States, copyright assignments must be in writing. 17 U.S.C. § 204.) A written copyright assignment is appropriate evidence of authenticity and authority to grant licenses to the original work. A *warranty of provenance* is justified in this situation.

3. The licensor may have received a license—perhaps an open source license or a contributor agreement—authorizing him or her to sublicense the contribution or derivative works to third parties. Such a license is reasonable proof that the software is being transferred legitimately

to third parties. Such a license may be proven by
written records or by the conduct of the contributor when he or she sent a contribution to the
project. A *warranty of provenance* is justified in
this situation.

Unfortunately, some open source projects may not have the
kinds of records of contributions that would allow them to
provide a warranty of provenance. Those projects cannot use
the OSL/AFL licenses.

It may come to pass that, despite careful record keeping and
formal licensing procedures, an open source project discovers
that a contribution is not authentic, a contribution agreement
has been breached, or a contributor has not been entirely hon-
est. The warranty of provenance is suddenly no longer appropriate. Continued distribution of the infringing contribution,
of course, must be stopped; that much is true even without a
warranty of provenance. But what is the licensor's potential
liability under that warranty for past breaches? I defer an
answer to this question to the discussion of section 8 of the
OSL/AFL, Limitation of Liability.

Note also that, even in the absence of a warranty of provenance, the intentional or reckless distribution of software for
which you don't have a license may be punishable as fraud or
an unfair business practice, or even as a criminal act of distributing stolen property.

The remainder of section 7 is a disclaimer of all other warranties, express or implied.

A warranty of "merchantability or fitness for a particular
purpose" promises that the software is fit for the ordinary purposes for which such software is used, and that it conforms to
the promises or affirmations of fact made in advertisements or
in the software documentation. Because open source software

is typically distributed without charge, it is expected that licensees will accept the risk that the software won't perform as designed or intended.

A warranty of "non-infringement" promises that the software does not infringe the copyrights or patents of third parties. Because it is generally impossible for any software distributor to determine whether copyright or patent claims from third parties will be made, and because the software is distributed at no charge, a warranty of noninfringement is not reasonable. The licensee is expected to accept that risk.

Note that a warranty of noninfringement is different from a warranty of provenance. The former is a promise that there will be no third party copyright or patent claims that may suddenly appear; the latter is a promise that the licensor's right to license the work is based on ownership or license.

The "including, without limitation" language in the warranty disclaimer indicates that the list of warranties (i.e., noninfringement, merchantability, and fitness for a particular purpose) is by way of example only. Any other express or implied warranties are also excluded.

There are no express warranties in the OSL/AFL except for the warranty of provenance. In all other respects, the software is "AS IS" and "WITHOUT WARRANTY."

Comparison to Other Licenses

No other open source licenses provide a warranty of provenance under that title. But other licenses contain similar representations. The MPL, in its section 3.4(c), and CPL, in its section 2(d), come closest.

All other open source licenses in this book provide a similar disclaimer of warranty. While the wording of those disclaimers differs among licenses, all include the *AS IS* phrase. Not all licenses specifically list the warranty of noninfringement, but it is implied by the "including, without limitation" language found in all warranty disclaimer provisions.

8. Limitation of Liability

> **Both OSL and AFL**
>
> Under no circumstances and under no legal theory, whether in tort (including negligence), contract, or otherwise, shall the Licensor be liable to any person for any direct, indirect, special, incidental, or consequential damages of any character arising as a result of this License or the use of the Original Work including, without limitation, damages for loss of goodwill, work stoppage, computer failure or malfunction, or any and all other commercial damages or losses. This limitation of liability shall not apply to liability for death or personal injury resulting from Licensor's negligence to the extent applicable law prohibits such limitation. Some jurisdictions do not allow the exclusion or limitation of incidental or consequential damages, so this exclusion and limitation may not apply to You.

Section 8 of the OSL/AFL disclaims liability for damages.

An attorney drafting a liability disclaimer on behalf of a licensor has an interesting challenge. The attorney must identify all possible ways in which a licensee may suffer damages (i.e., loss, detriment, or injury), and then the attorney must expressly announce that the licensor will pay for none of that. In that way, the limitation of liability provision in most licenses protects the licensor—not the licensee.

The OSL/AFL limitation of liability provision first identifies the possible legal theories under which a licensee may claim damages. *Tort (including negligence)* is the civil law that deals with private wrongs or injuries; *contract* is the civil law that deals with breaches of written or oral agreements. The phrase "under no circumstances and under no legal theory" at the beginning of the sentence, and the phrase "or otherwise" at the end of that list of legal theories, is intended to mean a total and complete limitation on liability.

As I shall explain, such a total and complete limitation isn't actually allowed by the law.

Liability can potentially extend *to any person.* For example, software may be incorporated into a commercial product that causes injuries to persons other than the licensee. Consider what might happen, for example, if defective software were used to run a nuclear power plant or control a space shuttle.

Although the OSL/AFL (and most other open source licenses) disclaim liability *to any person*, those third parties are not subject to the limitation because they have never agreed to the license—and they remain free to sue whoever they believe is liable for their injuries. The purpose of this language is to clarify that, as between the *licensor* and the *licensee*, it is the *licensee* who is potentially liable for injury to third parties. So if damages are ultimately assessed for injury to third parties, the *licensee* will pay them. (The effect on injured third parties of this limitation of liability provision is similar to an indemnification provision under which the licensee indemnifies the licensor for injuries to third parties.)

The OSL/AFL limitation of liability provision next identifies the types of damages that courts may potentially award. "Direct" damages are those that follow immediately upon the act done; in the case of a breach of contract, as one court put it, they are damages which, in the ordinary course of human experience, can be expected to result from breach. "Indirect" damages, of course, are those that are not direct. "Special" damages are those that do not arise from the wrongful act itself, but depend on circumstances peculiar to the injury or the parties; in contract law, they are damages that were not contemplated by the parties at the time the contract was made. "Incidental" damages are those expenses that result from an injured party taking commercially reasonable steps to deal with the wrongful act. "Consequential" damages are those that do not flow directly and immediately from the wrongful act, but only from some of the consequences or results of such act; anyone who deals with computer technology in modern commerce realizes the substantial potential financial consequences, for example, of replacing defective software.

As if that list were not enough, the OSL/AFL licenses then list specific examples of damages for which the licensor disclaims liability. Computer software can be such an integral part of a licensee's business that its failure risks the business itself. The OSL/AFL disclaim liability for that, mentioning specifically "loss of goodwill, work stoppage, computer failure or malfunction, or any and all other commercial damages or losses."

The intent of the first long sentence of this limitation of liability provision is to limit liability for absolutely everything the licensor can think of. Of course, the law doesn't really allow someone to simply write a liability disclaimer and then get away with outrageous commercial activities. Licensors always remain liable—regardless of a disclaimer of liability—for criminal activities, for unfair business practices (including antitrust), and for fraudulent behavior that induces licensees to accept the defective or dangerous software under the license.

Consider the effect of the *limitation of liability* provision in light of the express *warranty of provenance* in OSL/AFL section 7. Even in the event of a breach of that warranty of provenance, liability for damages may still be limited. Licensors may not have to pay damages even if it is discovered that the licensor didn't actually have authority to grant a sublicense to the software. For example, suppose a contributor lied about the provenance of his or her contribution to a project and the project, in reliance on that contributor's license, distributes the work under the OSL/AFL. The OSL/AFL disclaim liability for direct, indirect, etc., damages resulting from any such breach of warranty.

That liability disclaimer may not always be effective. In particular, in most jurisdictions, if a licensor provides a *warranty of provenance* with full knowledge that the promise he or she made is untrue or knowing that he or she does not have a reasonable basis for making the promise of provenance, that licensor may be liable for fraud despite his or her limitation of liability.

And so, the second and third sentences of the OSL/AFL *limitation of liability* provision remind licensees that *applicable law* may prohibit certain limitations of liability. That applicable law may be national, state, or local. In such situations, the licensor remains potentially liable regardless of what the OSL/AFL say. Only your own attorney can properly advise you of what that potential liability might be.

Once again, licensors should not rely on a limitation of liability provision to protect themselves from fraudulent or criminal or outrageous business behavior. They can, however, rely on limitation of liability provisions to protect them from the effects of accidental and unexpected breaches of the *warranty of provenance* or other implied or express warranties.

Comparison to Other Licenses

Every open source license in this book contains a limitation of liability clause.

The only time the specific wording will matter is if a licensee or third party suffers an injury and his or her attorney identifies a type of liability that the open source licensor's attorney forgot to disclaim. It requires that we speculate without bound about future events. For that reason, I'll leave any further discussion about liability to Chapter 12.

9. Acceptance and Termination

OSL	AFL
If You distribute copies of the Original Work or a Derivative Work, You must make a reasonable effort under the circumstances to obtain the express assent of recipients to the terms of this License. Nothing else but this License (or another written agreement between Licensor and You) grants You permission to create Derivative Works based upon the Original Work or to exercise any of the rights granted in Section 1 herein, and any attempt to do so except under the terms of this License (or another written agreement between Licensor and You) is expressly prohibited by U.S. copyright law, the equivalent laws of other countries, and by international treaty. Therefore, by exercising any of the rights granted to You in Section 1 herein, You indicate Your acceptance of this License and all of its terms and conditions. This License shall terminate immediately and you may no longer exercise any of the rights granted to You by this License upon Your failure to honor the proviso in Section 1(c) herein.	If You distribute copies of the Original Work or a Derivative Work, You must make a reasonable effort under the circumstances to obtain the express assent of recipients to the terms of this License. Nothing else but this License (or another written agreement between Licensor and You) grants You permission to create Derivative Works based upon the Original Work or to exercise any of the rights granted in Section 1 herein, and any attempt to do so except under the terms of this License (or another written agreement between Licensor and You) is expressly prohibited by U.S. copyright law, the equivalent laws of other countries, and by international treaty. Therefore, by exercising any of the rights granted to You in Section 1 herein, You indicate Your acceptance of this License and all of its terms and conditions.

The OSL/AFL licenses are designed to be enforced as contracts, and the law requires that parties to a contract expressly assent to its terms. Most courts don't really care what form that assent takes, as long as it is manifested by some definite action. For software, this often means a shrink-wrap or click-wrap procedure by which the licensee indicates awareness of the license and accepts it, but the OSL/AFL mandate neither procedure.

The OSL/AFL requires that downstream licenses for *Copies* and *Derivative Works* also be accepted as contracts. They mandate no particular method, but they require that downstream licensors exercise a "reasonable effort under the circumstances" to obtain assent. If those reasonable efforts are undertaken, the OSL/AFL will be enforceable as contracts.

But even ignoring contract law, the second and third sentences of section 9 make it clear that "nothing else but this license" allows anyone to use this software. This provision was taken from the GPL license, because it describes, in clear terms, the interdependence of copyright and contract law.

Here's how the argument goes: Anyone who copies, modifies, or distributes the licensor's software without a license is an *infringer*. The law punishing infringers is the U.S. copyright law, the equivalent laws of other countries, and international treaties. So anyone found using the software is either an infringer or a licensee. The OSL/AFL say that, by exercising the licensor's exclusive rights, either a user indicates acceptance of the license, or else the user is admitting that he or she is an infringer.

The final sentence of section 9 applies only to the OSL, because only the OSL contains a reciprocity provision. Once a contract is in effect it can be terminated. The OSL terminates if the licensee fails to honor the reciprocity condition in section 1(c). This puts teeth into the reciprocity bargain. A licensee cannot pick and choose which parts of this license to honor. Failure to distribute derivative works under the same

OSL is a breach of contract and grounds for terminating the license immediately.

Comparison to Other Licenses

The BSD, MIT, Apache, and Artistic licenses say nothing about contract formation or termination.

The basic concept for section 9 of the OSL/AFL came from the GPL. It uses similar language to assert the primacy of copyright law. However, the GPL is not intended to be enforced under contract law, so the first sentence of OSL/AFL section 9 (express assent) and the last sentence of OSL section 9 (termination for failure to honor the reciprocity provision) don't have analogues in the GPL.

The MPL says nothing about contract formation but it does include two termination clauses. The first says that the MPL license terminates:

> *...If You fail to comply with terms herein and fail to cure*
> *such breach within 30 days of becoming aware of the breach.*
> *(MPL section 8.1.)*

That termination provision is broader and applies in more situations than the termination provision of the OSL, which automatically terminates only for failure to honor the reciprocity provision. Terminating the OSL for other forms of breach would probably require the licensor to file a lawsuit. (See the discussion of the attorneys' fees provision in section 12, below.)

The second termination clause of the MPL will be discussed in section 10, termination for patent action.

The CPL also contains two termination provisions. One, relating to termination for patent action, will be discussed in section 10 below. The other is similar to the MPL:

All Recipient's rights under this Agreement shall terminate if it fails to comply with any of the material terms of conditions of this Agreement and does not cure such failure in a reasonable period of time after becoming aware of such noncompliance. (CPL section 7.)

Again, this is broader and applies in more situations than the OSL's termination for failure to honor the reciprocity condition, but in either situation a licensor may have to go to court to terminate the license. This is discussed in more detail in Chapter 12, Open Source Litigation.

10. Termination for Patent Action

Both OSL and AFL

This License shall terminate automatically and You may no longer exercise any of the rights granted to You by this License as of the date You commence an action, including a cross-claim or counterclaim, for patent infringement (i) against Licensor with respect to a patent applicable to software or (ii) against any entity with respect to a patent applicable to the Original Work (but excluding combinations of the Original Work with other software or hardware).

Patents are formidable property interests. Patents can be the basis for enormously profitable monopolies, and patents can bring infringing competitors to their knees. Like them or not, patents are enshrined in the Constitution of the United States (see Article I, section 8) and in the constitutions and laws of most countries around the world. We must deal with them for they are perceived by many to be a real threat to the openness of software.

Throughout this book I have described the ways that open source licenses deal—or don't deal—with the threat of third party patents. There aren't many reasonable options. Even if a licensor is thoroughly diligent to review patent databases, and almost regardless of the care that a licensor takes to avoid infringing other companies' patents, such submarines can appear suddenly and can stop an open source project dead in the water.

This has long been an issue in the software world. Proprietary software vendors deal with third party patent claims all the time. The big companies negotiate patent licenses and pay royalties where necessary. Those royalties are included in the cost of software. The price of software adjusts to compensate.

That isn't usually an option for free software, of course. Open source distributors don't have the same resources to simply bargain over the price of a royalty-bearing patent license, because they usually can't recover royalties in their own software prices. (See Open Source Principles # 2 and 3.)

Major software vendors often use defensive strategies to protect themselves from third party patents. The strategy of the biggest companies, it appears, is to create huge portfolios of intellectual property, which they can withhold from those people who threaten them. As an intellectual property defense it resembles the cold war threat that kept civilized countries from bombing each other into oblivion: "If you bomb me, I'll bomb you worse." Because their private intellectual property is so embedded in products used throughout the world, the mere threat to withdraw rights to valuable intellectual property is a deterrent to infringement lawsuits against these big patent owners.

Of course, if a third party doesn't actually benefit from the infringer's intellectual property, a threat to withdraw that intellectual property isn't worth much. Defensive use of intellectual property requires that the intellectual property that may be withdrawn be perceived as valuable. Thus defensive strategies are particularly valuable in software licenses. Licensees are presumed to need the licensor's software. A threat to withhold that software from the licensee may be enough to discourage a patent infringement lawsuit by that licensee.

Such a defensive strategy in the open source context also has the smell of justice being served. It just feels wrong to let a licensee benefit from free software and then turn around and sue that generous licensor for patent infringement. You shouldn't be allowed to have your cake and eat it too.

It feels right for a license to say: *If you sue me for patent infringement relating to software, or if you sue my customers for patent infringement by this licensed software, your license to this software terminates.*

Comparison to Other Licenses

It is perhaps easier to understand OSL/AFL section 10 by comparison to other licenses. For this we can ignore the other academic licenses (i.e., the BSD, MIT, Apache, and Artistic licenses) because none of them provide any form of patent defense.

Provisions for the defensive use of intellectual property are in the MPL and CPL licenses, and in most of the OSI-approved commercial open source licenses listed at *www.open-source.org*. Companies such as IBM, Nokia, Sun, Apple, and many others have released open source software under licenses containing defensive termination provisions.

Sections 8.2 and 8.3 of the MPL deal with license termination in the event of patent infringement. Here are the key differences between the OSL/AFL and MPL termination provisions:

- The MPL excludes *declaratory judgment actions.* Those are lawsuits in which a party seeks only to have the court declare that it is the owner of a patent, but doesn't seek damages. (MPL section 8.2.) The OSL/AFL do not draw this distinction.

- The MPL refers only to lawsuits against *Initial Developer* and *Contributor*. (MPL section 8.2.) The OSL/AFL also terminate the license if the licensee files an infringement lawsuit against a customer or user of the licensed software for infringement by the specific software being licensed.

- If someone sues for infringement by *Participant's Contributor Version*, then all *copyright and patent* licenses to that person in the MPL terminate. (MPL section 8.2[a].) If someone sues for infringement by *any software, hardware, or device, other than such Participant's Contributor Version*, then only the *patent* licenses to that person terminate. (MPL section 8.2[b].) Under the OSL/AFL, both *copyright and patent* license grants terminate.

- The MPL suggests settlement of the infringement dispute for a reasonable royalty and payment arrangement. The license can continue if the parties settle within a sixty-day period. (MPL section 8.2[a].) There is no equivalent provision in the OSL/AFL, but there are almost always advance notice and negotiation before companies undertake patent litigation.

- The *reasonable value of the license* is to offset the royalty for any patent license, which the parties negotiate. (MPL section 8.3.) There is no equivalent provision in the OSL/AFL.

The CPL's patent termination provision is in the second paragraph of its section 7. The major difference between the CPL's provision and the one in the OSL/AFL is that the CPL terminates only its patent license; the CPL's copyright license continues. If there are no licensor patents actually embodied in the software and licensed under the CPL, then the CPL license to the software does not terminate.

The CPL's provision makes sense when one considers that the author of that license, IBM, has the largest patent portfolio of any company in the world. That company has a tradition of using its patents portfolio to defend itself against patent infringement lawsuits. It generally hasn't needed to use its *copyrights* to protect against patent infringement lawsuits.

The OSL/AFL, on the other hand, by terminating both the *copyright and patent* licenses, use the entire intellectual property in the software—both its copyright component and its patent component—to protect that software and the licensor from patent infringement lawsuits. This is more appropriate than IBM's defensive strategy for open source contributors and distributors who, for the most part, don't have patents to license but who do have their copyrights.

The GPL's patent defense strategy is subtly different from all these others. Here is what the GPL says:

> *If, as a consequence of a court judgment or allegation of patent infringement or for any other reason (not limited to patent issues), conditions are imposed on you (whether by court order, agreement or otherwise) that contradict the conditions of this License, they do not excuse you from the con-*

ditions of this License. If you cannot distribute so as to satisfy
simultaneously your obligations under this License and any
other pertinent obligations, then as a consequence you may
not distribute the Program at all. For example, if a patent
license would not permit royalty-free redistribution of the
Program by all those who receive copies directly or indirectly
through you, then the only way you could satisfy both it and
this License would be to refrain entirely from distribution of
the Program. (GPL section 7.)

The GPL is incompatible with royalty-bearing patent licenses because they impose conditions *that contradict the conditions of this License*, in particular the *at no charge* requirement of GPL section 2(b). If such a license affects the software, then the software cannot be distributed under the GPL, and so a licensee may not distribute the Program at all.

There may be other license incompatibilities besides a requirement for patent royalties. A patent license that is limited as to *field of use* so that it prevents the creation of certain types of derivative works might ultimately turn out to be incompatible with the GPL. Any licensing incompatibilities *that contradict the conditions* of the GPL are sufficient to prevent further distribution under the GPL.

GPL section 7 effectively terminates only the license to distribute, not the license to copy and create derivative works. Those rights continue under the GPL. And GPL section 7 is designed to take effect when the *Program* infringes a patent, not every time the licensor is sued for patent infringement. In these ways it is very different from the termination provisions in the MPL, CPL, and OSL/AFL licenses. That GPL provision is unique among open source licenses.

What then happens if a GPL licensee wins a patent infringement lawsuit against a GPL licensor because the *Pro-*

gram infringes, and then the licensee refuses to license the patent royalty-free? The software can no longer be distributed by the licensee under the GPL license. (GPL section 7.) Can anyone else continue to distribute the software under the GPL? The GPL provides the following answer:

> *It is not the purpose of this section to induce you to infringe any patents or other property right claims or to contest validity of any such claims; this section has the sole purpose of protecting the integrity of the free software distribution system, which is implemented by public license practices. Many people have made generous contributions to the wide range of software distributed through that system in reliance on consistent application of that system; it is up to the author/donor to decide if he or she is willing to distribute software through any other system and a licensee cannot impose that choice. (GPL section 7.)*

Section 7 of the GPL is a form of patent defense, but it is unlike anything in any other open source license. Indeed, the GPL suggests that it is more than a license condition:

> *This section is intended to make thoroughly clear what is believed to be a consequence of the rest of this License. (GPL section 7.)*

The consequences of GPL section 7—indeed, the consequences of any of the patent defense provisions in any open source licensees—have never been tested in court.

Breaking News about OSL/AFL Version 2.1

The main criticism of section 10 of OSL/AFL version 2.0 is that it creates a substantial business risk to licensees who own patents. If they someday seek to assert one of their patents against the licensor, they may lose the right to the software being licensed. They risk nonenforceability of their present patents—and even perhaps their future patents—if they someday sue a licensor for patent infringement. That risk cannot easily be measured.

A difficult challenge in any license—open source or proprietary—is to balance the interests and rights of licensees who own patents with the interests and rights of licensors who own software. Parties to software licenses traditionally negotiate license terms and conditions and, through the process of negotiation, some balance is achieved between the interests of the licensor and the licensee. But mass-market software licenses are not negotiated and so, when you buy Windows or Linux, for example, you take the software under its license or leave it. It requires a sophisticated licensee to stand up to a mass-market software license and say, "This isn't a fair provision, and I won't accept the software under those terms."

The problem lies in subsection (i) of section 10 in OSL/AFL version 2.0. Here for easy reference is the provision again:

> *Termination for Patent Action. This License shall terminate automatically and You may no longer exercise any of the rights granted to You by this License as of the date You commence an action, including a cross-claim or counterclaim, for patent infringement (i) against Licensor with respect to a patent applicable to software or (ii) against any entity with respect to a patent applicable to the Original Work (but excluding combinations of the Original Work with other software or hardware). (OSL/AFL version 2.0, section 10.)*

Because of the phrase "patent applicable to software" in subsection (i), the licensor is conditioning the license for this "Original Work" on the licensee's not suing for patent infringement of *any patent* applicable to *any software*. For a licensee with a big patent portfolio, there is no easy way to assess that cost or to limit that risk. Such a company may come to discover that important *unrelated* patents in its portfolio have been emasculated because the company has in-licensed some software under an open source license containing this section 10. Its *other* patents relating to *other* software can no longer effectively be asserted against infringers who happen to be licensors of valuable open source software. Better, they say, given the uncertainty of the risk, not to accept *this* software under such licenses in the first place.

Note that the problem with section 10 of the OSL/AFL version 2.0 is virtually identical to the problem with MPL sections 8.2 and 8.3, CPL section 7, and several other approved commercial open source licenses. It is a major open source licensing problem that has adversely affected the acceptance of software under those licenses. Such license provisions are simply unacceptable to some licensees with large, diverse patent portfolios. They cannot assess the risk to unrelated patents in their portfolios if they in-license software under licenses containing such defensive provisions and so they refuse to in-license such software at all.

Here is the new language in section 10 in OSL/AFL version 2.1:

> *Termination for Patent Action. This License shall terminate automatically and You may no longer exercise any of the rights granted to You by this License as of the date You commence an action, including a cross-claim or counterclaim, against Licensor or any licensee alleging that the Original Work infringes a patent. This termination provision shall not apply for an action alleging patent infringement by combinations of the Original Work with other software or hardware. (OSL/AFL version 2.1, section 10.)*

This new section 10 defensive provision terminates the license to *this Original Work* only if the licensee asserts a patent claim against *this Original Work*. The condition relating to *unrelated software* is removed. The termination provision now applies if an infringement lawsuit is filed against "Licensor or any licensee"; the previous version included "any entity." These differences significantly reduce the scope of the patent termination provision and make it friendlier to patent-owning companies.

The whole point of this change is that such companies can now feel more comfortable in-licensing open source software. The community will grow, and more open source software will be created.

There is no such thing as a *fairest* license. As I have repeatedly suggested, each license in this book creates a legitimate open source bargain, albeit in sometimes vastly different ways from other licenses. But I personally agree with some who suggest that OSL/AFL version 2.1 is *fairer* to licensees than the earlier version. In the hope of mitigating some but not all of the patent risk, some of us have negotiated this compromise.

11. Jurisdiction, Venue, and Governing Law

Both OSL and AFL

Any action or suit relating to this License may be brought only in the courts of a jurisdiction wherein the Licensor resides or in which Licensor conducts its primary business, and under the laws of that jurisdiction excluding its conflict-of-law provisions. The application of the United Nations Convention on Contracts for the International Sale of Goods is expressly excluded. Any use of the Original Work outside the scope of this License or after its termination shall be subject to the requirements and penalties of the U.S. Copyright Act, 17 U.S.C. § 101 et seq., the equivalent laws of other countries, and international treaty. This section shall survive the termination of this License.

Potentially—perhaps inevitably—there will be litigation concerning the OSL/AFL. *Jurisdiction* determines which courts shall have the power to hear the case. *Venue* determines the location of that court. And *governing law* determines whose laws shall apply. There are only three choices for jurisdiction, venue, and governing law: (1) the licensor's home turf; (2) the licensee's home turf; or (3) some neutral territory (is there such a place?).

The OSL/AFL licenses forthrightly give the advantage to the licensor by specifying the licensor's jurisdiction, venue, and governing law. I believe that is appropriate considering that the licensor is the party giving away the open source software. It would be unfair to subject a licensor to the licensee's courts for something that he or she gave away for free.

The provision doesn't necessarily mean that litigation will take place in the licensor's resident state or country. A licensee may choose to bring litigation in any jurisdiction "in which Licensor conducts its primary business." A major distributor that conducts its *primary business* throughout the world is subject to being sued in any of those jurisdictions. That also seems to me to be a just way of softening what would otherwise be a licensor's unfair advantage.

The reference to the "United Nations Convention on Contracts for the International Sale of Goods" is intended to ensure that an OSL/AFL-licensed *Original Work* is treated as intellectual property, not as goods. The laws relating to goods are far more complex than I can deal with in this book.

The third sentence of this section is particularly important:

> *Any use of the Original Work outside the scope of this License or after its termination shall be subject to the requirements and penalties of the U.S. Copyright Act, 17 U.S.C. § 101 et seq., the equivalent laws of other countries, and international treaty.*

This ensures that the requirements and penalties of copyright law will be effective to punish anyone who copies, creates derivative works, distributes the *Original Work* without a license (i.e., if the formalities of offer, acceptance, or consideration fail), or after the license is terminated.

Comparison to Other Licenses

None of the academic licenses in this book (i.e., BSD, MIT, Apache, or Artistic) say anything about jurisdiction, venue, or governing law.

The authors of the GPL intend the governing law to be copyright law. The license itself says nothing about jurisdiction or venue.

Under the MPL, jurisdiction is the Federal Courts of the Northern District of California, venue is in Santa Clara County, California, and governing law is California. The MPL also excludes the application of the United Nations Convention on Contracts for the International Sale of Goods.

Under the CPL, jurisdiction and venue aren't specified, but governing law is the law of New York and the intellectual property laws of the United States of America. Jurisdiction and venue aren't specified. Any licensor intending to distribute software under the CPL should consult with an attorney to determine jurisdiction and venue in the absence of a license provision stating it.

12. Attorneys' Fees

Both OSL and AFL

In any action to enforce the terms of this License or seeking damages relating thereto, the prevailing party shall be entitled to recover its costs and expenses, including, without limitation, reasonable attorneys' fees and costs incurred in connection with such action, including any appeal of such action. This section shall survive the termination of this License.

Litigation over software licenses can be expensive. One tactic often used by litigation bullies is to file suit even if they may lose on the merits, because the cost of litigation alone will often force the other party to settle. In the United States (but not in all countries), each party is typically responsible for paying its own costs and attorneys' fees. Some important exceptions to this rule are:

- Certain statutes, such as the U.S. Copyright Act, provide that the prevailing party can recover attorneys' fees and costs at the discretion of the court. (17 U.S.C. § 505.)

- Under contract law, the contract itself can specify that the winner of a lawsuit is entitled to recover his or her attorneys' fees and costs from the loser.

The OSL/AFL licenses take the second approach.

Sometimes people avoid filing suit over a contract if they can't afford to hire an attorney. When attorneys' fees and costs can be recovered, however, some attorneys will offer to take such cases on a contingency basis. An attorneys' fees provision can help small contributors and distributors obtain access to attorneys.

For these same reasons, large companies often don't like attorneys' fees provisions. They fear that it tends to encourage litigation and makes them more vulnerable to lawsuit.

The OSL/AFL attorneys' fees and costs provision takes the side of the small contributor or distributor as against the large companies.

Comparison to Other Licenses

The academic licenses (i.e., BSD, MIT, Apache, and Artistic) and the GPL say nothing about attorneys' fees.

The *losing party* under the MPL is "responsible for costs, including without limitation, court costs and reasonable attorneys' fees and expenses." (MPL section 11.)

The CPL does not contain an attorneys' fees provision. This is as one would expect in a license by a large company (e.g., IBM) with a huge budget for attorneys.

13. Miscellaneous

> **Both OSL and AFL**
>
> This License represents the complete agreement concerning the subject matter hereof. If any provision of this License is held to be unenforceable, such provision shall be reformed only to the extent necessary to make it enforceable.

These provisions are common in professionally written licenses.

The first sentence avoids the confusion that can result when people say different things about a license than what the license itself says. I described one such situation in Chapter 6, where Linus Torvalds has written publicly that his interpretation of the GPL is different than that of the license's authors at the Free Software Foundation. The OSL/AFL handles such situations by saying that the words of the license prevail over extraneous statements by either party.

The second sentence may help to convince courts not to be too drastic in reforming the license when the license is found to be improper under some law. Judges are discouraged from radically reforming the license.

Comparison to Other Licenses

All the major reciprocal licenses in this book contain *miscellaneous* provisions. I leave those as an exercise for the reader.

14. Definition of "You" in This License

Both OSL and AFL

"You" throughout this License, whether in upper or lower case, means an individual or a legal entity exercising rights under, and complying with all of the terms of, this License. For legal entities, "You" includes any entity that controls, is controlled by, or is under common control with you. For purposes of this definition, "control" means (i) the power, direct or indirect, to cause the direction or management of such entity, whether by contract or otherwise, or (ii) ownership of fifty percent (50%) or more of the outstanding shares, or (iii) beneficial ownership of such entity.

Every license has to identify the parties. The first paragraph of the OSL/AFL identifies parties as the *Licensor* and *You*. Section 14 defines the word *You*.

Everyone understands that a licensee can be an individual. It can also be a *legal entity*, such as a corporation or partnership. The OSL is clear that all parts of an entity, the controlling parts, the controlled parts, or parts under common control (e.g., holding companies, subsidiaries, divisions of the same company) are collectively treated as a single licensee.

This has important legal consequences: The creation and distribution of derivative works strictly within the organizational parts of a single licensee company is not a distribution for purposes of the reciprocity obligation. All such parts are a single You.

Comparison to Other Licenses

This OSL/AFL provision is essentially copied from the MPL section 1.12, the definition of *You*.

The BSD license doesn't identify the second party to the license. It is assumed to be *everyone*.

The MIT license extends to *any person*.

The Apache license doesn't identify the second party to the license. It is assumed to be *everyone*.

The Artistic license defines *You* as "you, if you're thinking about copying or distributing this Package." As I snidely commented when discussing the Artistic license in Chapter 5, this provision is ridiculous.

The GPL states that *each licensee is addressed as "you".* (GPL section 0.)

The CPL refers to *Recipient*, defined as anyone who receives the *Program* under this *Agreement*.

15. Right to Use

Both OSL and AFL

You may use the Original Work in all ways not otherwise restricted or conditioned by this License or by law, and Licensor promises not to interfere with or be responsible for such uses by You.

This sentence is intended to accomplish two things. First, it declares that the *use* of the *Original Work* is a right of every licensee. It is a restatement of Open Source Principle # 1.

More important for the Licensor, it declares the Licensor's promise that he or she shall not *interfere with or be responsible for* such uses. *You*—not the Licensor—are responsible for complying with any local laws regarding the *Original Work*, such as the export control laws or the product safety laws. *You,* not the Licensor, have sole discretion to do what you want with the *Original Work*. Don't look to the Licensor for comfort or authority, and exercise your freedom responsibly.

Comparison to Other Licenses

Of the licenses discussed in this book, only the GPL contains a vaguely similar statement:

> *Activities other than copying, distribution and modification are not covered by this License; they are outside its scope. The act of running the Program is not restricted, and the output from the Program is covered only if its contents constitute a work based on the Program (independent of having been made by running the Program). Whether that is true depends on what the Program does. (GPL section 0.)*

This GPL provision is often read as a license to use, although it doesn't expressly say so.

Copyright and Licensing Notice

Most licenses identify their author and copyright owner. The OSL/AFL licenses do also.

Because of the risk of proliferation of different versions of the OSL and AFL licenses, I do not currently license others to modify them. I recognize that this conflicts in a subtle way with the Open Source Principles. But I am allowed, under the copyright laws, to do precisely that. I am merely exercising my exclusive right, under the copyright law, to control derivative works of my licenses.

This provision assumes that a software license is copyrightable subject matter, but it isn't clear to me that the *expression* of a license doesn't merge with its *ideas*, rendering it uncopyrightable. Anyone who has made it this far into this book and wants to engage in a philosophical discussion about that topic is invited to send me email about whether a license can be copyrighted.

Comparison to Other Licenses

The BSD, MIT, and Apache licenses say nothing about license ownership.

The Artistic license says nothing about license ownership. There are various versions of the Artistic license in use today. For example, notice that section 10 of the Artistic License doesn't appear in all versions of that license.

The GPL contains the following copyright and license notice:

> *Copyright (C) 1989, 1991 Free Software Foundation, Inc.,*
> *59 Temple Place, Suite 330, Boston, MA 02111-1307*
> *USA. Everyone is permitted to copy and distribute verbatim*
> *copies of this license document, but changing it is not al-*
> *lowed. (GPL first paragraph.)*

The MPL contains no copyright notice but it says this about the license:

> *If You create or use a modified version of this License (which*
> *you may only do in order to apply it to code which is not al-*
> *ready Covered Code governed by this License), You must (a)*
> *rename Your license so that the phrases "Mozilla",*
> *"MOZILLAPL", "MOZPL", "Netscape", "MPL", "NPL"*
> *or any confusingly similar phrase do not appear in your li-*

cense (except to note that your license differs from this License) and (b) otherwise make it clear that Your version of the license contains terms which differ from the Mozilla Public License and Netscape Public License. (Filling in the name of the Initial Developer, Original Code or Contributor in the notice described in Exhibit A shall not of themselves be deemed to be modifications of this License.) (MPL section 6.3.)

The CPL contains no copyright notice but it says this about the license:

Everyone is permitted to copy and distribute copies of this Agreement, but in order to avoid inconsistency the Agreement is copyrighted and may only be modified in the following manner. The Agreement Steward reserves the right to publish new versions (including revisions) of this Agreement from time to time. No one other than the Agreement Steward has the right to modify this Agreement. IBM is the initial Agreement Steward. IBM may assign the responsibility to serve as the Agreement Steward to a suitable separate entity. (CPL section 7.)

10

Choosing an Open Source License

How Licenses Are Chosen

I have been involved with the open source community long enough to recognize that decisions in projects about licensing strategy are almost always thoughtfully and carefully considered. Indeed, I learned far more about open source licensing from listening to those online licensing discussions than I ever learned about this topic in law school. The leaders of open source projects are knowledgeable about the law, committed to the principles of open source, and determined to create a commons of free software available to all. And so they write and choose licenses with intelligence and passion.

For many commercial companies, the discussion of which license to use, at least in the early stages, often centers on one or both of the following issues:

1. How can we make money from distributing this software under an open source license? In essence, can our license help us sell free software?

2. How can we prevent others from making money unfairly from our open source software? This is the so-called free-rider issue, where licensees reap

all the benefits of others' work with no return obligations.

These questions are addressed in reverse order in the next two sections of this chapter.

The Free-Rider Problem

The second question posed above is actually the easier one. Under Open Source Principles # 2 and 3, it is impossible to completely prevent free-riders in open source. All licensees are free to copy and create derivative works without payment of royalties to the licensor, and so a licensee can make as many copies of such software as possible without rewarding the licensor with even a peppercorn as payment.

If it is important to discourage free-riders who create and distribute derivative works, then a reciprocal license is often more effective than an academic license. At least with reciprocal licenses, everyone is a free-rider of everyone else's distributed derivative works, because that software is licensed under the same license. The pain of the free-rider problem is equally shared by all distributors of derivative works, not just by the original licensor, under reciprocal licenses.

But whether a licensor chooses to distribute under an academic or a reciprocal license, the growing commons of open source software that generally results from open source licensing is believed by most in the open source community to be sufficient reward for allowing everyone to be free-riders.

If after considering open source models you still want to prevent free-riders, you should consider adopting one of the non–open source licenses described in Chapter 11, or try instead to make money with a proprietary software distribution model.

Making Money from Open Source

The first question I posed above ("How do I make money at this?") is far more difficult to answer. Broad copyright and patent licenses such as those described in this book are certainly not consistent with business models that rely upon selling software at high per-copy prices. Anyone can become an open source distributor and compete on price. This inevitably drives the per-copy price downward toward its marginal cost of production and distribution.

But licensors can make money on what the open source license *doesn't grant*. For this reason, it is often more rewarding to consider the *exclusions from license* rather than the open source *grants of license* when looking for opportunities for profit.

The most important exclusion is trademark or brand identity. Trademarks are excluded from all open source licenses, either explicitly or implicitly. Under the law, for the licensor to do otherwise would risk loss of his or her trademarks. It would result in a dilution of the licensor's trademarks to the point that consumers wouldn't know what specific software it represents.

Despite their protestations that quality matters most, companies and individuals usually acquire software not by function but by reputation. Trademarks are thus very important factors in consumer decisions. Given consumer behavior, it is no surprise that Linux and Windows are valued trademarks in the software marketplace. By marketing software under a trademark, the licensor can sell perceived value even though the underlying software might be available elsewhere for free without the trademark.

As to what steps to take to turn trademarks into profit, that is an exercise best left to discussions between your business strategists and your own intellectual property attorney. Suffice it to say that customers are often willing to pay for brand-name software, particularly if it comes with support and other benefits. Most open source licenses don't adversely affect that business opportunity at all.

Also excluded from several open source licenses, for many of the same reasons, are the names and reputations of the licensors. Even though they grant licenses to their software, licensors can protect their names and reputations for personal profit. Many individual contributors whose names adorn copyright notices in valuable software are making a good living because their professional reputations were enhanced by those contributions. They essentially sell themselves and their expertise, rather than their software.

Most warranties are also excluded from the open source licenses in this book. A separate business can be made from selling such warranties—as well as other support and installation services—separate from the software itself.

Finally, the licensor of open source software is always free to license his or her software *also* under other terms and conditions. This means that a prospective licensee who prefers to accept the software under a different license than an open source one—and who is willing to pay for that "advantage"—may contact the licensor to determine if the software is also available under a different license. Chapter 11 discusses some examples of dual licensing.

In-Licensing

Consider first the process of software licensing from the perspective of the recipient of the license, the *licensee*. Of course, a licensee doesn't choose the license; open source software is usually offered on the licensor's terms, without negotiation. In some cases, even the licensor may actually have no choice in the license, as when an open source project uses a reciprocal license, as in the GPL, MPL, or OSL that mandates a license for modifications.

So since you probably can't negotiate the license, the main issues that should concern you if you in-license software is whether the terms and conditions of the license being offered are acceptable given your business goals.

These are the typical considerations:

- Do you understand the terms and conditions of the license, or are there ambiguities and uncertainties that might affect license interpretation by reasonable parties or by a court?

- Are you intending to create and distribute derivative works of the software? If so, can you accept the reciprocity obligation of the license? Are you willing to distribute your derivative works under the same license? Are you satisfied with the license's definition of derivative works?

- Does the license grant you sufficient patent rights to create derivative works? If not, what other patent licenses will you need to make, use, sell, offer to sell, or import derivative work software?

- Does the licensor actually provide source code? Will you actually ever need it?

- Will you need any additional rights not included in the license, such as the right to apply trademarks to your goods?

- Are you prepared to honor license conditions relating to copyright and other notices?

- Do you need broader warranty protection than is offered under the license? If you do, is additional warranty protection offered at a price?

- Do you accept the limitations of liability under which the software is offered?

- Are you prepared to accept the jurisdiction, venue, and governing law provisions of the license? If you ever have to litigate this license, where and how would it be done?

- Are you prepared to accept the license termination provisions? Assuming you are going to invest in adopting and using the software in important ways, what is the chance that your license to the software may terminate?

Notice that there is one consideration that has already been dealt with if you accept an approved license listed on the Open Source Initiative website, *www.opensource.org*. You may be certain that the software license meets the Open Source Definition and the five Open Source Principles listed in Chapter 1 of this book. You can copy, create derivative works, distribute, make, use, and sell the open source software that you in-license.

Out-Licensing

Licensors decide what license to use for their open source software. If at all possible, licensors should use an existing template license. Please don't invent your own. The open source community is not seeking new licenses to analyze and interpret.

The proliferation of open source licenses creates a serious problem: It risks additional fragmentation of the public commons of free software. While software under some academic licenses can be combined without restriction, combining software under different reciprocal licenses—particularly the more complex reciprocal licenses used by large companies—requires that lawyers or skilled licensing professionals review each of the licenses for incompatibilities. Even where the differences between licenses are trivial, such as their designation of governing law, a combinatorial analysis of open source licenses rapidly becomes a nontrivial exercise. For example, it is a nontrivial exercise to determine whether a work that combines two separately licensed programs requires a file-by-file, MPL-like comparison or the more general *work based on the Program* derivative work test of the GPL. I say more about this problem later in this chapter.

Without exception, leaders of the open source community discourage the submission of "yet another license." Any software company deciding to distribute its software under an open source license is fervently encouraged to select among the existing licenses rather than to create a new one.

- As before, the key licensing factor is whether to use a reciprocal or an academic license. As a licensor, do you want to be able to benefit from improvements made by others? Do you want derivative works created by your licensees to be distributed under the same license so that you can incorporate their improvements into your own software?

- If a reciprocal license is desirable, you should consider the scope of the reciprocity obligation. Licenses like the GPL contain vague provisions about derivative and collective works; some licensors prefer that ambiguity because it results in more software licensee contributions licensed under the GPL. Licenses like the MPL have a more narrow definition of derivative works, requiring only *files* that are changed to be distributed under the MPL; this can reduce resistance from licensees who want to retain the proprietary status of their own contributions. For a more balanced approach, the CPL or OSL leave the term *derivative works* to be defined by the courts under copyright law.

- Does the license define *distribution*? The OSL goes farther than the other licenses described in this book by defining *external deployment*, so that the reciprocity provision applies regardless of how the derivative work is distributed. (See also the even more dramatic definition of *external deployment* in the Real Networks Public Source License published on the OSI website at *www.opensource.org*.)

- Consider the scope of any patent licenses you will grant. Many licenses have only implied patent grants; the scope of those licenses is unclear. As for licenses with explicit patent grants (i.e., the Mozilla, CPL, and OSL/AFL licenses), decide whether you wish to allow your patents to be used for creating derivative works; these licenses have subtly different patent grants.

- Are you prepared to grant a warranty of provenance (e.g., the OSL/AFL licenses, and similar "representations" in the MPL and CPL licenses), or do you prefer to disclaim all warranties? Remember that a disclaimer of warranties is not always effective in every jurisdiction, so if you intend to distribute open source software in some countries you may have to accept warranties regardless of what your license says.

- Also consider your disclaimer of liability. You should consult an attorney to determine your potential liability in all countries in which you intend to do business.

- Do you want a defense against patent infringement lawsuits? If so, should the defensive strategy terminate only patent licenses (i.e., the Mozilla and CPL licenses) or both copyright and patent licenses (i.e., the OSL/AFL licenses) for patent infringement claims? Is it sufficient to mandate an express condition that the software cannot be distributed if there is a patent infringement claim against the software (i.e., the GPL license)?

- Do you want your license to be interpreted under copyright law only (i.e., the GPL) or under both copyright and contract law (i.e., almost all other open source licenses)? If the latter, don't forget that it isn't only the license terms but the license formation issues—offer, acceptance, and consideration—that must be dealt with.

- Does the template license you use select a convenient and comfortable jurisdiction, venue, and governing law? If not, ask your attorney what the defaults are in your jurisdiction.

- Do you want an attorneys' fees provision in your license? Remember that, in most jurisdictions, such provisions apply equally to all parties to a contract. You are usually subject to paying attorneys' fees if you lose a lawsuit under a license with an attorneys' fees provision regardless of whether you're the licensor or the licensee.

These questions are intended merely to get you thinking about licensing alternatives. Your attorney should be consulted before you actually craft or select a license.

Contributions to Projects

Some open source projects seek copyright assignment from their contributors. This serves two purposes:

1. A project that owns copyrights has standing to enforce those copyrights in court without needing the contributor's participation or approval.

2. The project, and not the contributor, now has the right to make licensing decisions about the software.

Many authors of software refuse to assign their copyrights. The experience of musicians, photographers, writers, and artists in past generations warns us not to lightly give away that which we create. And the experiences of literally thousands of open source projects give us reason to believe that open source projects can thrive quite nicely with mere licenses from contributors rather than copyright assignments.

Contributors can license their contributions to projects, knowing and intending that the projects will combine contributions from many people, modify them in some coherent way, and then distribute a resulting derivative or collective work to the public. The terms of the contributor's license determine what the project can do with the software.

Software licensed to a project under an academic license can generally be used for any purpose whatsoever. It can be treated as a contribution to any open source project. For example, if software were blood, contributors under at least some academic licenses would be universal donors.

Through reciprocity, the GPL creates a commons of software similarly licensed under the GPL. That software can be combined and modified under the terms of the GPL by anyone and everyone, and so the license doesn't classify people as contributors or anything else. The GPL refers to all licensees as "you." Again, if software were blood, GPL-licensed software would all be of one blood type.

All GPL-licensed software is available for reuse in all projects using the GPL license. No separate contributor agreement is needed. However, some open source licenses deal more directly with the special characteristics of contributors. For example, the MPL distinguishes an "Initial Developer Grant" (MPL section 2.1) and a "Contributor Grant" (MPL section 2.2). These two sections of the license are almost identical, except that the Initial Developer contributes the Original Code and the Contributor contributes Modifications. Section 3.1 of the MPL makes the license reciprocal for Contributors.

Later in the license, the MPL, which was written by the Initial Developer and thus reflects that company's interests, sets more stringent conditions for Contributors. For example, the latter accept obligations regarding Intellectual Property Matters that don't necessarily apply to the Initial Developer (MPL section 3.4). The MPL also allows the Initial Developer—but not the Contributor—to designate alternative licenses under which portions of the Covered Code can be distributed. (MPL section 13 and Exhibit A.)

The CPL is more balanced than the MPL. The person or company who starts the software development process is merely the "initial Contributor" and everyone later is a "subsequent Contributor." The license grant extends to Recipient, who is defined as "anyone who receives the Program under this Agreement, including all Contributors." (CPL section 1.) Under the CPL, Contributors are simply those who distribute the Program. (CPL section 1.)

If a project distributes its software under the CPL, it can accept contributions licensed under the CPL. No separate contributor agreement is needed.

The OSL/AFL licenses apply the GPL's approach to contributor licenses—there simply are no distinctions drawn among types of licensors or licensees and no need for a separate contributor agreement. The Licensor is the owner of an Original Work, and the licensee is You. If software were blood, contributors under the AFL would be universal donors, and

OSL-licensed software (because of its reciprocity provision) would all be of one blood type.

License Compatibility for Collective Works

I finally explain Open Source Principle # 5, which states that "licensees are free to combine open source and other software."

The word *combine* in this present context means to "bring together or to join." This is a common activity in the software world. We do that when we load a variety of software onto our hard disk, perhaps from different vendors, to perform useful tasks. For example, business owners often combine an accounting package to collect and store financial data with a tax package that is used at year-end to calculate the government's due based upon those financial data. Office productivity suites may include separate programs for word processing, spreadsheets, and electronic mail. These software packages may actually communicate with each other so that data need be entered only once.

Distributors of open source software often aggregate separately developed contributions onto their distribution disks as a convenience for their customers. These contributions may have been designed originally by their authors to interact with other programs in the aggregation, and the original authors or downstream aggregators may even have tested them for compatibility. Or they may be compatible simply because the contributions were designed to meet industry standards.

Computer hardware and software vendors often build turnkey systems, combining operating systems, drivers, data bases, server software, utilities, applications, and other "glue" to create comprehensive customer solutions. Such combinations, under copyright law, are *collective works*.

It matters not whether some of the contributions to collective works are open source and some are proprietary. No open source license can prohibit a licensee from using an open source accounting package in a collective work with a proprietary tax package, or a GPL-licensed operating system with an Apache-licensed server and an MPL-licensed browser. Users are free to select open source software based upon technical criteria without restrictions as to the uses—or combinations of uses—to which that software can be put.

The contributions to a collective work always retain their original copyrights and licenses. (17 U.S.C. § 103[b].) If they are open source, contributions to a collective work can be removed and reused in other collective works, subject to the terms and conditions of their original open source licenses, even without the permission of the author of the first collective work.

On the other hand, a collective work as a whole is also an original work, subject to its own copyrights and its own license. Here's a simple example outside the software field: You may copy each of the public domain poems in an anthology of Chinese poetry, but you may not copy the anthology itself without permission of its author.

So it is with software. While you may remove and reuse the original open source contributions in a collective work, you may not copy or modify the collective work itself without the permission of its owner. For example, you may remove and redistribute Linux from the Red Hat or SuSE distribution disk, but you may not simply copy and distribute those companies' entire distribution disks—unless, as is usually the case for these open source distributors, the licenses for the distribution disks permit you to do so.

There is nothing in any open source license that would prevent someone from creating a non–open source collective work of open source software, trying thereby to collect royalties for copies of the collective work or to prevent people from making copies of the collective work as a whole. Of course, that can't affect the open source character of the individual contributions themselves; the collective work, however—reflecting the creative aspects of the aggregation process—may be copyrightable and restricted.

The aggregator remains responsible for honoring the terms and conditions of the licenses to the individual contributions he or she has collected together including, if necessary, publishing the source code of those contributions and making available copies of the relevant licenses.

License Compatibility for Derivative Works

If there is one issue that causes the most confusion and angst in the open source licensing community it is this: How do open source licenses interact with each other when derivative works are created from multiple contributions?

For example, a GPL-licensed contribution may be offered for an Apache-licensed derivative work. Or an OSL-licensed contribution may be offered for a GPL-licensed derivative work. What license terms apply to the resulting derivative work? Can the contribution even be accepted, consistent with the terms of both the contribution and derivative works licenses?

I discussed in the previous section the simpler problem of incorporating a contribution into a *collective work*; that is always allowed under an open source license because of Open Source Principle # 5. And I leave until Chapter 12 the complex issue of how you determine whether something is actually a derivative work. For present purposes, all I ask is whether the open source licenses are compatible for creating derivative works, whatever that technical term of art means.

License Compatibility for Contributions under Reciprocal Licenses

It is easy to understand what happens when you in-license a contribution under a reciprocal license. You can't use it for a derivative work unless both the contribution and the derivative work are licensed under the same reciprocal license. That is the very principle of reciprocity, as represented in the chart below:

		DERIVATIVE WORK			
		GPL	MPL	CPL	OSL
CONTRIBUTION	GPL	yes	no	no	no
	MPL	no	yes	no	no
	CPL	no	no	yes	no
	OSL	no	no	no	yes

This chart suggests that once you start a contribution under the GPL, MPL, CPL, or OSL, that same license is the only one that can be used for subsequent derivative works. In reality, however, the reciprocity provisions in open source licenses are much more subtle than that.

Some licenses, such as the MPL and CPL, complicate the analysis by defining an iterative process by which contributions become part of a package that grows over time. Those contributions are not necessarily separately licensed, and you have to analyze the license carefully to determine whether it is possible to reuse contributions to those packages in other separately developed derivative works other than under the terms of the MPL or CPL license.

For example, the MPL expects contributions (Modifications or files) to be governed by the terms of the MPL. (MPL section 3.1.) But the MPL then allows contributions to be reused as part of a "Larger Work." (MPL section 2.2[a].) The term *Larger Work* is defined in terms reminiscent of a collective work. (MPL section 1.7.) I read this to mean that MPL-licensed contributions can be used for differently licensed collective works but not for derivative works, which appears to be consistent with the chart above.

The MPL license provides another potential escape from the license incompatibility problem by allowing licensees to distribute derivative works under the licensee's choice of the MPL or an alternative license specified by the Initial Developer in its Exhibit A. The website of the Free Software Foundation (*www.fsf.org*) suggests that if the alternative license is the GPL, then that part of the program has a compatible license. Note, however, that this choice is only available to the Initial Developer, and that it applies only because the alternative license is the GPL, not the MPL. According to the Free Software Foundation, the MPL itself remains incompatible with the GPL.

The OSL states the reciprocity provision succinctly:

> *[Licensor grants You a license] to distribute copies of the Original Work and Derivative Works to the public, with the proviso that copies of Original Work or Derivative Works that You distribute shall be licensed under the Open Software License. (OSL section 1[c].)*

There are no exceptions. Derivative works may only be distributed under the OSL, regardless of the license on the contribution. Of course, the license on that contribution must authorize that:

Licensor warrants that [the contributions] are sublicensed to You under the terms of this License with the permission of the contributor(s) of those copyrights and patent rights. (OSL section 7.)

Under the CPL, *Contributions* do not include "separate modules of software distributed in conjunction with the Program under their own license agreement." (CPL section 1.)

"Contribution" means: ... (b) in the case of each subsequent Contributor: i) changes to the Program, and ii) additions to the Program. (CPL section 1.)

So under the CPL, a derivative work is created not by accepting a separate Contribution and combining it in some way with another work, but by making changes or additions to that other work. Furthermore, the CPL requires that a Contributor be the author and distributor of his or her own Contributions, meaning that the CPL does not allow sublicensed Contributions at all.

The GPL license is widely considered to be the most restrictive in this respect, because of the interaction of the following provisions:

You must cause any work that you distribute or publish, that in whole or in part contains or is derived from the Program or any part thereof, to be licensed as a whole at no charge to all third parties under the terms of this License. (GPL section 2[b].)

You may not impose any further restrictions on the recipients' exercise of the rights granted herein. (GPL section 6.)

Derivative works of contributions submitted under the GPL *must* be distributed under the GPL, and you can't add any further restrictions. Once a chain of title is started for a contribution under the GPL, the GPL is the only license that can be used for subsequent derivative works.

License Compatibility for Contributions under Academic Licenses

What does it mean for the GPL to say that you can't add any further restrictions?

The BSD and MIT licenses are read to contain no conditions that could possibly interfere with any other license for derivative works. According to the Free Software Foundation, these licenses can be used for contributions to GPL-licensed derivative works, and I am aware of no open source project, under any license, that ever refuses BSD- and MIT-licensed contributions for creating derivative works. Such software can be used anywhere for any purpose.

The Free Software Foundation asserts that the Apache License, perhaps because of its provisions regarding the Apache trademark, is incompatible with the GPL. (But is a trademark exclusion, which states an essential rule under trademark law, an additional restriction that makes a license incompatible with the GPL?) Most contributors use the Apache license for contributions to Apache software and for nothing else. It is a shame that valuable Apache software is not being used for GPL-licensed derivative works simply because of the resistance to additional restrictions by the authors of the GPL.

The answer is not so simple for the Academic Free License. As I described in Chapter 9, the AFL contains several terms and conditions that are at least different from, if not contrary to, the provisions of other licenses. The AFL permits derivative works to be licensed under any license, but does that mean that AFL-licensed contributions can actually be so used without conflict with those other licenses?

Among the provisions of the AFL that are additional to those in the GPL are terms relating to the scope of the patent grant; the requirements regarding attribution rights; the warranty of provenance; provisions relating to jurisdiction, venue, governing law, and attorneys' fees; and, perhaps most contentious, the patent termination provision in AFL section 10.

Consider the effect on downstream licensees and sublicensees of a contribution originally licensed under the AFL with its patent termination provision. That provision protects the original Licensor, **A**, from patent infringement lawsuits by his or her licensees. Assume **A**'s contribution is used by another author, **D**, to create a derivative work. Obviously **D** is a licensee of **A**, and **D** cannot sue **A** for patent infringement without terminating the license. That much is straightforward under AFL section 10.

But the AFL is sublicensable, and so what happens when the derivative work is licensed by **D** to a downstream customer, **X**, under some different license that doesn't provide notice of the patent defense provision. That other license could be the GPL, one of the other open source licenses described in this book, or even a proprietary license. The AFL imposes no restrictions on that kind of downstream sublicensing. **A**'s contribution is effectively sublicensed to **X**.

Can **X** sue the author of **A** for patent infringement without risking termination of his license for **D**? Does **X** even have any way to know of the terms of **A**'s license? Does section 10 of the AFL extend through sublicensing to protect the author of **A** even against patent infringement lawsuits by downstream sublicensees like **X**? Similar questions could be framed about other potentially uncomfortable terms from **A**'s license, such as the AFL's attorneys' fees provision or the scope of its patent grant. Do such terms bind—via sublicensing—the recipients of derivative works of AFL-licensed contributions?

I find it hard to believe that any court would bind any downstream sublicensee of an open source contribution to any terms and conditions of a license of which he was not informed and didn't manifestly accept. That is certainly a basic tenet of contract law and a fair result in the context of mass-marketed open source software offered for free over the Internet. So to the extent that an AFL-licensed component was sublicensed by **D** as part of a derivative work, customer **X** at the end of the chain cannot be bound to the AFL but only to the license with **D** that he or she accepted.

This situation is not unfair to **A**. Remember that **A** could have avoided this result by distributing his or her contribution under a license that forbids sublicensing. Instead, **A** intended to contribute software under a license that was completely permissive about derivative works. **A**'s software can even be used in proprietary derivative works. License terms do not pass through via sublicensing unless **A** insists upon it in the software license, and the AFL does no such thing.

So it is unclear to me how an academic license such as the AFL can be incompatible with any other open source licenses. The AFL doesn't impose any conditions except upon the licensee of that software, and that licensee is permitted to sublicense the contribution under any license whatsoever.

Of course, these notions of fairness and the requirement that a licensee be informed of conditions to which he or she is bound apply only under contract law, not for a bare license under copyright law. I don't know how a court would decide such sublicensing issues for bare licenses.

The MPL license deals with license compatibility for derivative works by requiring a specific Contributor Grant. As long as the Contributor submits his or her Modification under the terms of that Contributor Grant, the MPL doesn't care about other licenses. It is up to the Contributor to ensure that whatever he or she contributes is Licensable by Contributor. (MPL section 2.2.)

> *"Licenseable" means having the right to grant, to the maximum extent possible, whether at the time of the initial grant or subsequently acquired, any and all of the rights conveyed herein. (MPL section 1.8.1.)*

The CPL permits only Contributions that are original to the Contributor. Sublicensed Contributions aren't accepted. (CPL section 1.)

The OSL does not expressly prohibit the imposition of "further restrictions," nor does it deal separately with contributors. But it does contain the following warranty of provenance that has the effect of promising compatibility of licensing for all contributions incorporated into the derivative work:

> *Licensor warrants that the copyright in and to the Original Work and to the patent rights granted herein by Licensor are owned by the Licensor or are sublicensed to You under the terms of this License with the permission of the contributor(s) of those copyrights and patent rights. (OSL/AFL section 7.)*

A licensor promises that he or she has permission (i.e., licenses) to distribute those contributions in an Original Work under the OSL. The OSL handles the license incompatibility problem by placing on the creator of a derivative work an obligation to ensure that whatever contributions he or she accepts are authorized for inclusion in that derivative work to be licensed under the OSL.

		DERIVATIVE WORK				
		GPL	MPL	CPL	OSL	Academic
CONTRIBUTION	BSD	yes	no[1]	no[2]	yes	yes[3]
	MIT	yes	no[1]	no[2]	yes	yes[3]
	Apache	yes[4]	no[1]	no[2]	yes	yes[3]
	AFL	yes[4]	no[1]	no[2]	yes	yes[3]

[1] MPL section 2.2 is a Contributor Grant that expresses the terms under which contributions can be accepted for MPL-licensed derivative works.

[2] CPL section 1 defines Contributor and Contribution. "Separate modules of software" are not Contributions.

[3] The Apache Software Foundation now requires a Contributor Agreement. (See *www.apache.org.*) Other projects using academic licenses may also require contributor agreements or specific contribution licenses.

[4] The Free Software Foundation says the Apache and AFL licenses are not compatible with the GPL. (See *www.fsf.org.*) I disagree with them, and so I wrote YES in these boxes.

The interrelationships between the contributions and derivative works are summarized in the preceding chart. But there are so many caveats in the footnotes that this chart should *not* be used in a mechanical fashion. Review the contributor and derivative works licenses carefully to ensure that the terms and conditions of both licenses are honored.

In summary, the creation of derivative works from contributions under academic licenses depends more on the license of the derivative work than on the terms of the academic license. Some licenses won't permit the incorporation of works licensed under an academic license regardless of what the academic license itself permits.

Relicensing

For some of us, the problem of combining software under different licenses into derivative works is a frustration. License incompatibilities prevent software from being freely used and combined. And with the proliferation of open source licenses, the problem is getting worse, not better.

But copyright and contract law is unambiguous: Open source distributors cannot simply relicense other people's copyrighted software unless they have permission to do so.

One way out is to convince contributors to make their works available under a different license. This might be possible for small projects where there are few contributors who need to agree on a licensing strategy. But convincing everyone in a large project to reconsider their licensing is very difficult.

Are projects, by virtue of the licenses under which they received contributions, prevented from relicensing their derivative works to replace licenses they no longer want in favor of different licenses? Can relicensing be done by projects to make their works compatible with other contributor licenses?

There is a legal answer and a political answer and, for this particular question, the political answer is far more significant. Open source must be a collaborative process. Any licensing change that is made by fiat is likely to result in a fracture of the community. A project may be left without some of its key contributors. Customers will face diverging product development strategies by different groups of developers, each competing for attention and support. Entire product lines may die.

Among the difficult options for software projects that won't relicense by consensus to accommodate contributions for derivative works is to avoid making derivative works. This is essentially what the Free Software Foundation suggests in order to live with Apache despite its incompatible license:

We urge you not to use the Apache licenses for software you write. However, there is no reason to avoid running programs that have been released under this license, such as Apache. (http://www.fsf.org/)

By merely aggregating software from different sources and treating such software as black boxes, one can technically avoid—sometimes with much clumsiness—creating derivative works. One can benefit from the software without actually having it available for internal modification and improvement.

This is not so different from what happens with proprietary software products. At some point, customers may demand different licensing terms than the licensor will provide. The choice is obvious: Live within the available license, or find different software.

Sometimes, where derivative works are prohibited, people write special plug-ins, drivers, or other complex workarounds to add functionality to programs they can't freely modify. When software vendors are particularly uncooperative with their licensing terms, creative people simply start from scratch and write the software anew under more favorable licenses.

License incompatibilities are inconveniences rather than barriers. Ultimately, one can get around almost all licensing restrictions to almost all intellectual property by being sufficiently creative and inventive.

11

Shared Source, Eventual Source, and Other Licensing Models

Alternatives to Open Source

There are many ways to license software. None is legally privileged. Contract law allows parties to license software under almost any terms and conditions that people can dream up. Copyright and patent law acts as a backstop, preventing anyone from copying, modifying, distributing, making, using, or selling protected software without the licensor's permission—but otherwise leaving to the parties themselves the terms and conditions of their licenses.

Open source software distribution is a young but maturing business model. Enormously successful software has been created and is available worldwide, usually for free. Despite this success, companies often refuse to "go all the way" with open source, afraid that giving software away for free is contrary to their profit motive.

At one extreme, of course, there is fully proprietary software that cannot be copied, modified, or distributed. Source code is not available, reverse engineering is forbidden, and none of the copyright rights are given away. (Remember, though, that you don't need a separate license to install a copy of software you own, and to make backup copies; see 17 U.S.C. 117.) This model remains quite successful in the market, as anyone can

255

plainly see. Proprietary software will doubtless continue to thrive.

In between fully proprietary and fully open source models there are other software distribution alternatives as well. This chapter describes some of those variations that pay homage to open source but don't quite go all the way. These licenses are, one might say, partly proprietary and partly open source.

Each of the licenses described in this chapter provides source code to licensees. You will remember from Chapter 1 that source code is but the means to an end; it is not an end itself. (Open Source Principle #4.) The real goal is software freedom, as reflected in the right to use for any purpose, to copy without payment of royalties, and to freely create and distribute derivative works. (Open Source Principles # 1, 2, and 3.)

The problem with all of the licenses described in this chapter is that they fail to fully promote software freedom. Their terms are far more reasonable than typical proprietary software licenses, but the software they license is not truly free.

That doesn't mean that you shouldn't accept software under them. Some of them are good licenses, just not good enough to be open source.

Shared Source

In response to the demands of its customers for access to source code, Microsoft created its shared source licensing program. This program allows Microsoft customers to read and examine certain of the company's source code.

The Microsoft Shared Source License is a dramatic leap forward for the world's largest proprietary software vendor, a company that has traditionally kept its source code secret for competitive reasons. At long last, Microsoft's customers may examine some of that company's source code and learn from it. Of course, from the perspective of open source licensing, the shared source concept is a weak alternative that doesn't go nearly far enough to provide software freedom.

The Microsoft Shared Source License has limited purposes:

> *You may use this Software for any non-commercial purpose, subject to the restrictions in this license. (Microsoft Shared Source CLI, C#, and JSCRIPT License.)*

By itself, the "non-commercial purpose" restriction of this license makes it incompatible with Open Source Principle # 1. But this license goes even further, making it also incompatible with Open Source Principles # 2 and 3. Open source software must be available to anyone for any purpose, to create derivative works, and to sell the software. The Microsoft software isn't so available:

> *You may not use or distribute this Software or any derivative works in any form for commercial purposes. Examples of commercial purposes would be running business operations, licensing, leasing, or selling the Software, or distributing the Software for use with commercial products. (Microsoft Shared Source CLI, C#, and JSCRIPT License.)*

In a more fundamental way, this is what the license says you may do—and what you are forbidden from doing—when you see Microsoft's shared source code:

> *You may use any information in intangible form that you re-member after accessing the Software. However, this right does not grant you a license to any of Microsoft's copyrights or patents for anything you might create using such information. (Microsoft Shared Source CLI, C#, and JSCRIPT License.)*

It is fascinating to consider whether an engineer with a photographic memory is allowed, without infringing Microsoft's copyrights, to re-create Microsoft's software from *intangible* information that he or she *remembers*. But that's not the legally interesting question for most engineers. Instead, the effect of this license provision is that engineers/licensees can use the information in some of Microsoft's source code to do practical things but they do not thereby obtain rights under copyright or patent. Source code can help licensees to design interfaces to Microsoft's products and to create programs that read and write Microsoft's data formats. It can be used to validate the security or reliability of Microsoft's products. For some of Microsoft's customers, this availability of source code for limited purposes is sufficient for their needs; they don't really need the software freedom provided by open source licenses.

So if you merely use intangibles that you remember, and if you base your software on those intangibles, you are allowed to do so. Microsoft's source code cannot be used, however, to write software that infringes Microsoft's copyrights or patents.

If you are a software developer who intends to write software that might potentially compete with Microsoft's copyrights or patents, there is great risk in looking at Microsoft's source code. Under the copyright law in the United States, if Microsoft proves that there is "substantial similarity" between your commercial software and theirs, you may be an infringer. You may have to prove that you saw and read Microsoft's source code but that you relied only on intangibles and only on your memory when you wrote your own software.

That's a difficult evidentiary burden. I'm not sure how even an experienced programmer can walk that fine line. Perhaps the best way is simply not to look at Microsoft's source code at all. At the very least, if you are directing corporate projects relating to products competing with Microsoft's shared source software, build a sturdy wall separating those who look at Microsoft's source code and those programmers who might otherwise—even inadvertently—create derivative works or any commercial products from that source code.

This risk is not unique to shared source software. Employees can be contaminated by proprietary source code they saw or wrote while working for previous employers. Even open source software contains intangibles that can contaminate the memory of a programmer.

The solution obviously is not to avoid source code entirely, but to build sturdy walls around those in your company who will create proprietary software. Make sure those engineers don't inadvertently create derivative works of any source code they read, because you must honor the conditions and limitations of those licenses.

As for those who create open source software, don't create derivative works of Microsoft's shared source software. The Microsoft Shared Source License—unlike open source licenses—doesn't give you software freedom.

Public Source

Many companies are willing to go much farther than Microsoft, allowing their source code to be used for more than just examination and interfacing. Licensees can make copies, create derivative works, and distribute their works.

They draw the line, though, at commercial uses of the resulting software. They argue that the free use of open source software for commercial purposes exacerbates the free-rider problem I described in Chapter 10. It reduces the incentives for contributors because profits from the software will go to large companies rather than to contributors. While not always prohibiting commercial uses, as the Microsoft Shared Source license does, public source licenses typically require the payment of royalties for commercial uses.

This form of license is referred to as *public source*, to indicate that the source code is published but that the software is not distributed under an open source license.

There can be many varieties of public source licenses, depending on the characteristics of the software being distributed and the business model of the licensor. For example, Ping Identity Corporation (see *www.pingid.com*) distributes some of its software under the following terms:

> *a. Without payment of royalty for unlimited Personal Use or Non-Commercial Distribution (as those terms are defined below);*

> *b. Without payment of royalty for other than Personal Use and Non-Commercial Distribution as long as Licensed Software will run on fewer than 100 processors (as that term is defined below); and*

> *c. Subject to the payment of one-time paid-up Royalty Fees for other than Personal Use and Non-Commercial Distribution on 100 or more processors. Licenses to run the Software on additional processors are subject to the Royalty Fees and payment terms as obtained at http://www.pingidentity.com and in effect on the date such additional licenses are obtained from Licensor. Royalty Fees to run the Software on additional processors are due and payable to Licensor prior to first use on those processors. (SourceID Public Source License section 1.)*

Unlike the CPL license, which leaves the term *commercial distribution* undefined, the SourceID Public Source License defines its terms precisely:

> As used in this License, the term *"Personal Use"* means the *functional use of software by an individual solely for his or her personal, private and non-commercial purposes. An individual's use of software in his or her capacity as an officer, employee, member, independent contractor or agent of a corporation, business or organization (commercial or non-commercial) does not qualify as Personal Use. (SourceID Public Source License section 3.)*

> As used in this License, the term *"Non-Commercial Distribution"* means the distribution of software to any third party for which no payment is made in connection with such distribution, whether directly (including, without limitation, payment for a copy of the software) or indirectly (including, without limitation, payment for a service related to the software, or payment for a product or service that includes a copy of the software "without charge"). (SourceID Public Source License section 3.)*

> As used in section 1 of this License, the term *"processors"* refers to a single processor running a single instance of Licensed Software. Each additional processor or instance of Licensed Software counts as an additional processor. (SourceID Public Source License section 3.)*

These distinctions among users are not permitted in open source licenses under Open Source Principle #1. Nor can there be conditions like these that require open source licensees to count processors or similar metrics of software use. Public source licenses like this one do not guarantee software freedom—they are not open source.

Dual and Multiple Licensing

The owner of a copyright can license his or her work any number of times. Distributors of proprietary software do that when they grant discounts to favored customers, issue blanket licenses for unlimited copies to large corporations, and apply shrink-wrap licenses to copies sold in stores.

The MPL license described in Chapter 7 offered one example of dual licensing. Under the MPL, the Initial Developer may designate portions of the Covered Code as Multiple-Licensed. This allows any licensee to choose to accept those portions under the MPL or a second license specified in "Exhibit A." Where that option is used, Initial Developers often choose the GPL.

More sophisticated examples than this of dual and multiple licensing are now widely used for important software. The owners of copyrights in open source software may simultaneously license that same software under non–open source licenses. This is particularly attractive for licensees who are reluctant to accept certain conditions of the available open source licenses and who are willing to pay extra license fees to relieve themselves of those conditions.

Such software, as originally licensed, *is* open source. It is available under an open source license. But it is also available under other licenses.

Consider the MySQL data base, which is distributed under the GPL and also under a separate commercial license. MySQL software is often incorporated into larger packages. Depending upon how the GPL is interpreted, such larger packages may become subject to the reciprocity condition of the GPL. This is unacceptable to some potential customers of MySQL who want to keep their derivative works proprietary.

The distributor of MySQL is also the owner of the copyrights in the software. It is thus free to license MySQL simultaneously under as many different licenses as it wants. In addition to the GPL, MySQL offers commercial licenses without reciprocity obligations—for a fee.

Mårten Mickos, the CEO of MySQL, describes his company's dual licensing commercial model this way:

> *Our paying customers get what they pay for: a commercially supported product with a level of assurance from the vendor and without any typical open source requirement that linked software must be open sourced as well.... Dual licensing allows companies to build viable long-term businesses while at the same time accommodating the needs of the open source/free software community. (See www.mysql.com.)*

Mickos explains the *quid pro quo* of this dual licensing bargain. He points out that their commercial customers benefit from the open source customers because open source software is inherently more reliable and effective. (He calls it "rigorous 'battle-testing.'") Meanwhile, their open source customers benefit from the commercial customers because the MySQL company "can afford to develop and improve the product at a fast pace."

One problem with this model is that contributions made by third parties to MySQL's GPL version must themselves be licensed under the GPL. (See GPL section 2[b].) The owners of the copyrights in the improvements *may* authorize dual licensing of their contributions under MySQL's commercial licenses, but nothing in the GPL requires them to do so. MySQL can try to avoid this problem by requesting that contributors assign their copyrights to the company, or by expressly accepting contributions under a license that permits MySQL to use the contributions as it sees fit.

Such dual licensing alternatives may have uses other than to avoid reciprocity obligations. Other conditions in an open source license may be unacceptable to prospective licensees. Some companies object to patent termination clauses (e.g., MPL section 8.2, CPL section 7, OSL/AFL section 10.) Some companies seek more elaborate warranties or forms of indemnification than are usually available under open source licenses. Licenses containing special waivers or additional benefits can sometimes be negotiated.

Any prospective licensee dealing with an unacceptable open source license should contact the licensor for other available licensing alternatives. Any licensor of open source software should consider dual licensing options as a way of attracting new customers.

Eventual Source and Scheduled Licensing

In business, timing is everything. A few months' lead developing and commercializing a product can mean the difference between commercial success and failure. For some commercial licensees, obtaining access to the source code now rather than eventually may justify paying for those license rights.

This business reality has encouraged companies to create licensing strategies that generate revenue from customers willing to pay extra for additional lead time to develop their products.

Artifex Software, the distributor of Ghostscript, uses such a scheduled licensing model. Initially new versions of Ghostscript are not fully open source, but at a later time they become open source under the GPL.

Ghostscript is intended to be embedded into printers to support industry-standard page description languages like PostScript and PDF. The lead time to introduce enhanced printers is short and the competition among printer vendors is fierce. Some of Artifex Software's customers seek a marketing advantage by getting new versions of Ghostscript early.

New versions of Ghostscript are distributed initially under the Aladdin Free Public License. They are also distributed under Artifex Software's commercial licenses.

Despite its confusing name, the Aladdin Free Public License is not an open source license. It prohibits commercial distribution of Ghostscript or of products containing Ghostscript. Commercial distribution of Ghostscript requires an Artifex commercial license—for which there is a royalty.

Peter Deutsch, the author of Ghostscript and the first practitioner of this scheduled licensing model by which commercial time-advantages can be paid for, describes the Aladdin Free Public License this way:

> This License is not an Open Source license: among other things, it places restrictions on distribution of the Program, specifically including sale of the Program. While Aladdin Enterprises respects and supports the philosophy of the Open Source Definition, and shares the desire of the GNU project to keep licensed software freely redistributable in both source and object form, we feel that Open Source licenses unfairly prevent developers of useful software from being compensated proportionately when others profit financially from their work. This License attempts to ensure that those who receive, redistribute, and contribute to the licensed Program according to the Open Source and Free Software philosophies have the right to do so, while retaining for the developer(s) of the Program the power to make those who use the Program to enhance the value of commercial products pay for the privilege of doing so. (Aladdin Free Public License.)

The Aladdin Free Public License imposes certain specific restrictions on distribution. Among other things, it prohibits the commercial distribution of Ghostscript software if any payment is made. The license describes (in section 2) some types of distribution that are not allowed:

- When payment is made directly for a copy of the Program.

- When payment is indirect, as for a service related to the Program.

- When payment is made for a product or service that includes a copy of the Program "without charge."

In many other respects, the Aladdin Free Public License reads like the GPL. Like the GPL it allows examination of the source code and the creation and distribution of derivative works. It even contains a reciprocity condition:

> *You must cause the Work to be licensed as a whole and at no charge to all third parties under the terms of this License. (Aladdin Free Public License section 2[c][ii].)*

Artifex Software, the commercial distributor of Ghostscript, simultaneously sells licenses to new versions of the program under commercial licenses. Those licenses allow customers to embed the most recent versions of Ghostscript into their printers. They also allow commercial licensees to use the source code in any way they wish, and they do not impose reciprocity obligations for derivative works.

Approximately one year after a version of Ghostscript is made available under the Aladdin Free Public License and its commercial licenses, Artifex Software re-releases that version under the GPL, at which point the software becomes truly open source.

The incentives for Artifex customers to buy commercial licenses are obvious. They can use the very latest versions of the software, with all the latest features. They can contract for the support of Artifex Software engineers to help them create their own products and derivative works. They can purchase warranties.

That extra time and those added-value services make scheduled licensing succeed as an open source business model. But such software isn't initially open source, and its licensors promise only that it eventually will be.

Combining Licensing Models

Nothing obliges a licensor to release all of its software under an open source license. Even companies that are friendly to open source may decide that some of their software should be kept proprietary.

A good example of this is Jabber, Inc., which creates and distributes instant messaging software. Jabber comes in both client and server versions. The client versions of Jabber's software are open source and the server versions of Jabber's software are not.

Jabber on user desktops is fostered by the easy availability of open source client software, available for free download from the *www.jabber.org* website. Meanwhile, companies can build proprietary instant messaging applications tailored to their needs on top of Jabber's commercial server software available from *www.jabber.com*. This convenient division into *.org* and *.com* distributors of related software highlights the distinction between open source and proprietary software, but it also demonstrates that the two worlds can actually support and encourage each other.

Just as they may choose to license different components of their software separately, software distributors may also offer advanced versions of their open source products only under commercial licenses. Red Hat sells its Red Hat Applications, a collective work optimized for Linux, in that way. (See *www.redhat.com.*) These products are supported by a range of Red Hat Services, offered for a fee.

Open source licensing is a successful model, but it is not a religion. Alternatives are possible, and some of those alternatives are not entirely unfriendly to open source. Licensing creativity can allow contributors and distributors to make money while still encouraging, creating, and sharing open source software.

12

Open Source Litigation

Owning a Cause of Action

The prospect of litigation over open source software is disturbing to all of us. Open source software cannot flourish in a litigious environment in which everyone is suing everybody else over perceived injustices relating to open source licenses.

Indeed, in practice, there is very little litigation over open source. After all, why would a licensor who is permitting everyone to copy, modify, and distribute his or her software need to complain about someone who did those things? And why would a licensee who receives software with essentially unlimited rights to it need to demand even more from the licensor? When the software is essentially *free* (i.e., zero price), and when software freedom is guaranteed by the license, why would anyone bother to sue?

But litigation can occur, and it is important for anyone involved with open source software to understand the risks.

The risks are low. If you honor the terms of the licenses for open source software you acquire, you probably won't be bothered. And whatever litigation risks you do accept with open source software are essentially the same risks as with proprietary software. If you live in a litigious society, you need to be prepared for lawsuits.

A *cause of action* is simply a matter for which a legal action may be maintained. In the open source context, causes of action can arise over intellectual property matters, such as ownership of copyrights or patents, and interpretation or enforceability of license and contract terms, and for business practices that are perceived by one party or another to be unfair. A cause of action is said to be *owned* by the party that has the right to maintain it in court.

When a licensee accepts software under an open source license, he or she acquires nonexclusive rights to intellectual property in the software, including the rights to make copies; to create and distribute derivative works; and to execute licenses to make, use, and sell products containing that software. The licensor, you will recall, has made promises (express or implied) to each licensee concerning the availability and quality of the software. A licensee may sue in court to enforce those promises, even if it means suing the licensor who gave him or her that software in the first place or suing third parties who improperly interfere with the practice of those rights. A licensee, then, can potentially own one or more causes of action and be the plaintiff in a lawsuit.

A licensor distributes software under an open source license containing certain terms and conditions that licensees must obey. Licensors may sue their licensees in court to enforce the terms and conditions of the license or to terminate it. A licensor, then, can potentially own one or more causes of action and be the plaintiff in a lawsuit.

A contributor participates in an open source project and submits his or her original works of authorship to the project. The contributor may sue to protect his or her copyrights and patents from those who use that software outside the scope of the license (express or implied) to the project. A contributor, then, can potentially own one or more causes of action and be the plaintiff in a lawsuit.

A stranger may own a copyright or patent that is embodied in open source software without the stranger's authorization. He or she may sue to have that infringing intellectual property removed from the software. A third party, then, can potentially own one or more causes of action and be the plaintiff in a lawsuit.

Finally, there are societal interests at stake in open source software. Governments may promulgate software export laws, mandate standards for security, and enforce antitrust rules. Bankruptcy laws may interfere with ownership of intellectual property. These interests may be enforced in court, sometimes directly by the government. Governments, or government agencies, can potentially own one or more causes of action and be plaintiffs in lawsuits.

Owning a cause of action, of course, doesn't necessarily mean that you will win in court. All you have is a right to institute judicial proceedings, and it will be the judge or jury that will decide, based on the facts and the law, whether the plaintiff or the defendant wins.

Damages

The main reason we worry about litigation is because of the consequences of losing. The other big reason is the cost of the litigation itself. For major battles between big companies, attorneys' fees of more than $300,000 per month are now commonplace in the United States. Ignoring attorneys' fees for the moment, though, what are the potential consequences of losing a lawsuit?

Calculating damages arising from cause of action in a software dispute is tricky. What is the value of software? Is it a function of the price paid for the software or the benefit derived from the software? Are damages a function of what was lost, such as business opportunity or sales? If the damages were caused by a part of the software but not the entire package, should damages be prorated?

There are no default damage calculation rules, although some licenses vaguely address this problem (e.g., MPL section 8.3; OSL/AFL section 11). There are also no standard royalty rates for copyrights or patents against which damages can be calculated.

The prospect of damages may encourage a company to file a lawsuit, but it probably shouldn't unless there is a reasonable prospect of recovering at least enough in damages to pay for its own attorneys' fees and costs.

I once represented a company that wanted to sue because a licensee hadn't complied with a provision of the GPL that requires the licensee to give recipients of the Program "a copy of this License along with the Program." (See GPL section 1.) While that was technically a violation of an express GPL condition, how should one calculate damages for its breach? How much would my client have to pay his own attorneys to force the licensee to either obey the GPL or pay damages for infringement? And then, how should a court calculate damages for the failure to publish a license that anyone can find instantly on the Internet? Our final problem was that, by the time we had discovered the licensee's failure to publish the GPL as required, the licensee had already stopped distributing his software. How can we calculate damages for *past* breaches of a license that are not ongoing?

Perhaps unfortunately for those who would welcome the clarity of a court decision, such questions were never answered because my client decided not to sue. No court has yet told us how to calculate damages for breaches of open source licenses.

Answers to these questions will depend upon the specific business and software facts of the case and upon local law.

All open source licenses—indeed, all software licenses of any kind from commercial companies—contain limitations of liability. This is to ensure that the maximum dollar exposure of a party for damages due to claims by the other party is strictly limited. (In some jurisdictions, class action lawsuits can aggregate the small damages of a large number of plaintiffs into one large claim on behalf of all members of the class; this possibility is well beyond the scope of this book.) As for the maximum dollar exposure for such claims, all open source licenses essentially contain provisions that say "no damages at all."

Limitation of liability provisions are not enforceable in all jurisdictions, despite what the license says. In some countries, consumer protection policies always trump a vendor liability disclaimer.

The limitation of liability provisions in the BSD, MIT, Apache, GPL and OSL/AFL licenses protect only the licensor; in the MPL and CPL, they protect both parties. Some limitation of liability provisions purport to limit liability to any person; see MPL section 6. It is difficult to see how such a limitation in a license between two parties would be binding on a third party.

So even where damages can be calculated, the limitation of liability provision may reduce the actual recovery.

Where actual damages are difficult to calculate, statutory damages may be prescribed by law. Statutory damages for copyright infringement in the United States can range from $750 to $30,000 "as the court considers just," and in cases of willful infringement the maximum statutory damages are increased to $150,000. Damages are calculated for the entire work and not for each copy made:

...For all infringements involved in the action, with respect
to any one work, for which any one infringer is liable indi-
vidually, or for which any two or more infringers are liable
jointly and severally.... For the purposes of this subsection, all
the parts of a compilation or derivative work constitute one
work. (17 U.S.C. § 504.)

The prospect of collecting statutory damages often isn't
enough to compensate for attorneys' fees and costs. For example, in the case I described earlier where a licensee had merely
failed to publish the license as required by GPL section 1, an
award of more than the minimum statutory damages of $750
is unlikely. After all, why would a court consider higher
amounts just under the circumstances?

Nor should a prospective litigant rely on a provision of a
license or of a statute that awards attorneys' fees to the prevailing party. Such awards are often limited to "reasonable"
attorneys' fees, and they may also be at the discretion of the
court.

In any civil action under this title, the court in its discretion
may allow the recovery of full costs by or against any party....
Except as otherwise provided by this title, the court may also
award a reasonable attorney's fee to the prevailing party as
part of the costs. (17 U.S.C. § 505.)

Injunctions

Usually an injunction is of far greater concern to a defendant than monetary damages. An injunction is:

A court order prohibiting someone from doing some specified
act or commanding someone to undo some wrong or injury.
(Black's Law Dictionary, 6th edition.)

Injunctions will be ordered by a court when economic damages are not adequate to compensate for the wrong. On the other hand, courts are reluctant to issue injunctions when monetary damages would be sufficient to redress the wrong.

Consider the financial repercussions to a company of being ordered by a court to stop using software that has become an essential component of that company's processes or products. Risks like these often make injunctions far more frightening than monetary damages.

In the previous section I described a situation in which a licensee had failed to publish a copy of the GPL with his software, in violation of GPL section 1. My client realized we might not recover much in damages, but at least we might be able to encourage a court to grant an injunction against any further use by that licensee of my client's software.

But would the court find that this was a "material condition" of the GPL whose breach could justify such a dramatic remedy as injunction? Such questions are particularly troublesome for bare licenses like the GPL, because the concept of materiality of a condition is found only in contract law. One would hope that courts would balance the equities in such situations so as to avoid terminating open source licenses for simple breaches that can easily be cured (i.e., by simply publishing the license).

On the other hand, the threat of an injunction can often cause licensees in breach to cure their breaches before the court acts.

In my client's situation, unfortunately, the licensee had already stopped using that GPL-licensed software, so an injunction was moot anyway. We ultimately never tested any of our damages or injunction theories in court.

Standing to Sue

Not everyone who perceives a wrong is allowed to sue to correct that wrong. Parties to litigation must have a suitable stake—a legally protectable and tangible interest—in the outcome of a dispute. *Standing* to sue deals only with the question of whether the litigant is the proper party to fight the lawsuit, not whether the issue itself is justiciable.

Open source licenses often elicit passionate support in the open source community. That passion does not necessarily translate, under the law, to *standing*. Only parties with a well-defined legal interest in the outcome may litigate an open source license. Even open source advocacy groups such as the Free Software Foundation and Open Source Initiative don't have standing to sue to protect software freedom or to protect software under open source licenses. Nor is the public an *intended beneficiary* of open source licenses, despite the open source goal to serve the public interest in software freedom. A mere member of the public can't sue to enforce an open source license.

Intellectual property laws narrowly limit standing. Only the owner of a copyright or patent may sue to enforce the copyright or patent. Distributors who don't own copyrights or patents can't sue under copyright or patent law to enforce their contributors' copyrights and patents, but they do have standing to enforce the copyrights and patents embodied in their own collective or derivative works.

Since the GPL is intended by its authors to be a copyright license but not a contract, and since there is usually no attempt to seek assent by licensees to the terms of the GPL, that license presumably cannot be enforced under contract law. All the other licenses described in this book are designed to be contracts and so the parties to those licenses can sue to enforce them as contracts. The parties to a contract have standing under contract law to enforce that contract. This means that licensors and licensees can enforce their licenses that are contracts, regardless of who owns the underlying copyrights or patents.

Burden of Proof

Consider first what would happen in a typical licensing dispute under copyright law for a bare license. (Refer to the comparison of bare licenses and contracts in Chapter 2.) A plaintiff will allege that the defendant is a copyright infringer and thus may not exercise any of the exclusive rights of the copyright owner.

1. The plaintiff will have to prove he or she is indeed the copyright owner. Only the copyright owner (or, in the United States, an exclusive licensee) has standing to sue to enforce the copyright.

2. The plaintiff has the initial burden of demonstrating that the defendant has undertaken one or more of the copyright owner's exclusive rights under the copyright law (e.g., made copies, created derivative works, or distributed). The defendant, as always, can defend him- or herself on this issue (i.e., not everything is a derivative work simply because a plaintiff calls it that; see the discussion of derivative works analysis later in this chapter).

3. The defendant can assert the license as a defense to infringement. In essence, the defen-

dant can admit to making the copy or creating the derivative work, but assert that the license authorizes this action. (If the defendant admits to the infringing acts but denies the existence of the license, of course, the defendant is an infringer.)

4. The plaintiff may then prove that the defendant breached a condition of the license, thus rendering it terminated or revoked. The conditions of the license will be interpreted by the court under local law standards as appropriate for bare licenses.

5. The plaintiff bears the burden of justifying injunctive relief and proving damages.

Notice that in a copyright dispute over a bare license, the plaintiff will almost certainly be the copyright owner. If a licensee were foolish enough to sue to enforce the terms and conditions of the license, the licensor can simply revoke the bare license, thus ending the dispute. Remember that a bare license in the absence of an interest is revocable.

It may be that bare licenses will be interpreted by the courts under contract law principles, even in the absence of the contract formalities of offer, acceptance, and consideration. After all, major software companies around the world distribute open source software as part of their products; those open source licenses may be technically and economically impossible to revoke. Furthermore, in commercial dealings of any significance worthy of being turned into litigation, there are almost certainly other aspects of *offer, acceptance,* and *consideration* that can be invoked by creative lawyers as proof that a contract was formed.

There are some important differences to this scenario if this becomes a contract dispute, where the license has been offered and accepted, and consideration has been paid. Now not only does the licensor have standing to be a plaintiff regardless of whether he or she owns the copyrights and patents, but also the licensee has standing to be a plaintiff to enforce the terms of the license and to prevent it from being revoked. The statutory and case law of contracts (at least in the United States) would guide the court to interpret the license and to determine whether there was breach of contract and, if so, what damages or injunctive relief should be granted.

The remedies of copyright and patent law are fairly broad-brush. The defendant is either an infringer or not, and must either obey the terms of the license or see it revoked. Damages are to be awarded as specified in the relevant copyright or patent statute.

Contract remedies can be more nuanced, however, and they may become very effective for open source license disputes. For example, one of the more interesting remedies available for contracts—but not for bare licenses—is "specific performance," by which the party breaching the contract may be ordered by the court to perform. Specific performance is not a remedy for a dispute over a bare license.

At the end of the day, the parties to an infringement dispute in court will often finally resolve it by drafting their own settlement agreement that allows the intellectual property to be used. Even if there was no contractual license initially, that settlement agreement will be a contract and license that is enforceable in court.

How much cheaper it would be to draft a good open source license up front, get the parties to agree to it as a contract, and proceed upon those agreed terms.

Enforcing the Terms of a Contract

Proving breach of contract has been the subject of literally millions of lawsuits. It would be impossible to summarize that body of case law and statutes effectively in this book. Indeed, contract enforcement depends in some ways on the jurisdiction in which the case is brought, and most such cases are fact-specific. I will list only the major rules that apply in many jurisdictions:

- Courts will generally try to give effect to the written contract of the parties. Parties are allowed to agree to almost anything as long as it is not against public policy.

- Aggrieved litigants are not allowed to back out of contracts they made simply because the terms are no longer to their liking. It usually doesn't generate sympathy if you complain after the fact that a contract you entered with your eyes open is now unfair.

- There are complex rules for resolving ambiguities of contract language, and the courts will often try to reword such ambiguities to make the contract enforceable. If the ambiguity is so profound that the parties probably didn't understand what they were agreeing to, the entire contract may become void. (In the absence of a contract, remember, copyright and patent laws remain in effect; a party who acts under authority of a void license is merely an infringer.)

- There are complex rules for filling gaps in contracts where the agreement is silent as to specific matters. Commercial relationships among countries have led to the development of consistent laws relating to the sale of goods. Whether software is goods depends on the laws in your jurisdiction. In many cases, though, courts will make an analogy between software licenses and contracts for the sale of goods, thereby developing case law where statutory law about software isn't complete.

- Contract terminology that is not defined will often be given its meaning as a term of art. In complex cases, courts may rely on expert witnesses to help them determine the effect of specific contract language. Among the terms of art relevant to software licenses are *collective work, derivative work, copy, distribution, file,* and *module.* Courts will apply case law and statutory interpretation processes to determine the meanings of such terms and their effects on specific licenses and software.

- Commercial parties are generally assumed to be sophisticated about the contracts they enter; they will find it difficult to argue that they didn't really know what they were agreeing to. Individual consumers, on the other hand, are not sophisticated; they probably didn't even read or understand the consequences of software licen-

ses they "agreed" to. Courts may protect individual consumers from unfair license conditions
where they wouldn't bother to protect a sophisticated company whose lawyers reviewed (or
should have reviewed) the licenses.

- Courts sometimes refuse to enforce specific provisions of contracts against ordinary consumers,
  particularly if those provisions are excessive burdens on unsophisticated licensees. For example,
  arbitration clauses, broad warranty and liability
  disclaimers, and biased selection of jurisdiction,
  venue, and governing law may not be enforced
  against naive licensees. No court case has yet
  tested whether a reciprocity provision can be asserted against an unsophisticated licensee, although big software companies can be presumed
  to know what those provisions mean.

I recognize that these guidelines don't provide much real
guidance for anyone who is considering suing for breach of
contract or who fears having to defend against such a lawsuit.
Fortunately, the open source community is not particularly
litigious. Licensors give away so many copyright and patent
rights that there's very little left of value worth suing over. And
licensees obtain almost everything they need to profit from the
software, so there's very little incentive to sue. Without damages, lawsuits aren't needed.

Nevertheless, licensees should be diligent in respecting the
intellectual property rights of contributors. Honor all the
terms and conditions. Little things often matter deeply to
open source licensors. For example, if a license requires that
you make available a copy of the license or of the source code

when you distribute the software or its derivative works, do so. The open source community generally believes that such license terms are really worth fighting over, so avoid such fights by obeying the license terms and conditions.

Disputes over Ownership of Intellectual Property

Licensors can only license software which they own or which they have received permission to license. That basic legal requirement is explicitly acknowledged in the OSL/AFL by the warranty of provenance and in the MPL and CPL by their representations. (OSL/AFL section 7; MPL section 3.4[c]; CPL section 2[d].) All open source licenses, regardless of their explicit language, at least imply that the software is being licensed under the authority of its copyright owner. A licensor who fails to abide by that implied or explicit promise can be guilty in some jurisdictions of fraud or gross negligence, regardless of warranty disclaimers.

A contributor who submits a contribution he or she doesn't own might be forced to pay damages to cover the cost to replace the infringing contribution or to buy a valid license from its rightful owner.

Companies that make contributions to open source projects are assumed to be sophisticated enough to take responsibility for the software they contribute. But sometimes employees make contributions that their employers do not approve or allow. That is really a dispute between the employee and his or her employer. Recipients of such unauthorized contributions may allege negligent supervision if employers fail to supervise properly their employees' participation in open source development.

This means that companies that participate in open source development should document their procedures and policies to their employees. Attorneys should review those procedures and policies to protect companies' intellectual property.

Recipients of open source software under apparently valid licenses may suddenly find their software challenged by third parties claiming ownership rights. This is in part what happened in the SCO *vs.* IBM litigation, where SCO claimed that IBM had no authority to license certain software under the GPL, software that ended up in Linux. Open source is not unique in this respect; such ownership disputes can also occur with proprietary software. Licensees are not direct parties to those intellectual property ownership disputes, although their licenses might ultimately be affected by the outcome.

There is little that downstream licensees can do in advance to avoid third party claims to intellectual property against their licensors. Some licensors are now offering to indemnify their customers against such claims, although any indemnification paid will often be worth far less than the infringing software those customers can no longer use.

When third parties prove their valid claims to ownership of open source software, only one response is appropriate: The software may no longer be used without a license from the true owner. Open source licensing depends on intellectual property law, and it would be hypocritical of open source distributors and customers to dishonor those laws by copying software to which they no longer have a license.

Disputes over Derivative Works

I left for last the most difficult legal question facing the open source software industry: What is a "derivative work" of software?

If an open source license doesn't have a reciprocity condition, derivative works simply don't cause problems. You can safely ignore this topic entirely if you license software under an academic open source license.

Early in this book I explained the complex problem of separating expressions from ideas, art from science, and right brain from left brain creations. To determine whether a software program is a derivative work of another software program, the courts need to disentangle these abstractions. The procedure that many courts use, called the *abstraction-filtration-comparison* test, is described below.

I previously took the easy way out. I said that you should treat derivative works as subsequent versions of an earlier work. But that easy way out no long suffices; works resemble each other in many subtle ways. For example, Microsoft Excel 2002 is probably a derivative work of Microsoft Excel 2000, but is it a derivative work of Lotus 1-2-3? Of Visicalc? Is Linux a derivative work of UNIX? Is the implementation of software conforming to an industry standard a derivative work of that specification? How much copying of source code is required to create a derivative work? How much copying of source code may you legitimately do before you create an infringing derivative work? Does linking create a derivative work?

These questions are important to some licensees because they want to avoid the reciprocity conditions of open source licenses, and they are important to licensors because they want to enforce those reciprocity conditions. Disputes over whether particular software is a derivative work of licensed software, and thus subject to reciprocity, are inevitable.

A derivative work, you will recall, is a work based upon a preexisting work. The preexisting work is modified, translated, recast, transformed, or adapted so as to create an improved (or at least different) derivative work. (17 U.S.C. § 101.)

In theory, different copyrightable works, including software, can be compared to determine whether one is a derivative work of the other. This may involve a comparison of the source code or the object code, depending upon the facts of the specific case.

Expert assistance may be needed. We may have to perform reverse translation or automated source code comparisons to identify similarities between two programs for presentation to a court. If we only have object code, we may have to compare object code versions or reverse-compile the software to create easy-to-read versions. This first step is itself complicated, because the parties to the dispute have to reduce the software similarities to simple constructs that can be recognized by nontechnical judges and juries.

In the simple case, two programs can be set side by side and their source code compared. A program that is substantially similar to a preexisting program is likely to be a derivative work. That is because such similarities rarely occur by coincidence, at least for substantial portions of the source code. But *substantial similarity* (a term of art in copyright litigation) is not enough to identify a derivative work.

Some similarities relating to the basic functioning of computer systems (e.g., subroutine entry and exit code, external interfaces) can occur by coincidence or intentionally because "that's the way computers have to work." Some snippets of software may be too small and ordinary to be copyrightable. In other cases program functions are coded in a particular way because that is the only (or most effective, or the industry standard) way to implement that specific function on that particular computer architecture. Such source code must be excluded from the comparison because it is not entitled to copyright protection; instead, it is idea that has merged into expression, and is thereby rendered uncopyrightable.

In practice, comparing two works of software is not as simple as a byte-by-byte or line-by-line scan. Software is often extensively modified between versions. Entirely new coding techniques, programming languages, and interface designs can make software appear to be very different at the source code level even when it is derived from an earlier version. Higher levels of abstraction may be needed to identify the similarities.

At those higher levels of abstraction, copyright protection:

- DOES NOT extend to any ideas, procedures, processes, systems, methods of operation, concepts, principles, or discoveries contained in the original program.

- MAY extend beyond the literal code of a program to its nonliteral aspects, such as its architecture, structure, sequence, organization, operational modules, and computer user interface.

These more abstract similarities are not always obvious to the naked eye; identifying them often requires expert guidance. In any event, once the noncopyrightable similarities are filtered out, only the remaining copyrightable similarities are compared. Substantial similarity of the copyrightable elements is evidence of copyright infringement, but substantial similarity of the noncopyrightable elements means nothing at all.

In Chapter 6, in the context of the GPL, I described the arguments that have raged in the open source community about whether linking between programs creates a derivative work. Nothing in the law of copyright suggests that linking between programs is a determinative factor in derivative work analyses by courts—except perhaps as evidence of one of the abstract, nonliteral, copyrightable aspects of the software, such as program architecture, structure, and organization.

In such cases, the burden usually rests on the licensor to explain to the court why the simple interaction of software modules—black boxes merely plugged into other software—creates a derivative work of the black boxes. Merely combining black boxes, I suggested earlier, creates collective works, not derivative works.

Substantial similarities, standing alone, are never enough to characterize a derivative work. An independent creation is not a derivative work no matter how much it resembles a preexisting work. Copyright only protects against copying, not against someone writing the same expression independently, by coincidence. So plaintiffs may still have to prove actual copying.

Evidence can sometimes be provided by a plaintiff to show that an alleged infringer had access to the preexisting work and an opportunity to copy it. For open source software, proving access and opportunity is relatively easy because the source code is published. The burden of proof then may shift to the defendant to show that the substantial similarities were an accidental byproduct of independent creation.

In practice, most infringing derivative works of software are blatant and not subtle because it usually takes more time to obscure an infringing work than to just write it anew from scratch. Nevertheless, when defendants intentionally set out to hide their copyright infringement, it can be difficult to prove.

Such extreme efforts to cheat open source software licensors by pretending not to have created derivative works is usually a waste of time. It is often less expensive just to write equivalent software from scratch. Why risk creating software with questionable provenance? It may result in an expensive infringement lawsuit—which you may lose. If you try to sell such software, your customers may reject it as risky even though it is not actually proven to have infringed.

The better plan is not to tread too close to the line separating collective and derivative works. Companies that create software should make sure their employees don't have access to preexisting software, and they should train their employees not to copy other software.

Instead of accepting the risk that their software will be called a derivative work, companies sometimes prefer to refuse software under licenses containing reciprocity obligations. Such software may then be available under dual licensing options, such as the ones described in Chapter 11.

Instead of avoiding the creation of derivative works, there's a more principled argument to be made that it is a public benefit to create derivative works and to distribute them under reciprocal open source licenses. That way everyone can profit from improvements to software.

Contributions to the software commons are always welcomed. So I encourage you to take a very broad view of your reciprocity obligations; don't be stingy about them. Contribute as many of your derivative works as possible to the community.

Patent Infringement Litigation

Patent infringement claims usually appear unexpectedly. They are serious matters, expensive, and potentially very damaging. When faced with a claim of infringement, you should consult an attorney. Fighting patent infringement litigation on your own is foolish.

You can't prevent patent infringement lawsuits, but your licenses can help you defend against them. Some open source licenses have very strong patent defense provisions (e.g., GPL section 7, MPL sections 8.2 and 8.3, CPL section 7, OSL/AFL section 10). These defensive termination provisions act by increasing the cost of suing an open source licensor for patent infringement. If the licensed software has value to the patent owner, he or she may prefer to forgo a patent infringement lawsuit rather than lose the license to the software.

Defensive termination provisions help protect open source licensors from infringement lawsuits by their own licensees. But there is no possible license provision that can protect a licensor—or anyone else—from lawsuits by third parties who are not licensees.

A collective approach to patents can also be helpful to encourage open source and proprietary software development. That is why companies cooperate, within the limitations of the antitrust law, to develop industry standards that are unencumbered by patents. The important role of open standards for the success of open source is the topic of the next and final chapter of this book.

SCO *vs.* Open Source

Anyone who has read the earlier section on standing will quickly recognize the incongruity of the title "SCO *vs.* Open Source." SCO is shorthand for The SCO Group, Inc., a Delaware corporation. *Open source* is a software development, business, and licensing model. Open source does not have standing to be a defendant in a lawsuit. Neither SCO, nor any other plaintiff, can sue an entire movement—particularly one that is so thoroughly grounded in intellectual property and contract law—over any cause of action worth litigating.

As this is written, The SCO Group is a party to several rancorous lawsuits against certain specific software companies, including IBM, Novell, and Red Hat, over intellectual property rights in the flagship open source product, Linux.

Initially, SCO's complaint alleged that it had licensed certain proprietary software to IBM and that IBM had then improperly contributed that software to open source Linux. The original lawsuit was framed in traditional breach of contract terms as a dispute over an agreement between IBM and SCO that purportedly required IBM to maintain the trade secret status of certain software licensed to it by SCO. IBM denied all material allegations and then, in turn, cross-complained against SCO, alleging breach of contract and patent infringement. SCO has since broadened its complaint to include allegations about the GPL under which Linux is licensed.

Then Red Hat sued SCO, alleging unfair business practices, among other business torts. Finally, SCO and Novell disputed the terms of the original contract under which SCO's predecessor-in-interest bought certain rights to UNIX from Novell.

The SCO litigation may be resolved by the time you read this book, in which event use the following opinion as a way of evaluating my prescience: The SCO cases are a legal mess, an unfortunate opportunity for companies to spend millions of dollars in attorneys' fees to defend their intellectual property and contractual rights and to argue about enormous damage claims. But they don't directly affect open source. All the licenses described in this book and all the software licensed under those licenses—with the possible exception of some small portion of Linux—will remain valid no matter what happens in the SCO lawsuits. As to that small portion of Linux, it may turn out after litigation to be no portion of Linux at all.

Like any other person, SCO has rights only to copyrightable works that it authored or acquired by assignment or license. The independently created copyrightable works of others, such as the contributions to Linux by Linus Torvalds and thousands of other programmers worldwide, are not owned by SCO. Nor can SCO own the unpatented ideas embodied in Linux. Given what I know about the history and evolution of operating systems (including UNIX and Linux), it is inconceivable to me that significant portions of Linux are copies or derivative works of any SCO software. Most Linux experts reassure me that, when the dust of this litigation settles, the courts will determine that SCO owns little or nothing of the intellectual property in Linux.

The SCO lawsuit reveals some interesting open source ironies. SCO itself distributed Linux open source software and, even after SCO had filed its first complaint against IBM, licensees could still obtain Linux under the GPL from an SCO website. I'm not aware of any important case—and Linux software is *important* in this sense—where commercially sophisticated licensors have been allowed to disavow their own licenses for the very software under dispute.

SCO's public arguments challenging the constitutionality of the GPL are particularly intriguing. (See the Open Letter from Darl McBride, president and CEO of SCO, dated December 4, 2003.) It would be truly exciting news if U.S. courts allowed a company to challenge the constitutionality of its own license.

But suppose the courts finally do step back from this entire open source phenomenon and ask, in the context of a legitimate lawsuit by parties with standing: "Is this licensing scheme to build a commons of open source software constitutional? Should licensors be allowed to turn copyright on its head this way, conditioning a license to software on a reciprocal obligation to contribute?"

There is absolutely no legal basis to argue that this scheme is unconstitutional. It is a basic legal principle that licensors can do what they wish with their intellectual property and set conditions for its use.

The public excitement about the SCO cases proves the point I've hinted at throughout this chapter. Litigation about open source software will be rare; if it were a common occurrence the public would be bored with the rather hysterical SCO litigation claims by now. The uniqueness of the SCO litigation, and its multi-billion dollar damage claims, makes it stand out.

The SCO litigation against Linux also marks a maturation of the open source movement, which is finally a big enough phenomenon for its software to be the object of a big lawsuit. Put simply, open source software is now important enough to sue over. The popularity and success of open source software and of Linux in particular inevitably draw litigation because there are important and valuable economic interests at stake.

The SCO litigation is an aberration. It is a big lawsuit about what most knowledgeable attorneys believe is a small issue between particular companies. It will eventually be resolved—and Linux and open source will continue to evolve. This too shall pass.

Many open source advocates have secretly longed for test cases so that the courts can clearly articulate the laws of open source licenses. There have thus far been very few such cases. Open source parties argue mostly about breach of contract, trademark infringement, occasionally patent infringement, and whether a derivative work has been created. Most such arguments are resolved informally, as is true for almost all commercial disputes in most civilized countries. Why would open source licensors and licensees sue each other if they can work out differences in a spirit of open source generosity?

It is difficult to imagine an important case where open source licensors and licensees will litigate about free software.

As long as open source projects act as responsible custodians of intellectual property, keeping careful track of the software they receive and the software they create, then licensees can rely on the continued availability of that software under open source rules. And as long as licensees honor the conditions of the licenses for software they accept, there is little reason to fear it will be taken away through litigation.

13

Open Standards

Defining Open Standards

The first presentation I ever attended about open source was actually supposed to be about *open standards*. A panel of representatives from some major software companies was trying to define *open standards* for the audience. They couldn't agree on a definition, and they kept confusing *open standards* with *open source*.

By then I had already started working with Open Source Initiative and I was smugly confident about the definition of *open source*. We had a published Open Source Definition to rely on (see Chapter 1). I understood the relationship between *open source* and *software freedom*. But I hadn't the slightest clue what the panelists really meant by *open standards*. Was it somehow also related to *software freedom*?

I believed then, even if this panel wasn't explaining it well, that at least the venerable standards bodies around the world must have found a way for standards to be "freely implemented" worldwide. It turns out that we were all a few years too early. Not until 2002 was an effective definition of *open standards* published by the World Wide Web Consortium (W3C) that was truly compatible with open source. I'll reprint that definition in full later in this chapter.

Standards are developed by industry consortia that, within the guidelines of the antitrust laws, cooperate to publish specifications for how products should interoperate. A common design or implementation is often essential to help prevent fragmented development of products that don't work with each other. Each participating company is expected to satisfy the agreed specifications in its products—and each company is encouraged to seek its own way to improve upon the specifications and to distinguish its own products from those of its competitors. As Scott Peterson from Hewlett Packard once described it to me, "Companies cooperate on standards and compete on implementations."

We couldn't live without industry standards. Standards allow telephones from one manufacturer to work on the communications switches of other manufacturers. All browsers (at least in theory) can display web pages identically if they meet industry standards. Electronic mail systems from different software vendors can exchange email. Without standards, this would truly be a Tower of Babel world.

Open Specifications

Suppose someone writes a book that teaches how to calculate income taxes, a specification for a yearly process that you hate to do manually. You read the book at your local library. You then implement the specification in computer software, creating your own original copyrightable work. You do not copy the book in your software, except perhaps in a few places where it says things like "subtract your deductions from your gross annual income" and you translate that into source code within your software. Are you a copyright infringer?

Colloquially, we often say things like "You *copied* the specification." But this has little to do with the definition of *copy* that I explained in Chapter 2. What we often mean to say is, "You read and understood what the specification told you about income tax rules and procedures and then, starting from scratch but relying on what you learned, you wrote your software." If you copied anything, it was the book's underlying ideas—what I have already described as "uncopyrightable subject matter."

In other words, the copying that you did when you implemented the standard is not necessarily copyright infringement. You do not appropriate the copyrightable intellectual property of the specification's author by implementing your software without directly copying the specification.

The specification document itself, of course, the book that was published by the standards organization, is copyrighted. That specification meets the definition of both "original work of authorship" and "copy" from the U.S. Copyright Act. (17 U.S.C. § 101.) The specification cannot be copied without the copyright owner's permission. (17 U.S.C. § 106.)

Simply because it describes an open standard does not mean that you can make copies or distribute that specification. You have to look separately to the specification license to determine whether you may do so. (This is no longer true in some jurisdictions for specifications that are incorporated by reference into laws and are enforceable under the law.) In general, the owner of the copyright to the specification—perhaps the standards organization itself, or one or more of its members—can license the specification in any way.

A specification license that prohibits people from reading the specification without paying a license fee to the licensor, or that restricts in any way the use of the information it contains, is not an open specification license. It is incompatible with Open Source Principle # 1. Such standards are not open standards.

A published specification describing an open standard, just like open source software, need not be distributed at zero price. (See Open Source Principle # 2.) Standards organizations can and some do sell copies of their specifications. Because the goal of most standards organizations is to maximize the implementation of their specifications, most often do not overcharge—or charge at all—for their documents.

Some standards organizations recover their costs by selling copies of their specifications and, when the cost is reasonable, most people will pay for official printed copies. Whichever the pricing model and whatever the price of a single copy of the specification of an open standard, any number of people can read that copy. So also may any number of people write software that implements that specification without any further payments to the copyright owner of the specification.

Enforcing the Standard by Copyright Restrictions

Some standards become laws that everyone must obey. For example, in the United States there are uniform codes regulating the building, electrical, and plumbing trades. Contractors may not build things that violate those industry standards.

Many state and local laws mandate industry standards without actually stating the standard; they incorporate the standard by reference to some specification published by a standards organization. These standards have the force of law and must be obeyed. Courts in the United States have only recently addressed the issue of standards organizations being able to charge fees for the public's right to copy industry standards that are enforceable under the law. In some jurisdictions, royalties for the right to make copies of laws are no longer allowed.

Some companies and other nongovernmental organizations also want to control industry standards. Since those industry standards are not adopted by legislatures as laws, they cannot be enforced like building, electrical, and plumbing codes. Private owners of the intellectual property in standards can enforce their standards privately, under contract law and through the application of copyright, patent, and trademark law, by controlling license rights to the specifications of the standards.

As described below, some of those copyright, patent, and trademark licenses are compatible with open source and open standards.

Licensing the Test Suite: The Open Group License

The Open Group is a standards organization that promotes, among other things, standards relating to UNIX. It also owns the UNIX certification mark that is registered around the world, and it manages a program to certify UNIX implementations by other companies. Versions of UNIX that meet the Open Group's specifications may carry the UNIX certification mark.

Certification requires testing. Under trademark law in most countries, the certifying organization must ensure that its certification marks are used only on tested and approved products. Otherwise the certification mark may be lost. A certifying organization (e.g., The Open Group) is responsible for verifying the quality of the certified goods.

The Open Group does this through published test suites, programs that are used to test versions of UNIX. If the test suites run successfully on the to-be-certified UNIX implementation, that UNIX version is certified.

The Open Group Test Suite License is for the test suite software itself, the Package. (See *www.opensource.org* for a copy of this license.) That Package is open source. The license does not require that the UNIX implementations that are tested against that Package themselves be open source.

The Open Group Test Suite License seeks to control the copyrightable elements of the test suite software sufficiently to protect the Open Group's certification marks. The preamble to the license calls it "artistic control" but this license actually has a much more practical objective. The Open Group is primarily concerned with the importance of testing to ensure conformance to the standards:

> *Since these are benchmark measures of conformance, we feel the integrity of test tools is of importance. In order to preserve the integrity of the existing conformance modes of this test package and to permit recipients of modified versions of this package to run the original test modes, this license requires that the original test modes be preserved. (Open Group Test Suite License Preamble.)*

This license conforms to the Open Source Principles. Licensees may copy, modify, and distribute copies of the Package. These are the important conditions:

- You must duplicate all of the original copyright notices and associated disclaimers from the Standard Version of this Package. (Open Group Test Suite License section 1.)

- You must insert a prominent notice in each changed file stating how and when you changed that file. (Open Group Test Suite License section 3.)

- You must rename any nonstandard executables and test cases and provide a separate manual page that clearly documents how it differs from the Standard Version. (Open Group Test Suite License section 3.)

- When you distribute your version, you must accompany your modifications with their corresponding Standard Version executables and test cases. (Open Group Test Suite License section 4.)

Through this open source license on its test suite Package, The Open Group is able to control the standards for its own certification mark while granting to everyone the software freedom to create derivative works of the Package. Those derivative works are not required to comply with the standard, but if they do not they cannot be called the *Standard Version*:

> *"Standard Version" refers to such a Package if it has not been modified, or has been modified in accordance with the wishes of the Copyright Holder. (Open Group Test Suite License Definitions.)*

Only those UNIX implementations that successfully past the Standard Version tests will be certified by the Open Group to call themselves UNIX.

Discouraging Forks: Sun's SISSL

Sun Microsystems wanted a more robust way to prevent the standard from being forked. *Forking* is a colloquial term used in the open source community to describe what happens when a cooperative project splits into two or more uncooperative separate projects. The result is either an opportunity or a problem, depending partly on whether you're the project being forked from or to, and partly on the ultimate success of the forked project's software in the marketplace. One of the risks of permitting derivative works of industry standard specifications and test suites is that competitors may move away from the standard. As I just described, The Open Group Test Suite License avoided that by requiring notice and documentation of such changes, and it prohibited calling derivative works the *Standard Version*. But that's only partially effective. Companies can diverge from the standard, or add new requirements, without having to return those contributions to the open standard.

An open source license cannot prohibit forks. (Refer to Open Source Principle # 3, which mandates the freedom to create derivative works.) But the license can set conditions, including a reciprocity condition, on such derivative works.

The Sun Industry Standards Source License (SISSL) is patterned largely on the MPL, with its emphasis on files rather than the broader concept of derivative works. (The full text of the SISSL is available at *www.opensource.org*.) You will recognize much of the MPL's structure, with this interesting addition to the reciprocity condition.

> *The Modifications which You create must comply with all requirements set out by the Standards body in effect one hundred twenty (120) days before You ship the Contributor Version. In the event that the Modifications do not meet such requirements, You agree to publish either*
>
> *(i) any deviation from the Standards protocol resulting from implementation of Your Modifications and a reference implementation of Your Modifications or*
>
> *(ii) Your Modifications in Source Code form, and to make any such deviation and reference implementation or Modifications available to all third parties under the same terms*

as this license on a royalty free basis within thirty (30) days
of Your first customer shipment of Your Modifications.
(SISSL license section 3.1.)

Like all reciprocity provisions in open source licenses, the SISSL requires no more of the licensee than the licensor already gave. It permits forks of the standard, but any Modifications that break compatibility with the standard will be available on a reciprocal basis for all to adopt. It also imposes timing constraints on the creation of derivative works that allow the standards organization—in this case Sun Microsystems—an opportunity to react to attempted forks.

Sun uses the SISSL license for the file format and application programming interface specifications of its version of Open Office software, and the GPL for the Open Office software itself.

Patents on Open Standards

What happens when someone owns patents that are necessary to implement the specification for an open standard? You will recall that the owner of a patent can prevent you from making, using, or selling his or her patented invention regardless of how you learned to do it, even if you invented it yourself subsequently.

If someone owns a patent claim necessary to practice an open standard, you will need a license from the patent owner to practice that standard in your own software. Your freedom to practice the standard in your software is subject to the license terms from the patent owner.

Standards organizations recognize this. That is why they have focused in recent years on designing patent policies that are compatible with open source. The key to open standards is a patent policy that encourages the widespread adoption of the standard in all kinds of software—including open source software.

Patent claims necessary to practice an industry standard can suddenly appear. The story is often written about the eccentric scientist who, while puttering in his garage, secretly invents and perhaps tries to delay the publication of an essential patent to valuable technology. There is nothing that a standards organization, or anyone else, can do to prevent such surprise patents that are published by the Patent Office after a standard is promulgated.

But far more typically, important patents are owned by the same companies that participate in the standards organizations. Who, after all, is more likely to want to file patents in a particular industry technology than the companies that have special expertise in that field? Those companies have the talent and resources to create a wealth of patents surrounding the field of the standards.

Standards organizations need ways to protect their members from each others' private patents. The latest technique, the development of agreed patent policies that limit the options of their members to enforce private patents, is one important solution to the patent problem for industry standards. The patent policy of the W3C is the leader in this new area of open standards; the W3C Patent License is described in the last section of this chapter.

Reasonable and Nondiscriminatory

Most standards organizations demand that their members agree to license any of their patent claims necessary to practice their standards on "reasonable and nondiscriminatory terms." Here is a typical license grant from one company, Cisco, to one standards organization, the Internet Engineering Task Force:

> *Cisco has a pending patent application relating to the subject*
> *matter of draft-ietf-mobileip-nat-traversal-06.txt, "Mobile*
> *IP NAT/NAPT Traversal using UDP Tunneling". If a*
> *standard relating to this subject matter is adopted by IETF*
> *and any claims of any issued Cisco patents are necessary for*
> *practicing this standard, any party will be able to obtain a*
> *license from Cisco to use any such patent claims under rea-*
> *sonable, nondiscriminatory terms, with reciprocity, to imple-*
> *ment and fully comply with the standard. (From*
> *www.ietf.org.)*

The key words in this letter are *reasonable* and *nondiscrimi-natory*. You will see these words in most patent grants to most standards organizations worldwide. This is just one example; Cisco and the IETF are not unique. I'm not picking on them by reprinting this letter.

The word *reasonable* is impossible to define precisely. It always depends on the facts of the specific case. So, for example, there is no single reasonable price for a car or a house, no agreement on what constitutes reasonable warranty terms, and perhaps for some companies there is no reasonable way at all to accept a reciprocity provision. What is the reasonable juris-diction and venue for litigation against an open source pro-grammer who lives in Africa or Europe?

The word *nondiscriminatory* is also ambiguous. Does it mean that both rich and poor will not be discriminated against? (It is difficult to set any price other than very near zero that doesn't discriminate against at least some of the poor.) Or does the promise not to discriminate merely extend to the forms of discrimination already outlawed by law, such as age, race, and sex? As some have complained about the GPL and other reciprocal open source licenses, aren't all reciprocity pro-visions discriminatory against those who won't or can't accept a reciprocity obligation?

In practice, the reasonable and nondiscriminatory promises simply mean that everyone will pay the same price, and be subject to the same terms and conditions, for the same patent license rights—even if those terms and conditions are onerous and incompatible with free software. That is not open source, any more than saying that Microsoft Windows is open source because everyone pays the same price and agrees to the same End User License Agreement. As I have noted throughout this book, the devil is in the detailed license terms and conditions that must be agreed to.

Another ambiguous phrase in the Cisco letter is *with reciprocity*. The scope of the reciprocal license expected from implementers or users of the standard is unknown until the precise license terms are revealed by Cisco. Is reciprocity in this case benign?

An open source licensor can take little comfort when a company issues vague promises of reasonable and nondiscriminatory licenses for its patents. We need to be certain that the patent licenses are actually compatible with open source.

Royalty Free

Software freedom doesn't require zero price for a copy of the specification describing how to write software. But it does require zero royalties for a license to those patent claims necessary to make, use, and sell open source implementations of that software. A price other than zero for the right to make copies conflicts directly with Open Source Principle # 2.

Therefore, the only reasonable royalty for a patent license for an open standard that can be implemented in open source is zero. The term of art for such a license is *royalty free*.

Very few of the reasonable and nondiscriminatory patent licenses for industry standards actually charge a royalty. As a practical matter, the word *reasonable* mostly means *zero*. But not always, and when a license requires payment of a royalty, it poses a problem for open source software developers who can't recover that royalty through license fees.

It would be a mistake, though, to just focus on price. As I have described throughout this book, there are many other characteristics of open source software that matter much more, such as the right to create derivative works. An open standard patent license that is compatible with open source must include more than a promise of a zero royalty.

The term *royalty free* is now potentially as confusing as the term *free* was for software. Perhaps it would be better if we called standards that satisfy the W3C Royalty-Free Patent License requirements *open standards*?

The W3C Patent License

The World Wide Web Consortium was the first software industry standards organization to confront directly the problem of patent licenses for open source software. In May 2003, following several years of internal debate among W3C members (including representatives from all the major software companies and open source organizations), W3C published its patent policy. The effort was characterized by W3C director Tim Burners-Lee as "the most thorough ... to date in defining a basic patent policy for standard-setting." (See *www.w3.org*.)

One of their major goals was to make W3C standards (what they call *Recommendations*) fully compatible with open source software.

As a condition for participating on a specific W3C standard-setting working group, W3C member companies and their representatives undertake to disclose and/or license their patents relating to that working group to everyone under an open source compatible patent license. A member company can refuse to license its patents for a W3C standard. But if it fails to disclose the existence of those patents, or if it decides to issue licenses, it must license its patents under a license compatible with the W3C Patent Policy.

These are the requirements for such patent licenses:

> *With respect to a Recommendation developed under this policy, a W3C Royalty-Free license shall mean a non-assignable, non-sublicensable license to make, have made, use, sell, have sold, offer to sell, import, and distribute and dispose of implementations of the Recommendation that:*
>
> *1. shall be available to all, worldwide, whether or not they are W3C Members;*
>
> *2. shall extend to all Essential Claims owned or controlled by the licensor;*
>
> *3. may be limited to implementations of the Recommendation, and to what is required by the Recommendation;*
>
> *4. may be conditioned on a grant of a reciprocal RF license (as defined in this policy) to all Essential Claims owned or controlled by the licensee. A reciprocal license may be required to be available to all, and a reciprocal license may itself be conditioned on a further reciprocal license from all.*
>
> *5. may not be conditioned on payment of royalties, fees or other consideration;*
>
> *6. may be suspended with respect to any licensee when licensor is sued by licensee for infringement of claims essential to implement any W3C Recommendation;*
>
> *7. may not impose any further conditions or restrictions on the use of any technology, intellectual property rights, or other restrictions on behavior of the licensee, but may include rea-*

*sonable, customary terms relating to operation or mainte-
nance of the license relationship such as the following: choice
of law and dispute resolution;*

*8. shall not be considered accepted by an implementer who
manifests an intent **not** to accept the terms of the W3C Royalty-Free license as offered by the licensor.*

License term:

*9. The RF license conforming to the requirements in this pol-
icy shall be made available by the licensor as long as the Recommendation is in effect. The term of such license shall be
for the life of the patents in question, subject to the limitations of 5(10).*

*10. If the Recommendation is rescinded by W3C, then no
new licenses need be granted but any licenses granted before
the Recommendation was rescinded shall remain in effect.
(See www.w3.org.)*

Of particular importance, of course, are items 1, 5, and 7,
which allow everyone to make, use, or sell standard open
source software, and which prevent the imposition of patent
license conditions that would restrict its creation or distribution. Such licenses are compatible with the Open Source Principles from Chapter 1.

The W3C Royalty-Free license is a model for open standards patent licenses that are compatible with open source.
Other standards organizations are beginning to consider similar licensing models.

Not every requirement of the W3C Royalty-Free license
policy is friendly to open source, however. For example,
because such licenses are "non-assignable" and "non-subli-
censeable," each licensee theoretically must obtain a license
directly from the patent owner. In practice hardly anybody

does, and because of the W3C member commitments to each other, nobody needs to fear that a royalty-free patent license wouldn't be available to anyone who actually wanted one.

Item 3 allows the imposition of a field of use restriction in a patent license. Everyone should recognize that in some situations this field of use restriction may limit the creation of certain types of derivative works. This is not a unique problem for the W3C patent license; remember that open source licenses such as the MPL and CPL also contain subtle but important field of use restrictions.

Item 6 allows the patent being licensed to be used for defensive purposes. Anyone who sues the patent owner for patent infringement risks having patent licenses to "this and other W3C specifications" suspended (or terminated). Similar provisions in many open source licenses have already been discussed in this book. Open source licensors are allowed to use their intellectual property to defend against infringement lawsuits by others.

Justifying Open Standards and Open Source

Item 5 of the W3C Royalty-Free license, the requirement that a patent license "may not be conditioned on payment of royalties, fees or other consideration," is the most significant factor for most companies. They face the prospect of licensing some of their patented intellectual property at zero price if they contribute to the development of an industry standard.

How could contributing patents at zero price for open standards ever be justified to company shareholders?

Somehow it must be justified over and over again, because very few companies actually charge royalties for their patent licenses relating to industry standards. Zero price is typical even though it is not yet generally the rule. Companies have long recognized that charging royalties for some things will impede the beneficial cooperation for which they joined industry consortia in the first place. It is better to forego small royalty profits for a small number of patents in exchange for the prospect of long term financial gain in a vibrant, competitive marketplace.

This is the same economic tradeoff that confronts a copyright licensor who is considering licensing software under an open source license. The licensor's customers will be able to make unlimited free copies of this copyrighted intellectual property. How can a licensor make money that way?

You will find many examples of profitable open source business models among the major software companies and open source projects worldwide. We now see huge collections of open source software being created and contributed to around the world under the licenses described in this book. The price of software copyright and patent licenses isn't always the most important characteristic or advantage of open source software.

Open source and open standards are an enormous reality even if this book doesn't fully explain why people and companies do it. I could only describe licensing in this book. I could not also help you to justify the underlying open source business models. That is for someone else's book.

The simple fact is that many companies and individuals now contribute to a growing commons of intellectual property. They have discovered that more value is derived by distributing this intellectual property freely to others and sharing in the growing public commons of free software.

The Open Source Paradigm

The open source paradigm is transforming software development and distribution around the world. More and more consumers, companies, and government agencies are now demanding that they be allowed software freedom as enunciated in the five Open Source Principles from Chapter 1: The freedom to use, copy, modify, and distribute software, to have the source code, and to combine open source software with other software.

I used the word *paradigm* because it has an appropriately broad definition:

> *Paradigm: A set of assumptions, concepts, values, and practices that constitutes a way of viewing reality for the community that shares them, especially in an intellectual discipline. (The American Heritage Dictionary of the English Language, Fourth Edition.)*

Open source licenses formalize the "assumptions, concepts, values and practices" of open source developers, distributors, and customers. They provide a legal framework for software generosity (sometimes coupled with reciprocity) that makes open source so tempting and so rewarding.

Paradigms evolve over time. The software world is not what it was in 1989 when the GPL and BSD licenses were first

313

introduced. I have no doubt that, starting shortly after this book is published, new open source licenses and new open source business models not currently anticipated will be introduced by creative people around the world. Indeed, that is the very foundational concept of the open source paradigm, which requires that people be free to learn from their predecessors and to create "derivative works."

I fully expect that there will be new versions of at least some of the licenses described in this book. There are long running rumors of a GPL version 3, for example, and the Apache project just announced a new license. Version 2.1 of the OSL and AFL licenses were recently approved by Open Source Initiative. But I doubt that there will soon be an entirely different paradigm to replace this one, and so the legal underpinnings of these licenses that I have described are likely to be the most important ones to concern us for the foreseeable future.

What will probably happen is that some of those legal underpinnings—the definitions of *collective* and *derivative works* in the context of software, for example, or the laws regarding contract formation when software is distributed for free, or the policies toward software patents for industry standards—will be articulated by courts and legislatures. The complicated questions raised in this book may eventually be answered, making the choices among alternatives more obvious.

But those answers aren't yet at hand, and so I must repeat a warning I gave at the beginning of this book. I have described only a few of the available open source licenses, open source business models, and open source legal issues that are before us today. New ones are appearing constantly. To rely on these few hints as the basis for important software business decisions would be foolhardy. Ask your own attorney for advice.

Appendices

BSD License

The following is a BSD license template. To generate your own license, change the values of OWNER, ORGANIZATION, and YEAR from their original values as given here, and substitute your own.

Note: The advertising clause in the license appearing on BSD UNIX files was officially rescinded by the Director of the Office of Technology Licensing of the University of California on July 22, 1999. He states that clause 3 is "hereby deleted in its entirety." (See copy of rescission letter below.)

<OWNER> = Regents of the University of California

<ORGANIZATION> = University of California, Berkeley

<YEAR> = 1998

In the original BSD license, both occurrences of the phrase "COPYRIGHT HOLDERS AND CONTRIBUTORS" in the disclaimer read "REGENTS AND CONTRIBUTORS."

Here is the license template:

Copyright (c) <YEAR>, <OWNER>

All rights reserved.

Redistribution and use in source and binary forms, with or without modification, are permitted provided that the following conditions are met:

Redistributions of source code must retain the above copyright notice, this list of conditions and the following disclaimer.

Redistributions in binary form must reproduce the above copyright notice, this list of conditions and the following disclaimer in the documentation and/or other materials provided with the distribution.

Neither the name of the <ORGANIZATION> nor the names of its contributors may be used to endorse or promote products derived from this software without specific prior written permission.

THIS SOFTWARE IS PROVIDED BY THE COPYRIGHT HOLDERS AND CONTRIBUTORS "AS IS" AND ANY EXPRESS OR IMPLIED WARRANTIES, INCLUDING, BUT NOT LIMITED TO, THE IMPLIED WARRANTIES OF MERCHANTABILITY AND FITNESS FOR A PARTICULAR PURPOSE ARE DISCLAIMED. IN NO EVENT SHALL THE COPYRIGHT OWNER OR CONTRIBUTORS BE LIABLE FOR ANY DIRECT, INDIRECT, INCIDENTAL, SPECIAL, EXEMPLARY, OR CONSEQUENTIAL DAMAGES (INCLUDING, BUT NOT LIMITED TO, PROCUREMENT OF SUBSTITUTE GOODS OR SERVICES; LOSS OF USE, DATA, OR PROFITS; OR BUSINESS INTERRUPTION) HOWEVER CAUSED AND ON ANY THEORY OF LIABILITY, WHETHER IN CONTRACT, STRICT LIABILITY, OR TORT (INCLUDING NEGLIGENCE OR OTHERWISE) ARISING IN ANY WAY OUT OF THE USE OF THIS SOFTWARE, EVEN IF ADVISED OF THE POSSIBILITY OF SUCH DAMAGE.

*(This is the rescission letter referred to
n the BSD license. —LR)*

July 22, 1999

To All Licensees, Distributors of Any Version of BSD:

As you know, certain of the Berkeley Software Distribution ("BSD") source code files require that further distributions of products containing all or portions of the software, acknowledge within their advertising materials that such products contain software developed by UC Berkeley and its contributors.

Specifically, the provision reads:

  3. All advertising materials mentioning features or use of this software must display the following acknowledgement: "This product includes software developed by the University of California, Berkeley and its contributors."

Effective immediately, licensees and distributors are no longer required to include the acknowledgement within advertising materials. Accordingly, the foregoing paragraph of those BSD UNIX files containing it is hereby deleted in its entirety.

William Hoskins
Director, Office of Technology Licensing
University of California, Berkeley

MIT License

Copyright (c) <year> <copyright holders>

Permission is hereby granted, free of charge, to any person obtaining a copy of this software and associated documentation files (the "Software"), to deal in the Software without restriction, including without limitation the rights to use, copy, modify, merge, publish, distribute, sublicense, and/or sell copies of the Software, and to permit persons to whom the Software is furnished to do so, subject to the following conditions:

The above copyright notice and this permission notice shall be included in all copies or substantial portions of the Software.

THE SOFTWARE IS PROVIDED "AS IS," WITHOUT WARRANTY OF ANY KIND, EXPRESS OR IMPLIED, INCLUDING BUT NOT LIMITED TO THE WARRANTIES OF MERCHANTABILITY, FITNESS FOR A PARTICULAR PURPOSE AND NONINFRINGEMENT. IN NO EVENT SHALL THE AUTHORS OR COPYRIGHT HOLDERS BE LIABLE FOR ANY CLAIM, DAMAGES OR OTHER LIABILITY, WHETHER IN AN ACTION OF CONTRACT, TORT OR OTHERWISE, ARISING FROM, OUT OF OR IN CONNECTION WITH THE SOFTWARE OR THE USE OR OTHER DEALINGS IN THE SOFTWARE.

Apache License

Version 1.1

Copyright (c) 2000 The Apache Software Foundation. All rights reserved.

Redistribution and use in source and binary forms, with or without modification, are permitted provided that the following conditions are met:

1. Redistributions of source code must retain the above copyright notice, this list of conditions and the following disclaimer.

2. Redistributions in binary form must reproduce the above copyright notice, this list of conditions and the following disclaimer in the documentation and/or other materials provided with the distribution.

3. The end-user documentation included with the redistribution, if any, must include the following acknowledgment:

   "This product includes software developed by the Apache Software Foundation (http://www.apache.org/)."

   Alternately, this acknowledgment may appear in the software itself, if and wherever such third-party acknowledgments normally appear.

4. The names "Apache" and "Apache Software Foundation" must not be used to endorse or promote products derived from this software without prior written permission. For written permission, please contact apache@apache.org.

5. Products derived from this software may not be called "Apache," nor may "Apache" appear in their name,

without prior written permission of the Apache Software Foundation.

THIS SOFTWARE IS PROVIDED "AS IS" AND ANY EXPRESSED OR IMPLIED WARRANTIES, INCLUDING, BUT NOT LIMITED TO, THE IMPLIED WARRANTIES OF MERCHANTABILITY AND FITNESS FOR A PARTICULAR PURPOSE ARE DISCLAIMED. IN NO EVENT SHALL THE APACHE SOFTWARE FOUNDATION OR ITS CONTRIBUTORS BE LIABLE FOR ANY DIRECT, INDIRECT, INCIDENTAL, SPECIAL, EXEMPLARY, OR CONSEQUENTIAL DAMAGES (INCLUDING, BUT NOT LIMITED TO, PROCUREMENT OF SUBSTITUTE GOODS OR SERVICES; LOSS OF USE, DATA, OR PROFITS; OR BUSINESS INTERRUPTION) HOWEVER CAUSED AND ON ANY THEORY OF LIABILITY, WHETHER IN CONTRACT, STRICT LIABILITY, OR TORT (INCLUDING NEGLIGENCE OR OTHERWISE) ARISING IN ANY WAY OUT OF THE USE OF THIS SOFTWARE, EVEN IF ADVISED OF THE POSSIBILITY OF SUCH DAMAGE.

The Apache Contributor License Agreement

Thank you for your interest in The Apache Software Foundation (the "Foundation"). In order to clarify the intellectual property license granted with contributions of software from any person or entity (the "Contributor"), the Foundation would like to have a Contributor License Agreement on file that has been signed by the Contributor, indicating agreement to the license terms below. This license is for your protection as a Contributor of software to the Foundation and does not change your right to use your own contributions for any other purpose.

If you have not already done so, please complete this Agreement and send it by facsimile to the Foundation at +1-410-803-2258, or send a photocopy by regular mail to The Apache Software Foundation, 1901 Munsey Drive, Forest Hill, MD 21050-2747, U.S.A. Please read this document carefully before signing and keep the original for your records.

You and the Foundation hereby accept and agree to the following terms and conditions:

1. Your "Contributions" means all of your past, present and future contributions of object code, source code and documentation to the Foundation, however submitted to the Foundation, excluding any submissions that are conspicuously marked or otherwise designated in writing by You as "Not a Contribution."

2. You hereby grant to the Foundation a non-exclusive, irrevocable, worldwide, no-charge, transferable copyright license to use, execute, prepare derivative works of, and distribute (internally and externally, in object code and, if included in your Contributions, source code

form) your Contributions. Except for the rights granted to the Foundation in this paragraph, You reserve all right, title and interest in and to your Contributions.

3. You represent that you are legally entitled to grant the above license. If your employer(s) have rights to intellectual property that you create, you represent that you have received permission to make the Contributions on behalf of that employer, or that your employer has waived such rights for your Contributions to the Foundation.

4. You represent that, except as disclosed in your Contribution submission(s), each of your Contributions is your original creation. You represent that your Contribution submission(s) include complete details of any license or other restriction (including, but not limited to, related patents and trademarks) associated with any part of your Contribution(s) (including a copy of any applicable license agreement). You agree to notify the Foundation of any facts or circumstances of which you become aware that would make Your representations in this Agreement inaccurate in any respect.

5. You are not expected to provide support for your Contributions, except to the extent you desire to provide support. You may provide support for free, for a fee, or not at all. Your Contributions are provided as-is, with all faults defects and errors, and without warranty of any kind (either express or implied) including, without limitation, any implied warranty of merchantability and fitness for a particular purpose and any warranty of non-infringement.

Please sign: _____Date: _____

Artistic License

Preamble

The intent of this document is to state the conditions under which a Package may be copied, such that the Copyright Holder maintains some semblance of artistic control over the development of the package, while giving the users of the package the right to use and distribute the Package in a more-or-less customary fashion, plus the right to make reasonable modifications.

Definitions

"Package" refers to the collection of files distributed by the Copyright Holder, and derivatives of that collection of files created through textual modification.

"Standard Version" refers to such a Package if it has not been modified, or has been modified in accordance with the wishes of the Copyright Holder.

"Copyright Holder" is whoever is named in the copyright or copyrights for the package.

"You" is you, if you're thinking about copying or distributing this Package.

"Reasonable copying fee" is whatever you can justify on the basis of media cost, duplication charges, time of people involved, and so on. (You will not be required to justify it to the Copyright Holder, but only to the computing community at large as a market that must bear the fee.)

"Freely Available" means that no fee is charged for the item itself, though there may be fees involved in handling the item. It also means that recipients of the item may redistribute it under the same conditions they received it.

1. You may make and give away verbatim copies of the source form of the Standard Version of this Package without restriction, provided that you duplicate all of the original copyright notices and associated disclaimers.

2. You may apply bug fixes, portability fixes and other modifications derived from the Public Domain or from the Copyright Holder. A Package modified in such a way shall still be considered the Standard Version.

3. You may otherwise modify your copy of this Package in any way, provided that you insert a prominent notice in each changed file stating how and when you changed that file, and provided that you do at least ONE of the following:

   a. place your modifications in the Public Domain or otherwise make them Freely Available, such as by posting said modifications to Usenet or an equivalent medium, or placing the modifications on a major archive site such as ftp.uu.net, or by allowing the Copyright Holder to include your modifications in the Standard Version of the Package.

   b. use the modified Package only within your corporation or organization.

   c. rename any non-standard executables so the names do not conflict with standard executables, which must also be provided, and provide a separate manual page for each non-standard executable that clearly documents how it differs from the Standard Version.

   d. make other distribution arrangements with the Copyright Holder.

4. You may distribute the programs of this Package in object code or executable form, provided that you do at least ONE of the following:

   e. distribute a Standard Version of the executables and library files, together with instructions (in the manual page or equivalent) on where to get the Standard Version.

   f. accompany the distribution with the machine-readable source of the Package with your modifications.

   g. accompany any non-standard executables with their corresponding Standard Version executables, giving the non-standard executables non-standard names, and clearly documenting the differences in manual pages (or equivalent), together with instructions on where to get the Standard Version.

   h. make other distribution arrangements with the Copyright Holder.

5. You may charge a reasonable copying fee for any distribution of this Package. You may charge any fee you choose for support of this Package. You may not charge a fee for this Package itself. However, you may distribute this Package in aggregate with other (possibly commercial) programs as part of a larger (possibly commercial) software distribution provided that you do not advertise this Package as a product of your own.

6. The scripts and library files supplied as input to or produced as output from the programs of this Package do not automatically fall under the copyright of this Package, but belong to whomever generated them, and may

be sold commercially, and may be aggregated with this Package.

7. C or perl subroutines supplied by you and linked into this Package shall not be considered part of this Package.

8. The name of the Copyright Holder may not be used to endorse or promote products derived from this software without specific prior written permission.

9. THIS PACKAGE IS PROVIDED "AS IS" AND WITHOUT ANY EXPRESS OR IMPLIED WARRANTIES, INCLUDING, WITHOUT LIMITATION, THE IMPLIED WARRANTIES OF MERCHANTIBILITY AND FITNESS FOR A PARTICULAR PURPOSE.

   (Some versions of the Artistic License contain the following clause.—LR)

10. Aggregation of this Package with a commercial distribution is always permitted provided that the use of this Package is embedded; that is, when no overt attempt is made to make this Package's interfaces visible to the end user of the commercial distribution. Such use shall not be construed as a distribution of this Package.

General Public License (GPL)

Version 2, June 1991

Copyright (C) 1989, 1991 Free Software Foundation, Inc., 59 Temple Place, Suite 330, Boston, MA 02111-1307 USA

Everyone is permitted to copy and distribute verbatim copies of this license document, but changing it is not allowed.

Preamble

The licenses for most software are designed to take away your freedom to share and change it. By contrast, the GNU General Public License is intended to guarantee your freedom to share and change free software—to make sure the software is free for all its users. This General Public License applies to most of the Free Software Foundation's software and to any other program whose authors commit to using it. (Some other Free Software Foundation software is covered by the GNU Library General Public License instead.) You can apply it to your programs, too.

When we speak of free software, we are referring to freedom, not price. Our General Public Licenses are designed to make sure that you have the freedom to distribute copies of free software (and charge for this service if you wish), that you receive source code or can get it if you want it, that you can change the software or use pieces of it in new free programs; and that you know you can do these things.

To protect your rights, we need to make restrictions that forbid anyone to deny you these rights or to ask you to surrender the rights. These restrictions translate to certain responsibilities for you if you distribute copies of the software, or if you modify it.

For example, if you distribute copies of such a program, whether gratis or for a fee, you must give the recipients all the rights that you have. You must make sure that they, too, receive or can get the source code. And you must show them these terms so they know their rights.

We protect your rights with two steps: (1) copyright the software, and (2) offer you this license which gives you legal permission to copy, distribute and/or modify the software.

Also, for each author's protection and ours, we want to make certain that everyone understands that there is no warranty for this free software. If the software is modified by someone else and passed on, we want its recipients to know that what they have is not the original, so that any problems introduced by others will not reflect on the original authors' reputations.

Finally, any free program is threatened constantly by software patents. We wish to avoid the danger that redistributors of a free program will individually obtain patent licenses, in effect making the program proprietary. To prevent this, we have made it clear that any patent must be licensed for everyone's free use or not licensed at all.

The precise terms and conditions for copying, distribution and modification follow.

TERMS AND CONDITIONS FOR COPYING, DISTRIBUTION AND MODIFICATION

1. This License applies to any program or other work which contains a notice placed by the copyright holder saying it may be distributed under the terms of this General Public License. The "Program," below, refers to any such program or work, and a "work based on the Program" means either the Program or any derivative work

under copyright law: that is to say, a work containing the Program or a portion of it, either verbatim or with modifications and/or translated into another language. (Hereinafter, translation is included without limitation in the term "modification.") Each licensee is addressed as "you."

Activities other than copying, distribution and modification are not covered by this License; they are outside its scope. The act of running the Program is not restricted, and the output from the Program is covered only if its contents constitute a work based on the Program (independent of having been made by running the Program). Whether that is true depends on what the Program does.

You may charge a fee for the physical act of transferring a copy, and you may at your option offer warranty protection in exchange for a fee **1**. You may copy and distribute verbatim copies of the Program's source code as you receive it, in any medium, provided that you conspicuously and appropriately publish on each copy an appropriate copyright notice and disclaimer of warranty; keep intact all the notices that refer to this License and to the absence of any warranty; and give any other recipients of the Program a copy of this License along with the Program.

2. You may modify your copy or copies of the Program or any portion of it, thus forming a work based on the Program, and copy and distribute such modifications or work under the terms of Section 1 above, provided that you also meet all of these conditions:

   a) You must cause the modified files to carry prominent notices stating that you changed the files and the date of any change.

b) You must cause any work that you distribute or publish, that in whole or in part contains or is derived from the Program or any part thereof, to be licensed as a whole at no charge to all third parties under the terms of this License.

c) If the modified program normally reads commands interactively when run, you must cause it, when started running for such interactive use in the most ordinary way, to print or display an announcement including an appropriate copyright notice and a notice that there is no warranty (or else, saying that you provide a warranty) and that users may redistribute the program under these conditions, and telling the user how to view a copy of this License. (Exception: if the Program itself is interactive but does not normally print such an announcement, your work based on the Program is not required to print an announcement.)

3. You may copy and distribute the Program (or a work based on it, under Section 2) in object code or executable form under the terms of Sections 1 and 2 above provided that you also do one of the following:

a) Accompany it with the complete corresponding machine-readable source code, which must be distributed under the terms of Sections 1 and 2 above on a medium customarily used for software interchange; or,

b) Accompany it with a written offer, valid for at least three years, to give any third party, for a charge no more than your cost of physically performing source distribution, a complete machine-readable copy of the corresponding source code, to be distributed under the terms of Sections 1 and 2 above on a medium customarily used for software interchange; or,

c) Accompany it with the information you received as to the offer to distribute corresponding source code. (This alternative is allowed only for noncommercial distribution and only if you received the program in object code or executable form with such an offer, in accord with Subsection b above.)

The source code for a work means the preferred form of the work for making modifications to it. For an executable work, complete source code means all the source code for all modules it contains, plus any associated interface definition files, plus the scripts used to control compilation and installation of the executable. However, as a special exception, the source code distributed need not include anything that is normally distributed (in either source or binary form) with the major components (compiler, kernel, and so on) of the operating system on which the executable runs, unless that component itself accompanies the executable.

If distribution of executable or object code is made by offering access to copy from a designated place, then offering equivalent access to copy the source code from the same place counts as distribution of the source code, even though third parties are not compelled to copy the source along with the object code.

4. You may not copy, modify, sublicense, or distribute the Program except as expressly provided under this License. Any attempt otherwise to copy, modify, sublicense or distribute the Program is void, and will automatically terminate your rights under this License. However, parties who have received copies, or rights, from you under this License will not have their licenses terminated so long as such parties remain in full compliance.

5. You are not required to accept this License, since you have not signed it. However, nothing else grants you permission to modify or distribute the Program or its derivative works. These actions are prohibited by law if you do not accept this License. Therefore, by modifying or distributing the Program (or any work based on the Program), you indicate your acceptance of this License to do so, and all its terms and conditions for copying, distributing or modifying the Program or works based on it.

6. Each time you redistribute the Program (or any work based on the Program), the recipient automatically receives a license from the original licensor to copy, distribute or modify the Program subject to these terms and conditions. You may not impose any further restrictions on the recipients' exercise of the rights granted herein. You are not responsible for enforcing compliance by third parties to this License.

7. If, as a consequence of a court judgment or allegation of patent infringement or for any other reason (not limited to patent issues), conditions are imposed on you (whether by court order, agreement or otherwise) that contradict the conditions of this License, they do not excuse you from the conditions of this License. If you cannot distribute so as to satisfy simultaneously your obligations under this License and any other pertinent obligations, then as a consequence you may not distribute the Program at all. For example, if a patent license would not permit royalty-free redistribution of the Program by all those who receive copies directly or indirectly through you, then the only way you could satisfy both it and this License would be to refrain entirely from distribution of the Program.

If any portion of this section is held invalid or unenforceable under any particular circumstance, the balance of the section is intended to apply and the section as a whole is intended to apply in other circumstances.

It is not the purpose of this section to induce you to infringe any patents or other property right claims or to contest validity of any such claims; this section has the sole purpose of protecting the integrity of the free software distribution system, which is implemented by public license practices. Many people have made generous contributions to the wide range of software distributed through that system in reliance on consistent application of that system; it is up to the author/donor to decide if he or she is willing to distribute software through any other system and a licensee cannot impose that choice.

This section is intended to make thoroughly clear what is believed to be a consequence of the rest of this License.

8. If the distribution and/or use of the Program is restricted in certain countries either by patents or by copyrighted interfaces, the original copyright holder who places the Program under this License may add an explicit geographical distribution limitation excluding those countries, so that distribution is permitted only in or among countries not thus excluded. In such case, this License

incorporates the limitation as if written in the body of this License.

9. The Free Software Foundation may publish revised and/or new versions of the General Public License from time to time. Such new versions will be similar in spirit to the present version, but may differ in detail to address new problems or concerns.

   Each version is given a distinguishing version number. If the Program specifies a version number of this License which applies to it and "any later version," you have the option of following the terms and conditions either of that version or of any later version published by the Free Software Foundation. If the Program does not specify a version number of this License, you may choose any version ever published by the Free Software Foundation.

10. If you wish to incorporate parts of the Program into other free programs whose distribution conditions are different, write to the author to ask for permission. For software which is copyrighted by the Free Software Foundation, write to the Free Software Foundation; we sometimes make exceptions for this. Our decision will be guided by the two goals of preserving the free status of all derivatives of our free software and of promoting the sharing and reuse of software generally.

NO WARRANTY

11. BECAUSE THE PROGRAM IS LICENSED FREE OF CHARGE, THERE IS NO WARRANTY FOR THE PROGRAM, TO THE EXTENT PERMITTED BY APPLICABLE LAW. EXCEPT WHEN OTHERWISE STATED IN WRITING THE COPYRIGHT HOLDERS AND/OR OTHER PARTIES PROVIDE

THE PROGRAM "AS IS" WITHOUT WARRANTY OF ANY KIND, EITHER EXPRESSED OR IMPLIED, INCLUDING, BUT NOT LIMITED TO, THE IMPLIED WARRANTIES OF MERCHANTABILITY AND FITNESS FOR A PARTICULAR PURPOSE. THE ENTIRE RISK AS TO THE QUALITY AND PERFORMANCE OF THE PROGRAM IS WITH YOU. SHOULD THE PROGRAM PROVE DEFECTIVE, YOU ASSUME THE COST OF ALL NECESSARY SERVICING, REPAIR OR CORRECTION.

12. IN NO EVENT UNLESS REQUIRED BY APPLICABLE LAW OR AGREED TO IN WRITING WILL ANY COPYRIGHT HOLDER, OR ANY OTHER PARTY WHO MAY MODIFY AND/OR REDISTRIBUTE THE PROGRAM AS PERMITTED ABOVE, BE LIABLE TO YOU FOR DAMAGES, INCLUDING ANY GENERAL, SPECIAL, INCIDENTAL OR CONSEQUENTIAL DAMAGES ARISING OUT OF THE USE OR INABILITY TO USE THE PROGRAM (INCLUDING BUT NOT LIMITED TO LOSS OF DATA OR DATA BEING RENDERED INACCURATE OR LOSSES SUSTAINED BY YOU OR THIRD PARTIES OR A FAILURE OF THE PROGRAM TO OPERATE WITH ANY OTHER PROGRAMS), EVEN IF SUCH HOLDER OR OTHER PARTY HAS BEEN ADVISED OF THE POSSIBILITY OF SUCH DAMAGES.

END OF TERMS AND CONDITIONS

How to Apply These Terms to Your New Programs

If you develop a new program, and you want it to be of the greatest possible use to the public, the best way to achieve this is to make it free software which everyone can redistribute and change under these terms.

To do so, attach the following notices to the program. It is safest to attach them to the start of each source file to most effectively convey the exclusion of warranty; and each file should have at least the "copyright" line and a pointer to where the full notice is found.

one line to give the program's name and a brief idea of what it does.

Copyright (C) <year> <name of author>

This program is free software; you can redistribute it and/or modify it under the terms of the GNU General Public License as published by the Free Software Foundation; either version 2 of the License, or (at your option) any later version.

This program is distributed in the hope that it will be useful, but WITHOUT ANY WARRANTY; without even the implied warranty of MERCHANTABILITY or FITNESS FOR A PARTICULAR PURPOSE. See the GNU General Public License for more details.

You should have received a copy of the GNU General Public License along with this program; if not, write to the Free Software Foundation, Inc., 59 Temple Place, Suite 330, Boston, MA 02111-1307 USA

Also add information on how to contact you by electronic and paper mail.

If the program is interactive, make it output a short notice like this when it starts in an interactive mode:

Gnomovision version 69, Copyright (C) <year> <name of author> Gnomovision comes with ABSOLUTELY NO WARRANTY; for details type 'show w'. This is free software, and you are welcome to redistribute it under certain conditions; type 'show c' for details.

The hypothetical commands 'show w' and 'show c' should show the appropriate parts of the General Public License. Of course, the commands you use may be called something other than 'show w' and 'show c'; they could even be mouse-clicks or menu items—whatever suits your program.

You should also get your employer (if you work as a programmer) or your school, if any, to sign a "copyright disclaimer" for the program, if necessary. Here is a sample; alter the names:

Yoyodyne, Inc., hereby disclaims all copyright interest in the program 'Gnomovision' (which makes passes at compilers) written by James Hacker.

signature of Ty Coon, 1 April 1989

Ty Coon, President of Vice

This General Public License does not permit incorporating your program into proprietary programs. If your program is a subroutine library, you may consider it more useful to permit linking proprietary applications with the library. If this is what you want to do, use the GNU Library General Public License instead of this License.

Lesser General Public License (LGPL)

Version 2.1, February 1999

Copyright (C) 1991, 1999 Free Software Foundation, Inc.

59 Temple Place, Suite 330, Boston, MA 02111-1307 USA

Everyone is permitted to copy and distribute verbatim copies of this license document, but changing it is not allowed.

(This is the first released version of the Lesser GPL. It also counts as the successor of the GNU Library Public License, version 2, hence the version number 2.1.)

TERMS AND CONDITIONS FOR COPYING, DISTRIBUTION AND MODIFICATION

1. This License Agreement applies to any software library or other program which contains a notice placed by the copyright holder or other authorized party saying it may be distributed under the terms of this Lesser General Public License (also called "this License"). Each licensee is addressed as "you."

A "library" means a collection of software functions and/or data prepared so as to be conveniently linked with application programs (which use some of those functions and data) to form executables.

The "Library," below, refers to any such software library or work which has been distributed under these terms. A "work based on the Library" means either the Library or any derivative work under copyright law: that is to say, a work containing the Library or a portion of it, either verbatim or with modifications and/or translated straightforwardly into another language. (Hereinafter, translation is included without limitation in the term "modification.")

"Source code" for a work means the preferred form of the work for making modifications to it. For a library, complete source code means all the source code for all modules it contains, plus any associated interface definition files, plus the scripts used to control compilation and installation of the library.

Activities other than copying, distribution and modification are not covered by this License; they are outside its scope. The act of running a program using the Library is not restricted, and output from such a program is covered only if its contents constitute a work based on the Library (independent of the use of the Library in a tool for writing it). Whether that is true depends on what the Library does and what the program that uses the Library does.

2. You may copy and distribute verbatim copies of the Library's complete source code as you receive it, in any medium, provided that you conspicuously and appropriately publish on each copy an appropriate copyright notice and disclaimer of warranty; keep intact all the notices that refer to this License and to the absence of any warranty; and distribute a copy of this License along with the Library.

   You may charge a fee for the physical act of transferring a copy, and you may at your option offer warranty protection in exchange for a fee.

3. You may modify your copy or copies of the Library or any portion of it, thus forming a work based on the Library, and copy and distribute such modifications or work under the terms of Section 1 above, provided that you also meet all of these conditions:

a) The modified work must itself be a software library.

b) You must cause the files modified to carry prominent notices stating that you changed the files and the date of any change.

c) You must cause the whole of the work to be licensed at no charge to all third parties under the terms of this License.

d) If a facility in the modified Library refers to a function or a table of data to be supplied by an application program that uses the facility, other than as an argument passed when the facility is invoked, then you must make a good faith effort to ensure that, in the event an application does not supply such function or table, the facility still operates, and performs whatever part of its purpose remains meaningful.

(For example, a function in a library to compute square roots has a purpose that is entirely well-defined independent of the application. Therefore, Subsection 2d requires that any application-supplied function or table used by this function must be optional: if the application does not supply it, the square root function must still compute square roots.)

These requirements apply to the modified work as a whole. If identifiable sections of that work are not derived from the Library, and can be reasonably considered independent and separate works in themselves, then this License, and its terms, do not apply to those sections when you distribute them as separate works. But when you distribute the same sections as part of a whole which is a work based on the Library, the distribution of the whole must be on the terms of this License, whose permissions for other licensees extend to the entire whole, and thus to each and every part regardless of who wrote it.

Thus, it is not the intent of this section to claim rights or contest your rights to work written entirely by you; rather, the intent is to exercise the right to control the distribution of derivative or collective works based on the Library.

In addition, mere aggregation of another work not based on the Library with the Library (or with a work based on the Library) on a volume of a storage or distribution medium does not bring the other work under the scope of this License.

4. You may opt to apply the terms of the ordinary GNU General Public License instead of this License to a given copy of the Library. To do this, you must alter all the notices that refer to this License, so that they refer to the ordinary GNU General Public License, version 2, instead of to this License. (If a newer version than version 2 of the ordinary GNU General Public License has appeared, then you can specify that version instead if you wish.) Do not make any other change in these notices.

Once this change is made in a given copy, it is irreversible for that copy, so the ordinary GNU General Public License applies to all subsequent copies and derivative works made from that copy.

This option is useful when you wish to copy part of the code of the Library into a program that is not a library.

5. You may copy and distribute the Library (or a portion or derivative of it, under Section 2) in object code or executable form under the terms of Sections 1 and 2 above provided that you accompany it with the complete corresponding machine-readable source code, which must be distributed under the terms of Sections 1 and 2 above on a medium customarily used for software interchange.

   If distribution of object code is made by offering access to copy from a designated place, then offering equivalent access to copy the source code from the same place satisfies the requirement to distribute the source code, even though third parties are not compelled to copy the source along with the object code.

6. A program that contains no derivative of any portion of the Library, but is designed to work with the Library by being compiled or linked with it, is called a "work that uses the Library." Such a work, in isolation, is not a derivative work of the Library, and therefore falls outside the scope of this License.

   However, linking a "work that uses the Library" with the Library creates an executable that is a derivative of the Library (because it contains portions of the Library), rather than a "work that uses the library." The executable is therefore covered by this License. Section 6 states terms for distribution of such executables.

   When a "work that uses the Library" uses material from a header file that is part of the Library, the object code for the work may be a derivative work of the Library even though the source code is not. Whether this is true is especially significant if the work can be linked without the Library, or if the work is itself a library. The threshold for this to be true is not precisely defined by law.

Otherwise, if the work is a derivative of the Library, you may distribute the object code for the work under the terms of Section 6. Any executables containing that work also fall under Section 6, whether or not they are linked directly with the Library itself. If such an object file uses only numerical parameters, data structure layouts and accessors, and small macros and small inline functions (ten lines or less in length), then the use of the object file is unrestricted, regardless of whether it is legally a derivative work. (Executables containing this object code plus portions of the Library will still fall under Section 6.)

7. As an exception to the Sections above, you may also combine or link a "work that uses the Library" with the Library to produce a work containing portions of the Library, and distribute that work under terms of your choice, provided that the terms permit modification of the work for the customer's own use and reverse engineering for debugging such modifications.

You must give prominent notice with each copy of the work that the Library is used in it and that the Library and its use are covered by this License. You must supply a copy of this License. If the work during execution displays copyright notices, you must include the copyright notice for the Library among them, as well as a reference directing the user to the copy of this License. Also, you must do one of these things:

a) Accompany the work with the complete corresponding machine-readable source code for the Library including whatever changes were used in the work (which must be distributed under Sections 1 and 2 above); and, if the work is an executable linked with the Library, with the complete machine-readable "work that uses the Library," as object code and/or source code, so that the user can modify the Library and then relink to produce a modified executable containing the modified Library. (It is understood that the user who changes the contents of definitions files in the Library will not necessarily be able to recompile the application to use the modified definitions.)

b) Use a suitable shared library mechanism for linking with the Library. A suitable mechanism is one that (1) uses at run time a copy of the library already present on the user's computer system, rather than copying library functions into the executable, and (2) will operate properly with a modified version of the library, if the user installs one, as long as the modified version is interface-compatible with the version that the work was made with.

c) Accompany the work with a written offer, valid for at least three years, to give the same user the materials specified in Subsection 6a, above, for a charge no more than the cost of performing this distribution.

d) If distribution of the work is made by offering access to copy from a designated place, offer equivalent access to copy the above specified materials from the same place.

e) Verify that the user has already received a copy of these materials or that you have already sent this user a copy.

For an executable, the required form of the "work that uses the Library" must include any data and utility programs needed for reproducing the executable from it. However, as a special exception, the materials to be distributed need not include anything that is normally distributed (in either source or binary form) with the major components (compiler, kernel, and so on) of the operating system on which the executable runs, unless that component itself accompanies the executable.

It may happen that this requirement contradicts the license restrictions of other proprietary libraries that do not normally accompany the operating system. Such a contradiction means you cannot use both them and the Library together in an executable that you distribute.

8. You may place library facilities that are a work based on the Library side-by-side in a single library together with other library facilities not covered by this License, and distribute such a combined library, provided that the separate distribution of the work based on the Library and of the other library facilities is otherwise permitted, and provided that you do these two things:

a) Accompany the combined library with a copy of the same work based on the Library, uncombined with any other library facilities. This must be distributed under the terms of the Sections above.

b) Give prominent notice with the combined library of the fact that part of it is a work based on the Library, and explaining where to find the accompanying uncombined form of the same work.

9. You may not copy, modify, sublicense, link with, or distribute the Library except as expressly provided under this License. Any attempt otherwise to copy, modify, sublicense, link with, or distribute the Library is void, and will automatically terminate your rights under this License. However, parties who have received copies, or rights, from you under this License will not have their licenses terminated so long as such parties remain in full compliance.

10. You are not required to accept this License, since you have not signed it. However, nothing else grants you permission to modify or distribute the Library or its derivative works. These actions are prohibited by law if you do not accept this License. Therefore, by modifying or distributing the Library (or any work based on the Library), you indicate your acceptance of this License to do so, and all its terms and conditions for copying, distributing or modifying the Library or works based on it.

11. Each time you redistribute the Library (or any work based on the Library), the recipient automatically receives a license from the original licensor to copy, distribute, link with or modify the Library subject to these terms and conditions. You may not impose any further restrictions on the recipients' exercise of the rights granted herein. You are not responsible for enforcing compliance by third parties with this License.

12. If, as a consequence of a court judgment or allegation of patent infringement or for any other reason (not limited to patent issues), conditions are imposed on you (whether by court order, agreement or otherwise) that contradict the conditions of this License, they do not excuse you from the conditions of this License. If you cannot distribute so as to satisfy simultaneously your obligations under this License and any other pertinent obligations, then as a consequence you may not distribute the Library at all. For example, if a patent license would not permit royalty-free redistribution of the Library by all those who receive copies directly or indirectly through you, then the only way you could satisfy both it and this License would be to refrain entirely from distribution of the Library.

If any portion of this section is held invalid or unenforceable under any particular circumstance, the balance of the section is intended to apply, and the section as a whole is intended to apply in other circumstances.

It is not the purpose of this section to induce you to infringe any patents or other property right claims or to contest validity of any such claims; this section has the sole purpose of protecting the integrity of the free software distribution system which is implemented by public license practices. Many people have made generous contributions to the wide range of software distributed through that system in reliance on consistent application of that system; it is up to the author/donor to decide if he or she is willing to distribute software through any other system and a licensee cannot impose that choice.

This section is intended to make thoroughly clear what is believed to be a consequence of the rest of this License.

13. If the distribution and/or use of the Library is restricted in certain countries either by patents or by copyrighted interfaces, the original copyright holder who places the Library under this License may add an explicit geographical distribution limitation excluding those countries, so that distribution is permitted only in or among countries not thus excluded. In such case, this License incorporates the limitation as if written in the body of this License.

14. The Free Software Foundation may publish revised and/or new versions of the Lesser General Public License from time to time. Such new versions will be similar in spirit to the present version, but may differ in detail to address new problems or concerns.

    Each version is given a distinguishing version number. If the Library specifies a version number of this License which applies to it and "any later version," you have the option of following the terms and conditions either of that version or of any later version published by the Free Software Foundation. If the Library does not specify a license version number, you may choose any version ever published by the Free Software Foundation.

15. If you wish to incorporate parts of the Library into other free programs whose distribution conditions are incompatible with these, write to the author to ask for permission. For software which is copyrighted by the Free Software Foundation, write to the Free Software Foundation; we sometimes make exceptions for this. Our decision will be guided by the two goals of preserving the free status of all derivatives of our free software and of promoting the sharing and reuse of software generally.

NO WARRANTY

16. BECAUSE THE LIBRARY IS LICENSED FREE OF CHARGE, THERE IS NO WARRANTY FOR THE LIBRARY, TO THE EXTENT PERMITTED BY APPLICABLE LAW. EXCEPT WHEN OTHERWISE STATED IN WRITING THE COPYRIGHT HOLDERS AND/OR OTHER PARTIES PROVIDE THE LIBRARY "AS IS" WITHOUT WARRANTY OF ANY KIND, EITHER EXPRESSED OR IMPLIED, INCLUDING, BUT NOT LIMITED TO, THE IMPLIED WARRANTIES OF MERCHANTABILITY AND FITNESS FOR A PARTICULAR PURPOSE. THE ENTIRE RISK AS TO THE QUALITY AND PERFORMANCE OF THE LIBRARY IS WITH YOU. SHOULD THE LIBRARY PROVE DEFECTIVE, YOU ASSUME THE COST OF ALL NECESSARY SERVICING, REPAIR OR CORRECTION.

17. IN NO EVENT UNLESS REQUIRED BY APPLICABLE LAW OR AGREED TO IN WRITING WILL ANY COPYRIGHT HOLDER, OR ANY OTHER PARTY WHO MAY MODIFY AND/OR REDISTRIBUTE THE LIBRARY AS PERMITTED ABOVE, BE LIABLE TO YOU FOR DAMAGES, INCLUDING ANY GENERAL, SPECIAL, INCIDENTAL OR CONSEQUENTIAL DAMAGES ARISING OUT OF THE USE OR INABILITY TO USE THE LIBRARY (INCLUDING BUT NOT LIMITED TO LOSS OF DATA OR DATA BEING RENDERED INACCURATE OR LOSSES SUSTAINED BY YOU OR THIRD PARTIES OR A FAILURE OF THE LIBRARY TO OPERATE WITH ANY OTHER SOFTWARE), EVEN IF SUCH HOLDER OR OTHER PARTY HAS BEEN ADVISED OF THE POSSIBILITY OF SUCH DAMAGES.

Mozilla Public License (MPL)

Version 1.1

1. Definitions.

1.0. **"Commercial Use"** means distribution or otherwise making the Covered Code available to a third party.

1.1. **"Contributor"** means each entity that creates or contributes to the creation of Modifications.

1.2. **"Contributor Version"** means the combination of the Original Code, prior Modifications used by a Contributor, and the Modifications made by that particular Contributor.

1.3. **"Covered Code"** means the Original Code or Modifications or the combination of the Original Code and Modifications, in each case including portions thereof.

1.4. **"Electronic Distribution Mechanism"** means a mechanism generally accepted in the software development community for the electronic transfer of data.

1.5. **"Executable"** means Covered Code in any form other than Source Code.

1.6. **"Initial Developer"** means the individual or entity identified as the Initial Developer in the Source Code notice required by Exhibit A.

1.7. **"Larger Work"** means a work which combines Covered Code or portions thereof with code not governed by the terms of this License.

1.8. **"License"** means this document.

1.8.1. **"Licensable"** means having the right to grant, to the maximum extent possible, whether at the time of the initial grant or subsequently acquired, any and all of the rights conveyed herein.

1.9. **"Modifications"** means any addition to or deletion from the substance or structure of either the Original Code or any previous Modifications. When Covered Code is released as a series of files, a Modification is:

A. Any addition to or deletion from the contents of a file containing Original Code or previous Modifications.

B. Any new file that contains any part of the Original Code or previous Modifications.

1.10. **"Original Code"** means Source Code of computer software code which is described in the Source Code notice required by Exhibit A as Original Code, and which, at the time of its release under this License is not already Covered Code governed by this License.

> **1.10.1.** **"Patent Claims"** means any patent claim(s), now owned or hereafter acquired, including without limitation, method, process, and apparatus claims, in any patent Licensable by grantor.

1.11. **"Source Code"** means the preferred form of the Covered Code for making modifications to it, including all modules it contains, plus any associated interface definition files, scripts used to control compilation and installation of an Executable, or source code differential comparisons against either the Original Code or another well known, available Covered Code of the Contributor's choice. The Source Code can be in a compressed or archival form, provided the appropriate decompression or de-archiving software is widely available for no charge.

1.12. **"You"** (or **"Your"**) means an individual or a legal entity exercising rights under, and complying with all of the terms of, this License or a future version of this License issued under Section 6.1. For legal entities, "You" includes any entity which controls, is controlled by, or is under common control with You. For purposes of this definition, "control" means (a) the power, direct or indirect, to cause the direction or management of such entity, whether by contract or otherwise, or (b) ownership of more than fifty percent (50%) of the outstanding shares or beneficial ownership of such entity.

2. Source Code License.

2.1. The Initial Developer Grant.

The Initial Developer hereby grants You a world-wide, royalty-free, non-exclusive license, subject to third party intellectual property claims:

(a) under intellectual property rights (other than patent or trademark) Licensable by Initial Developer to use, reproduce, modify, display, perform, sublicense and distribute the Original Code (or portions thereof) with or without Modifications, and/or as part of a Larger Work; and

(b) under Patents Claims infringed by the making, using or selling of Original Code, to make, have made, use, practice, sell, and offer for sale, and/or otherwise dispose of the Original Code (or portions thereof).

(c) the licenses granted in this Section 2.1(a) and (b) are effective on the date Initial Developer first distributes Original Code under the terms of this License.

(d) Notwithstanding Section 2.1(b) above, no patent license is granted: 1) for code that You delete from the Original Code; 2) separate from the Original Code; or 3) for infringements caused by: i) the modification of the Original Code or ii) the combination of the Original Code with other software or devices.

2.2. Contributor Grant.

Subject to third party intellectual property claims, each Contributor hereby grants You a world-wide, royalty-free, non-exclusive license

(a) under intellectual property rights (other than patent or trademark) Licensable by Contributor, to use, reproduce, modify, display, perform, sublicense and distribute the Modifications created by such Contributor (or portions thereof) either on an unmodified basis, with other Modifications, as Covered Code and/or as part of a Larger Work; and

(b) under Patent Claims infringed by the making, using, or selling of Modifications made by that Contributor either alone and/or in combination with its Contributor Version (or portions of such combination), to make, use, sell, offer for sale, have made, and/or otherwise dispose of: 1) Modifications made by that Contributor (or portions thereof); and 2) the combination of Modifications made by that Contributor with its Contributor Version (or portions of such combination).

(c) the licenses granted in Sections 2.2(a) and 2.2(b) are effective on the date Contributor first makes Commercial Use of the Covered Code.

(d) Notwithstanding Section 2.2(b) above, no patent license is granted: 1) for any code that Contributor has deleted from the Contributor Version; 2) separate from the Contributor Version; 3) for infringements caused by: i) third party modifications of Contributor Version or ii) the combination of Modifications made by that Contributor with other software (except as part of the Contributor Version) or other devices; or 4) under Patent Claims infringed by Covered Code in the absence of Modifications made by that Contributor.

3. Distribution Obligations.

3.1. Application of License.

The Modifications which You create or to which You contribute are governed by the terms of this License, including without limitation Section 2.2. The Source Code version of Covered Code may be distributed only under the terms of this License or a future version of this License released under Section 6.1, and You must include a copy of this License with every copy of the Source Code You distribute. You may not offer or impose any terms on any Source Code version that alters or restricts the applicable version of this License or the recipients' rights hereunder. However, You may include an additional document offering the additional rights described in Section 3.5.

3.2. Availability of Source Code.

Any Modification which You create or to which You contribute must be made available in Source Code form under the terms of this License either on the same media as an Executable version or via an accepted Electronic Distribution Mechanism to anyone to whom you made an Executable version available; and if made available via Electronic Distribution Mechanism, must remain available for at least twelve (12) months after the date it initially became available, or at least six (6) months after a subsequent version of that particular Modification has been made available to such recipients. You are responsible for ensuring that the Source Code version remains available even if the Electronic Distribution Mechanism is maintained by a third party.

3.3. Description of Modifications.

You must cause all Covered Code to which You contribute to contain a file documenting the changes You made to create that Covered Code and the date of any change. You must include a prominent statement that the Modification is derived, directly or indirectly, from Original Code provided by the Initial Developer and including the name of the Initial Developer in (a) the Source Code, and (b) in any notice in an Executable version or related documentation in which You describe the origin or ownership of the Covered Code.

3.4. Intellectual Property Matters

(a) Third Party Claims.

If Contributor has knowledge that a license under a third party's intellectual property rights is required to exercise the rights granted by such Contributor under Sections 2.1 or 2.2, Contributor must include a text file with the Source Code distribution titled "LEGAL" which describes the claim and the party making the claim in sufficient detail that a recipient will know whom to contact. If Contributor obtains such knowledge after the Modification is made available as described in Section 3.2, Contributor shall promptly modify the LEGAL file in all copies Contributor makes available thereafter and shall take other steps (such as notifying appropriate mailing lists or newsgroups) reasonably calculated to inform those who received the Covered Code that new knowledge has been obtained.

(b) Contributor APIs.

If Contributor's Modifications include an application programming interface and Contributor has knowledge of patent licenses which are reasonably necessary to implement that API, Contributor must also include this information in the LEGAL file.

(c) Representations.

Contributor represents that, except as disclosed pursuant to Section 3.4(a) above, Contributor believes that Contributor's Modifications are Contributor's original creation(s) and/or Contributor has sufficient rights to grant the rights conveyed by this License.

3.5. Required Notices.

You must duplicate the notice in Exhibit A in each file of the Source Code. If it is not possible to put such notice in a particular Source Code file due to its structure, then You must include such notice in a location (such as a relevant directory) where a user would be likely to look for such a notice. If You created one or more Modification(s) You may add your name as a Contributor to the notice described in Exhibit A. You must also duplicate this License in any documentation for the Source Code where You describe recipients' rights or ownership rights relating to Covered Code. You may choose to offer, and to charge a fee for, warranty, support, indemnity or liability obligations to one or more recipients of Covered Code. However, You may do so only on Your own behalf, and not on behalf of the Initial Developer or any Contributor. You must make it absolutely clear than any such warranty, support, indemnity or liability obligation is offered by You alone, and You hereby agree to indemnify the Initial Developer and every Contributor for any liability incurred by the Initial Developer or such Contributor as a result of warranty, support, indemnity or liability terms You offer.

3.6. Distribution of Executable Versions.

You may distribute Covered Code in Executable form only if the requirements of Section 3.1–3.5 have been met for that Covered Code, and if You include a notice stating that the Source Code version of the Covered Code is available under the terms of this License, including a description of how and where You have fulfilled the obligations of Section 3.2. The notice must be conspicuously included in any notice in an Executable version, related documentation or collateral in which You describe recipients' rights relating to the Covered Code. You may distribute the Executable version of Covered Code or ownership rights under a license of Your choice, which may contain terms different from this License, provided that You are in compliance with the terms of this License and that the license for the Executable version does not attempt to limit or alter the recipient's rights in the Source Code version from the rights set forth in this License. If You distribute the Executable version under a different license You must make it absolutely clear that any terms which differ from this License are offered by You alone, not by the Initial Developer or any Contributor. You hereby agree to indemnify the Initial Developer and every Contributor for any liability incurred by the Initial Developer or such Contributor as a result of any such terms You offer.

3.7. Larger Works.

You may create a Larger Work by combining Covered Code with other code not governed by the terms of this License and distribute the Larger Work as a single product. In such a case, You must make sure the requirements of this License are fulfilled for the Covered Code.

4. Inability to Comply Due to Statute or Regulation.

If it is impossible for You to comply with any of the terms of this License with respect to some or all of the Covered Code due to statute, judicial order, or regulation then You must: (a) comply with the terms of this License to the maximum extent possible; and (b) describe the limitations and the code they affect. Such description must be included in the LE-GAL file described in Section 3.4 and must be included with all distributions of the Source Code. Except to the extent prohibited by statute or regulation, such description must be sufficiently detailed for a recipient of ordinary skill to be able to understand it.

5. Application of this License.

This License applies to code to which the Initial Developer has attached the notice in **Exhibit A** and to related Covered Code.

6. Versions of the License.

6.1. New Versions.

Netscape Communications Corporation ("Netscape") may publish revised and/or new versions of the License from time to time. Each version will be given a distinguishing version number.

6.2. Effect of New Versions.

Once Covered Code has been published under a particular version of the License, You may always continue to use it under the terms of that version. You may also choose to use such Covered Code under the terms of any subsequent version of the License published by Netscape. No one other than Netscape has the right to modify the terms applicable to Covered Code created under this License.

6.3. Derivative Works.

If You create or use a modified version of this License (which you may only do in order to apply it to code which is not already Covered Code governed by this License), You must (a) rename Your license so that the phrases "Mozilla," "MOZILLAPL," "MOZPL,"

"Netscape," "MPL," "NPL" or any confusingly similar phrase do not appear in your license (except to note that your license differs from this License) and (b) otherwise make it clear that Your version of the license contains terms which differ from the Mozilla Public License and Netscape Public License. (Filling in the name of the Initial Developer, Original Code or Contributor in the notice described in Exhibit A shall not of themselves be deemed to be modifications of this License.)

7. DISCLAIMER OF WARRANTY.

COVERED CODE IS PROVIDED UNDER THIS LICENSE ON AN "AS IS" BASIS, WITHOUT WARRANTY OF ANY KIND, EITHER EXPRESSED OR IMPLIED, INCLUDING, WITHOUT LIMITATION, WARRANTIES THAT THE COVERED CODE IS FREE OF DEFECTS, MERCHANTABLE, FIT FOR A PARTICULAR PURPOSE OR NON-INFRINGING. THE ENTIRE RISK AS TO THE QUALITY AND PERFORMANCE OF THE COVERED CODE IS WITH YOU. SHOULD ANY COVERED CODE PROVE DEFECTIVE IN ANY RESPECT, YOU (NOT THE INITIAL DEVELOPER OR ANY OTHER CONTRIBUTOR) ASSUME THE COST OF ANY NECESSARY SERVICING, REPAIR OR CORRECTION. THIS DISCLAIMER OF WARRANTY CONSTITUTES AN ESSENTIAL PART OF THIS LICENSE. NO USE OF ANY COVERED CODE IS AUTHORIZED HEREUNDER EXCEPT UNDER THIS DISCLAIMER.

8. TERMINATION.

8.1. This License and the rights granted hereunder will terminate automatically if You fail to comply with terms herein and fail to cure such breach within 30 days of becoming aware of the breach. All sublicenses to the Covered Code which are properly granted shall survive any termination of this License. Provisions which, by their nature, must remain in effect beyond the termination of this License shall survive.

8.2. If You initiate litigation by asserting a patent infringement claim (excluding declaratory judgment actions) against Initial Developer or a Contributor (the Initial Developer or Contributor against whom You file such action is referred to as "Participant") alleging that:

(a) such Participant's Contributor Version directly or indirectly infringes any patent, then any and all rights granted by such Participant to You under Sections 2.1 and/or 2.2 of this License shall, upon 60 days notice from Participant terminate prospectively, unless if within 60 days after receipt of notice You either: (i) agree in writing to pay Participant a mutually agreeable reasonable royalty for Your past and future use of Modifications made by such Participant, or (ii) withdraw Your litigation claim with respect to the Contributor Version against such Participant. If within 60 days of notice, a reasonable royalty and payment arrangement are not mutually agreed upon in writing by the parties or the litigation claim is not withdrawn, the rights granted by Participant to You under Sections 2.1 and/or 2.2 automatically terminate at the expiration of the 60 day notice period specified above.

(b) any software, hardware, or device, other than such Participant's Contributor Version, directly or indirectly infringes any patent, then any rights granted to You by such Participant under Sections 2.1(b) and 2.2(b) are revoked effective as of the date You first made, used, sold, distributed, or had made, Modifications made by that Participant.

8.3. If You assert a patent infringement claim against Participant alleging that such Participant's Contributor Version directly or indirectly infringes any patent where such claim is resolved (such as by license or settlement) prior to the initiation of patent infringement litigation, then the reasonable value of the licenses granted by such Participant under Sections 2.1 or 2.2 shall be taken into account in determining the amount or value of any payment or license.

8.4. In the event of termination under Sections 8.1 or 8.2 above, all end user license agreements (excluding distributors and resellers) which have been validly granted by You or any distributor hereunder prior to termination shall survive termination.

9. LIMITATION OF LIABILITY.

UNDER NO CIRCUMSTANCES AND UNDER NO LEGAL THEORY, WHETHER TORT (INCLUDING NEGLIGENCE), CONTRACT, OR OTHERWISE, SHALL YOU, THE INITIAL DEVELOPER, ANY OTHER CONTRIBUTOR, OR ANY DISTRIBUTOR OF COVERED CODE, OR ANY SUPPLIER OF ANY OF SUCH PARTIES, BE LIABLE TO ANY PERSON FOR ANY INDIRECT, SPECIAL, INCIDENTAL, OR CONSEQUENTIAL DAMAGES OF ANY CHARACTER IN-

CLUDING, WITHOUT LIMITATION, DAMAGES FOR LOSS OF GOODWILL, WORK STOPPAGE, COMPUTER FAILURE OR MALFUNCTION, OR ANY AND ALL OTHER COMMERCIAL DAMAGES OR LOSSES, EVEN IF SUCH PARTY SHALL HAVE BEEN INFORMED OF THE POSSIBILITY OF SUCH DAMAGES. THIS LIMITATION OF LIABILITY SHALL NOT APPLY TO LIABILITY FOR DEATH OR PERSONAL INJURY RESULTING FROM SUCH PARTY'S NEGLIGENCE TO THE EXTENT APPLICABLE LAW PROHIBITS SUCH LIMITATION. SOME JURISDICTIONS DO NOT ALLOW THE EXCLUSION OR LIMITATION OF INCIDENTAL OR CONSEQUENTIAL DAMAGES, SO THIS EXCLUSION AND LIMITATION MAY NOT APPLY TO YOU.

10. U.S. GOVERNMENT END USERS.

The Covered Code is a "commercial item," as that term is defined in 48 C.F.R. 2.101 (Oct. 1995), consisting of "commercial computer software" and "commercial computer software documentation," as such terms are used in 48 C.F.R. 12.212 (Sept. 1995). Consistent with 48 C.F.R. 12.212 and 48 C.F.R. 227.7202-1 through 227.7202-4 (June 1995), all U.S. Government End Users acquire Covered Code with only those rights set forth herein.

11. MISCELLANEOUS.

This License represents the complete agreement concerning subject matter hereof. If any provision of this License is held to be unenforceable, such provision shall be reformed only to the extent necessary to make it enforceable. This License shall be governed by California law provisions (except to the extent applicable law, if any, provides otherwise), excluding its conflict-of-law provisions. With respect to disputes in which at least one party is a citizen of, or an entity chartered or registered to do business in the United States of America, any litigation relating to this License shall be subject to the jurisdiction of the Federal Courts of the Northern District of California, with venue lying in Santa Clara County, California, with the losing party responsible for costs, including without limitation, court costs and reasonable attorneys' fees and expenses. The application of the United Nations Convention on Contracts for the International Sale of Goods is expressly excluded. Any law or regulation which provides that the language of a contract shall be construed against the drafter shall not apply to this License.

12. RESPONSIBILITY FOR CLAIMS.

As between Initial Developer and the Contributors, each party is responsible for claims and damages arising, directly or indirectly, out of its utilization of rights under this License and You agree to work with Initial Developer and Contributors to distribute such responsibility on an equitable basis. Nothing herein is intended or shall be deemed to constitute any admission of liability.

13. MULTIPLE-LICENSED CODE.

Initial Developer may designate portions of the Covered Code as "Multiple-Licensed." "Multiple-Licensed" means that the Initial Developer permits you to utilize portions of the Covered Code under Your choice of the MPL or the alternative licenses, if any, specified by the Initial Developer in the file described in Exhibit A.

EXHIBIT A—Mozilla Public License

The contents of this file are subject to the Mozilla Public License Version 1.1 (the "License"); you may not use this file except in compliance with the License. You may obtain a copy of the License at

http://www.mozilla.org/MPL/

Software distributed under the License is distributed on an "AS IS" basis, WITHOUT WARRANTY OF ANY KIND, either express or implied. See the License for the specific language governing rights and limitations under the License.

The Original Code is _____.

The Initial Developer of the Original Code is _____.

Portions created by _____ are Copyright (C) _____ _____.

All Rights Reserved.

Contributor(s):

_____.

Alternatively, the contents of this file may be used under the terms of the _____ license (the "(___) License"), in which case the provisions of (_____) License are applicable instead of those above. If you wish to allow use of your version of this file only under the terms of the (___) License and not to allow others to use your version of this file under the MPL, indicate your decision by deleting the provisions above and replace them with the notice and other provisions required by the (___) License. If you do not delete the provisions above, a recipient may use your version of this file under either the MPL or the (___) License.

(NOTE: The text of this Exhibit A may differ slightly from the text of the notices in the Source Code files of the Original Code. You should use the text of this Exhibit A rather than the text found in the Original Code Source Code for Your Modifications.)

Common Public License (CPL)

THE ACCOMPANYING PROGRAM IS PROVIDED UNDER THE TERMS OF THIS COMMON PUBLIC LICENSE ("AGREEMENT"). ANY USE, REPRODUCTION OR DISTRIBUTION OF THE PROGRAM CONSTITUTES RECIPIENT'S ACCEPTANCE OF THIS AGREEMENT.

1. DEFINITIONS

"Contribution" means:

a) in the case of the initial Contributor, the initial code and documentation distributed under this Agreement, and

b) in the case of each subsequent Contributor:

i) changes to the Program, and

ii) additions to the Program;

where such changes and/or additions to the Program originate from and are distributed by that particular Contributor. A Contribution 'originates' from a Contributor if it was added to the Program by such Contributor itself or anyone acting on such Contributor's behalf. Contributions do not include additions to the Program which: (i) are separate modules of software distributed in conjunction with the Program under their own license agreement, and (ii) are not derivative works of the Program.

"Contributor" means any person or entity that distributes the Program.

"Licensed Patents" mean patent claims licensable by a Contributor which are necessarily infringed by the use or sale of its Contribution alone or when combined with the Program.

"Program" means the Contributions distributed in accordance with this Agreement.

"Recipient" means anyone who receives the Program under this Agreement, including all Contributors.

2. GRANT OF RIGHTS

a) Subject to the terms of this Agreement, each Contributor hereby grants Recipient a non-exclusive, worldwide, royalty-free copyright license to reproduce, prepare derivative works of, publicly display, publicly perform, distribute and sublicense the Contribution of such Contributor, if any, and such derivative works, in source code and object code form.

b) Subject to the terms of this Agreement, each Contributor hereby grants Recipient a non-exclusive, worldwide, royalty-free patent license under Licensed Patents to make, use, sell, offer to sell, import and otherwise transfer the Contribution of such Contributor, if any, in source code and object code form. This patent license shall apply to the combination of the Contribution and the Program if, at the time the Contribution is added by the Contributor, such addition of the Contribution causes such combination to be covered by the Licensed Patents. The patent license shall not apply to any other combinations which include the Contribution. No hardware per se is licensed hereunder.

c) Recipient understands that although each Contributor grants the licenses to its Contributions set forth herein, no assurances are provided by any Contributor that the Program does not infringe the patent or other intellectual property rights of any other entity. Each Contributor disclaims any liability to Recipient for claims brought by any other entity based on infringement of intellectual property rights or otherwise. As a condition to exercising the rights and licenses granted hereunder, each Recipient hereby assumes sole responsibility to secure any other intellectual property rights needed, if any. For example, if a third party patent license is required to allow Recipient to distribute the Program, it is Recipient's responsibility to acquire that license before distributing the Program.

d) Each Contributor represents that to its knowledge it has sufficient copyright rights in its Contribution, if any, to grant the copyright license set forth in this Agreement.

3. REQUIREMENTS

A Contributor may choose to distribute the Program in object code form under its own license agreement, provided that:

a) it complies with the terms and conditions of this Agreement; and

b) its license agreement:

i) effectively disclaims on behalf of all Contributors all warranties and conditions, express and implied, including warranties or conditions of title and non-infringement, and implied warranties or conditions of merchantability and fitness for a particular purpose;

ii) effectively excludes on behalf of all Contributors all liability for damages, including direct, indirect, special, incidental and consequential damages, such as lost profits;

iii) states that any provisions which differ from this Agreement are offered by that Contributor alone and not by any other party; and

iv) states that source code for the Program is available from such Contributor, and informs licensees how to obtain it in a reasonable manner on or through a medium customarily used for software exchange.

When the Program is made available in source code form:

a) it must be made available under this Agreement; and

b) a copy of this Agreement must be included with each copy of the Program.

Contributors may not remove or alter any copyright notices contained within the Program.

Each Contributor must identify itself as the originator of its Contribution, if any, in a manner that reasonably allows subsequent Recipients to identify the originator of the Contribution.

4. COMMERCIAL DISTRIBUTION

Commercial distributors of software may accept certain responsibilities with respect to end users, business partners and the like. While this license is intended to facilitate the commercial use of the Program, the Contributor who includes the Program in a commercial product offering should do so in a manner which does not create potential liability for other Contributors. Therefore, if a Contributor includes the Program in a commercial product offering, such Contributor ("Commercial Contributor") hereby agrees to defend and indemnify every other Contributor ("Indemnified Contributor") against any losses, damages and costs (collectively "Losses") arising from claims, lawsuits and other legal actions brought by a third party against the Indemnified Contributor to the extent caused by the acts or omissions of such Commercial Contributor in connection with its distribution of the Program in a commercial product offering. The obligations in this section do not apply to any claims or Losses relating to any actual or alleged intellectual property infringement. In order to qualify, an Indemnified Contributor must: a) promptly notify the Commercial Contributor in writing of such claim, and b) allow the Commercial Contributor to control, and cooperate with the Commercial Contributor in, the defense and any related settlement negotiations. The Indemnified Contributor may participate in any such claim at its own expense.

5. NO WARRANTY

For example, a Contributor might include the Program in a commercial product offering, Product X. That Contributor is then a Commercial Contributor. If that

Commercial Contributor then makes performance claims, or offers warranties related to Product X, those performance claims and warranties are such Commercial Contributor's responsibility alone. Under this section, the Commercial Contributor would have to defend claims against the other Contributors related to those performance claims and warranties, and if a court requires any other Contributor to pay any damages as a result, the Commercial Contributor must pay those damages.

EXCEPT AS EXPRESSLY SET FORTH IN THIS AGREEMENT, THE PROGRAM IS PROVIDED ON AN "AS IS" BASIS, WITHOUT WARRANTIES OR CONDITIONS OF ANY KIND, EITHER EXPRESS OR IMPLIED INCLUDING, WITHOUT LIMITATION, ANY WARRANTIES OR CONDITIONS OF TITLE, NON-INFRINGEMENT, MERCHANTABILITY OR FITNESS FOR A PARTICULAR PURPOSE. Each Recipient is solely responsible for determining the appropriateness of using and distributing the Program and assumes all risks associated with its exercise of rights under this Agreement, including but not limited to the risks and costs of program errors, compliance with applicable laws, damage to or loss of data, programs or equipment, and unavailability or interruption of operations.

6. DISCLAIMER OF LIABILITY

EXCEPT AS EXPRESSLY SET FORTH IN THIS AGREEMENT, NEITHER RECIPIENT NOR ANY CONTRIBUTORS SHALL HAVE ANY LIABILITY FOR ANY DIRECT, INDIRECT, INCIDENTAL, SPECIAL, EXEMPLARY, OR CONSEQUENTIAL

DAMAGES (INCLUDING WITHOUT LIMITA-
TION LOST PROFITS), HOWEVER CAUSED
AND ON ANY THEORY OF LIABILITY,
WHETHER IN CONTRACT, STRICT LIABILI-
TY, OR TORT (INCLUDING NEGLIGENCE OR
OTHERWISE) ARISING IN ANY WAY OUT OF
THE USE OR DISTRIBUTION OF THE PRO-
GRAM OR THE EXERCISE OF ANY RIGHTS
GRANTED HEREUNDER, EVEN IF ADVISED
OF THE POSSIBILITY OF SUCH DAMAGES.

7. GENERAL

If any provision of this Agreement is invalid or unenforceable under applicable law, it shall not affect the validity or enforceability of the remainder of the terms of
this Agreement, and without further action by the parties hereto, such provision shall be reformed to the
minimum extent necessary to make such provision valid and enforceable.

If Recipient institutes patent litigation against a Contributor with respect to a patent applicable to software
(including a cross-claim or counterclaim in a lawsuit),
then any patent licenses granted by that Contributor to
such Recipient under this Agreement shall terminate as
of the date such litigation is filed. In addition, if Recipient institutes patent litigation against any entity (including a cross-claim or counterclaim in a lawsuit)
alleging that the Program itself (excluding combinations of the Program with other software or hardware)
infringes such Recipient's patent(s), then such Recipient's rights granted under Section 2(b) shall terminate
as of the date such litigation is filed.

All Recipient's rights under this Agreement shall terminate if it fails to comply with any of the material terms or conditions of this Agreement and does not cure such failure in a reasonable period of time after becoming aware of such noncompliance. If all Recipient's rights under this Agreement terminate, Recipient agrees to cease use and distribution of the Program as soon as reasonably practicable. However, Recipient's obligations under this Agreement and any licenses granted by Recipient relating to the Program shall continue and survive.

Everyone is permitted to copy and distribute copies of this Agreement, but in order to avoid inconsistency the Agreement is copyrighted and may only be modified in the following manner. The Agreement Steward reserves the right to publish new versions (including revisions) of this Agreement from time to time. No one other than the Agreement Steward has the right to modify this Agreement. IBM is the initial Agreement Steward. IBM may assign the responsibility to serve as the Agreement Steward to a suitable separate entity. Each new version of the Agreement will be given a distinguishing version number. The Program (including Contributions) may always be distributed subject to the version of the Agreement under which it was received. In addition, after a new version of the Agreement is published, Contributor may elect to distribute the Program (including its Contributions) under the new version. Except as expressly stated in Sections 2(a) and 2(b) above, Recipient receives no rights or licenses to the intellectual property of any Contributor under this Agreement, whether expressly, by implication, estoppel or otherwise. All rights in the Program not expressly granted under this Agreement are reserved.

This Agreement is governed by the laws of the State of New York and the intellectual property laws of the United States of America. No party to this Agreement will bring a legal action under this Agreement more than one year after the cause of action arose. Each party waives its rights to a jury trial in any resulting litigation.

Open Software License (OSL)
and Academic Free License (AFL)

Version 2.0

This Open Software License (the "License") applies to any original work of authorship (the "Original Work") whose owner (the "Licensor") has placed the following notice immediately following the copyright notice for the Original Work:

Licensed under the Open Software License version 2.0

(The name of the license is changed to "Academic Free License" in the first paragraph and the notice in the AFL.—LR)

1) **Grant of Copyright License.** Licensor hereby grants You a world-wide, royalty-free, non-exclusive, perpetual, sublicenseable license to do the following:

   a) to reproduce the Original Work in copies;

   b) to prepare derivative works ("Derivative Works") based upon the Original Work;

   c) to distribute copies of the Original Work and Derivative Works to the public,

   with the proviso that copies of Original Work or Derivative Works that You distribute shall be licensed under the Open Software License;

   (The Academic Free License omits the underlined proviso.—LR)

   d) to perform the Original Work publicly; and

   e) to display the Original Work publicly.

2) **Grant of Patent License.** Licensor hereby grants You a world-wide, royalty-free, non-exclusive, perpetual, sublicenseable license, under patent claims owned or controlled by the Licensor that are embodied in the Original Work as furnished by the Licensor, to make, use, sell and offer for sale the Original Work and Derivative Works.

3) **Grant of Source Code License.** The term "Source Code" means the preferred form of the Original Work for making modifications to it and all available documentation describing how to modify the Original Work. Licensor hereby agrees to provide a machine-readable copy of the Source Code of the Original Work along with each copy of the Original Work that Licensor distributes. Licensor reserves the right to satisfy this obligation by placing a machine-readable copy of the Source Code in an information repository reasonably calculated to permit inexpensive and convenient access by You for as long as Licensor continues to distribute the Original Work, and by publishing the address of that information repository in a notice immediately following the copyright notice that applies to the Original Work.

4) **Exclusions From License Grant.** Neither the names of Licensor, nor the names of any contributors to the Original Work, nor any of their trademarks or service marks, may be used to endorse or promote products derived from this Original Work without express prior written permission of the Licensor. Nothing in this License shall be deemed to grant any rights to trademarks, copyrights, patents, trade secrets or any other intellectual property of Licensor except as expressly

stated herein. No patent license is granted to make, use, sell or offer to sell embodiments of any patent claims other than the licensed claims defined in Section 2. No right is granted to the trademarks of Licensor even if such marks are included in the Original Work. Nothing in this License shall be interpreted to prohibit Licensor from licensing under different terms from this License any Original Work that Licensor otherwise would have a right to license.

5) **External Deployment.** The term "External Deployment" means the use or distribution of the Original Work or Derivative Works in any way such that the Original Work or Derivative Works may be used by anyone other than You, whether the Original Work or Derivative Works are distributed to those persons or made available as an application intended for use over a computer network. As an express condition for the grants of license hereunder, You agree that any External Deployment by You of a Derivative Work shall be deemed a distribution and shall be licensed to all under the terms of this License, as prescribed in section 1(c) herein.

(The Academic Free License deletes this section 5 in its entirety. —LR)

6) **Attribution Rights.** You must retain, in the Source Code of any Derivative Works that You create, all copyright, patent or trademark notices from the Source Code of the Original Work, as well as any notices of licensing and any descriptive text identified therein as an "Attribution Notice." You must cause the Source Code for any Derivative Works that You create to carry a prominent Attribution Notice reasonably calculated to

inform recipients that You have modified the Original Work.

7) **Warranty of Provenance and Disclaimer of Warranty.** Licensor warrants that the copyright in and to the Original Work and the patent rights granted herein by Licensor are owned by the Licensor or are sublicensed to You under the terms of this License with the permission of the contributor(s) of those copyrights and patent rights. Except as expressly stated in the immediately proceeding sentence, the Original Work is provided under this License on an "AS IS" BASIS and WITHOUT WARRANTY, either express or implied, including, without limitation, the warranties of NON-INFRINGEMENT, MERCHANTABILITY or FITNESS FOR A PARTICULAR PURPOSE. THE ENTIRE RISK AS TO THE QUALITY OF THE ORIGINAL WORK IS WITH YOU. This DISCLAIMER OF WARRANTY constitutes an essential part of this License. No license to Original Work is granted hereunder except under this disclaimer.

8) **Limitation of Liability.** Under no circumstances and under no legal theory, whether in tort (including negligence), contract, or otherwise, shall the Licensor be liable to any person for any direct, indirect, special, incidental, or consequential damages of any character arising as a result of this License or the use of the Original Work including, without limitation, damages for loss of goodwill, work stoppage, computer failure or malfunction, or any and all other commercial damages or losses. This limitation of liability shall not apply to liability for death or personal injury resulting from Licensor's negligence to the extent applicable law prohib-

its such limitation. Some jurisdictions do not allow the exclusion or limitation of incidental or consequential damages, so this exclusion and limitation may not apply to You.

9) **Acceptance and Termination.** If You distribute copies of the Original Work or a Derivative Work, You must make a reasonable effort under the circumstances to obtain the express assent of recipients to the terms of this License. Nothing else but this License (or another written agreement between Licensor and You) grants You permission to create Derivative Works based upon the Original Work or to exercise any of the rights granted in Section 1 herein, and any attempt to do so except under the terms of this License (or another written agreement between Licensor and You) is expressly prohibited by U.S. copyright law, the equivalent laws of other countries, and by international treaty. Therefore, by exercising any of the rights granted to You in Section 1 herein, You indicate Your acceptance of this License and all of its terms and conditions. This License shall terminate immediately and you may no longer exercise any of the rights granted to You by this License upon Your failure to honor the proviso in Section 1(c) herein.

(The Academic Free License deletes the last sentence of section 9.—LR)

10) **Termination for Patent Action.** This License shall terminate automatically and You may no longer exercise any of the rights granted to You by this License as of the date You commence an action, including a cross-claim or counterclaim, for patent infringement (i) against Licensor with respect to a patent applicable to

software or (ii) against any entity with respect to a patent applicable to the Original Work (but excluding combinations of the Original Work with other software or hardware).

(Version 2.1 of the OSL/AFL contains the following language instead.—LR)

10) **Termination for Patent Action.** This License shall terminate automatically and You may no longer exercise any of the rights granted to You by this License as of the date You commence an action, including a cross-claim or counterclaim, against Licensor or any licensee alleging that the Original Work infringes a patent. This termination provision shall not apply for an action alleging patent infringement by combinations of the Original Work with other software or hardware.

11) **Jurisdiction, Venue and Governing Law.** Any action or suit relating to this License may be brought only in the courts of a jurisdiction wherein the Licensor resides or in which Licensor conducts its primary business, and under the laws of that jurisdiction excluding its conflict-of-law provisions. The application of the United Nations Convention on Contracts for the International Sale of Goods is expressly excluded. Any use of the Original Work outside the scope of this License or after its termination shall be subject to the requirements and penalties of the U.S. Copyright Act, 17 U.S.C. § 101 et seq., the equivalent laws of other countries, and international treaty. This section shall survive the termination of this License.

12) **Attorneys' Fees.** In any action to enforce the terms of this License or seeking damages relating thereto, the

prevailing party shall be entitled to recover its costs and expenses, including, without limitation, reasonable attorneys' fees and costs incurred in connection with such action, including any appeal of such action. This section shall survive the termination of this License.

13) **Miscellaneous.** This License represents the complete agreement concerning the subject matter hereof. If any provision of this License is held to be unenforceable, such provision shall be reformed only to the extent necessary to make it enforceable.

14) **Definition of "You" in This License.** "You" throughout this License, whether in upper or lower case, means an individual or a legal entity exercising rights under, and complying with all of the terms of, this License. For legal entities, "You" includes any entity that controls, is controlled by, or is under common control with you. For purposes of this definition, "control" means (i) the power, direct or indirect, to cause the direction or management of such entity, whether by contract or otherwise, or (ii) ownership of fifty percent (50%) or more of the outstanding shares, or (iii) beneficial ownership of such entity.

15) **Right to Use.** You may use the Original Work in all ways not otherwise restricted or conditioned by this License or by law, and Licensor promises not to interfere with or be responsible for such uses by You.

Index

About the Author

Lawrence Rosen is both an attorney and a computer specialist. He is founding partner of Rosenlaw & Einschlag, a technology law firm with offices in Los Altos Hills and Ukiah, California, that specializes in intellectual property, licensing, and business transactions for technology companies.

Rosen is general counsel and secretary of the nonprofit Open Source Initiative (OSI), which promotes the Open Source Definition for the good of the community, reviews and approves major open source licenses, and manages the "OSI Certified" certification mark for open source software.

Before he became an attorney Rosen was a computer technologist. He managed computing activities and taught computer programming and database design at Stanford University, later going into industry where he coordinated the design, development, manufacturing, and marketing of data communications products. He received his bachelor's degree from Dartmouth College, pursued a master of computer science degree at the University of North Carolina at Chapel Hill, and received his law degree from Santa Clara University.

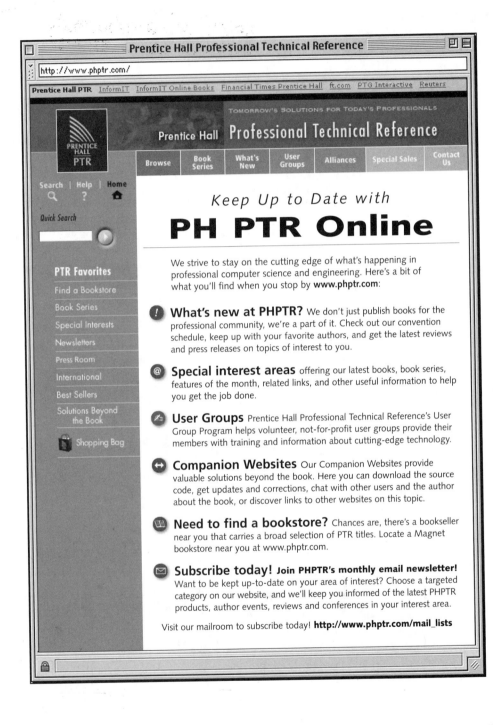

Prentice Hall Professional Technical Reference

http://www.phptr.com/

Prentice Hall PTR   InformIT   InformIT Online Books   Financial Times Prentice Hall   ft.com   PTG Interactive   Reuters

TOMORROW'S SOLUTIONS FOR TODAY'S PROFESSIONALS

Prentice Hall Professional Technical Reference

| Browse | Book Series | What's New | User Groups | Alliances | Special Sales | Contact Us |

Search | Help | Home

Quick Search

PTR Favorites

Find a Bookstore

Book Series

Special Interests

Newsletters

Press Room

International

Best Sellers

Solutions Beyond the Book

Shopping Bag

Keep Up to Date with
PH PTR Online

We strive to stay on the cutting edge of what's happening in professional computer science and engineering. Here's a bit of what you'll find when you stop by **www.phptr.com**:

What's new at PHPTR? We don't just publish books for the professional community, we're a part of it. Check out our convention schedule, keep up with your favorite authors, and get the latest reviews and press releases on topics of interest to you.

Special interest areas offering our latest books, book series, features of the month, related links, and other useful information to help you get the job done.

User Groups Prentice Hall Professional Technical Reference's User Group Program helps volunteer, not-for-profit user groups provide their members with training and information about cutting-edge technology.

Companion Websites Our Companion Websites provide valuable solutions beyond the book. Here you can download the source code, get updates and corrections, chat with other users and the author about the book, or discover links to other websites on this topic.

Need to find a bookstore? Chances are, there's a bookseller near you that carries a broad selection of PTR titles. Locate a Magnet bookstore near you at www.phptr.com.

Subscribe today! Join PHPTR's monthly email newsletter! Want to be kept up-to-date on your area of interest? Choose a targeted category on our website, and we'll keep you informed of the latest PHPTR products, author events, reviews and conferences in your interest area.

Visit our mailroom to subscribe today! **http://www.phptr.com/mail_lists**